KU-392-933

DATABASE TECHNOLOGY
A Software Engineering Approach

John G. Hughes
Queen's University of Belfast

PRENTICE HALL

NEW YORK   LONDON   TORONTO   SYDNEY   TOKYO   SINGAPORE

First published 1988 by
Prentice Hall International (UK) Ltd,
Campus 400, Maylands Avenue, Hemel Hempstead,
Hertfordshire, HP2 7EZ
A division of
Simon & Schuster International Group

© 1988 Prentice Hall International (UK) Ltd

All rights reserved. No part of this publication may be
reproduced, stored in a retrieval system, or transmitted,
in any form, or by any means, electronic, mechanical,
photocopying, recording or otherwise, without the prior
permission, in writing, from the publisher.
For permission within the United States of America
contact Prentice Hall Inc., Englewood Cliffs, NJ07632.

Printed in Great Britain by
Antony Rowe Ltd, Chippenham, Wiltshire

Library of Congress Cataloging-in-Publication Data

Hughes, John G., 1953–
  Database technology.
  (Prentice Hall international series
  in computer science)
  Includes index.
  1. Data base management.   2. Software
  engineering.
  I. Title   II. Series.
  QA76.9.D3H844   1988   005.74   88-6000
  ISBN 0-13-197914-0

British Library Cataloguing in Publication Data

Hughes, John G., 1953–
  Database technology: a software engineering
  approach – (Prentice Hall international series
  in computer science).
  1. Machine-readable files
  I. Title
  005.74
  ISBN 0-13-197914-0
  ISBN 0-13-197906-X Pbk

4 5 95 94

ISBN 0-13-197914-0
ISBN 0-13-197906-X PBK

Contents

8 Database Administration

9 Commercial Systems and Database Machines

Preface

This book is primarily intended for undergraduate and postgraduate students at universities and polytechnics who use a language such as Pascal as their principal programming language. One of the main aims of the book is to cover the principal aspects of Database Technology within the framework of a modern well-structured language, so giving the subject its rightful place in the mainstream of computer science, alongside topics such as Software Engineering and Concurrent Systems.

It is unfortunately the case that commercial database management systems have for the most part remained unaffected by the significant developments that have taken place in programming languages over the past 15 years. Thus, most modern systems still offer rather primitive programming facilities. Typically, data manipulation statements may be embedded in programs written in languages such as COBOL, FORTRAN or Pascal, but the database constructs are themselves rather loosely coupled with the programming language and little or no advantage can be taken of the facilities in the language for data structuring.

In recent years, however, a number of database programming languages have emerged which integrate the relational model of data with a well-structured programming language. These languages offer a unified approach to database management which recognises the fact that database design and program development are two closely interrelated disciplines. Unfortunately few of these languages are as yet widely available, and thus Modula-2 has been chosen to illustrate the ideas presented in the book.

The language Modula-2, through its module construct, offers much more powerful facilities for type definition than those found, for example, in Pascal. In addition Modula-2 is suitable for both high- and low-level programming and possesses many excellent facilities for designing and implementing large software systems. On the practical side, Modula-2 is quite a small language and implementations exist for a wide range of computers ranging from microcomputers to mainframes.

The module facility of Modula-2 is particularly attractive for implementing database systems. Modules provide a mechanism by which types may be mapped, step by step, from higher user-oriented levels to lower levels, ending with the details of a particular machine. At each level, the view of the data may be abstracted from those details which are unnecessary for data usage, namely details with regard to representation, constraints, access rights, etc. Database systems have always required a multi-level approach and clearly great advantages are to be gained from implementing such systems in high-level programming languages which offer powerful and well-controlled data modelling facilities and a methodology for programming multilevel systems.

Chapters 1 to 4 of the book introduce the reader to the basic concepts of database technology and in particular to data modelling. The emphasis is very much on the relational model of data, firstly since this model forms the basis for most new commercial systems, and secondly since the basic concepts of the relational model are easily incorporated into modern high-level programming languages. Chapter 5 introduces database programming languages and demonstrates, through the use of Modula-2, how software engineering concepts such as data abstraction and modularisation may be applied in the construction of database software. Chapters 6 and 7 deal with implementation issues and once again Modula-2 is used to illustrate the concepts involved in the physical storage organisation of databases and in the efficient implementation of relational database operations. Chapter 8 gives an overview of some of the most important administrative issues in database technology, including the problems associated with recovery, integrity, security, and concurrent access to database systems. The important aspects of distributed databases are also described in this chapter. The final chapter describes the principal features of some of the most popular commercial database management systems, fourth generation languages, and database machines.

It is expected that the reader will have an elementary knowledge of programming languages and data structures. No prior knowledge of Database Technology is assumed, and an overview of Modula-2 is provided in Appendix 1.

I should like to thank John Elder and Dave Bustard for many useful discussions and for permission to adapt some of their programs for use in this text. I am also grateful to the staff of Prentice Hall, and in particular to Helen Martin, for their advice and encouragement during the preparation of the book.

Belfast   J.G.H.
January 1988

1

Database   Concepts

1.1   INTRODUCTION

For many years there has been a continual and rapid growth in database
systems, not only with respect to the sheer number of such systems, but
also with regard to the amount of information being stored and the complexity of applications being developed. This growing demand for systems
of ever-increasing complexity and precision has stimulated the need for
higher level concepts, tools, and techniques for database design and development. Thus database design methodologies developed over the last
decade provide the designer with the means for modelling an enterprise at a
high level of abstraction, before proceeding with the detailed logical and
physical database design.

   During the same period, programming languages have developed
sophisticated abstraction mechanisms which permit, for example, the
specification of data types and objects independent of their implementation.
To a large extent however, these significant developments in database technology and programming languages have proceeded independently. This
fact tends to be reflected in database courses at universities, which are often
treated in isolation and bear little relevance to the mainstream computer science topics such as Software Engineering, Data Structures, and Concurrent
Systems. In this book we attempt to bridge the gap between database technology and programming languages by demonstrating how the facilities in
programming languages for data abstraction may be applied to database
description, manipulation and implementation.

   In this chapter we describe the basic concepts behind database management systems. We look at the architecture of a database system, in particular at the levels of abstraction involved, and the kinds of software
required to define and manipulate such a system. We also describe the
database life cycle and relate the various phases of this life cycle to the now
well-established principles of software engineering.

1

1.2   THE AIMS OF DATABASE TECHNOLOGY

A database may be defined as a computerised collection of *interrelated* data stored such that:

1. The data are *shared* among different users and applications, but a common and controlled approach is used for inserting, deleting, modifying and retrieving data.
2. Terminal users and application programs which access the data do not need to be aware of the detailed storage structure.

A Database Management System (DBMS) is a software system capable of supporting and managing any number of independent databases.

The data in a database are usually logically organised according to some *data model*. Data models are central to database systems. They provide a conceptual basis for design, a formal basis for defining unambiguously the items of data and their interrelationships, and a framework for implementation. Database systems are generally based on one of three data models, namely:

1. *The relational data model*
   This model is based on the mathematical notion of a relation. In this model both the data objects and their interrelationships are represented by two dimensional tables.

2. *The network data model*
   In this model the database is represented by a directed graph, the nodes of which represent the data objects (record types), and the arcs of which define the relationships among the data objects.

3. *The hierarchical data model*
   In this model the database is represented by tree structures. If the data are not naturally hierarchical (as is usually the case) then this model imposes quite severe restrictions on the data modeller.

In this book we shall concentrate primarily on the relational model of data. Although a network or hierarchical approach might have the edge on performance for certain applications, these models impose too many restrictions at the data modelling level, and lead to databases which are difficult to maintain, modify and upgrade.

The main difficulty is that network and hierarchical systems provide only a minimal amount of *data independence*, whereby the logical database structure is buffered from the physical database organisation. In contrast, the relational specification of a logical data model is independent of implementation considerations. The relative advantages and disadvantages of the three data models are discussed in more detail in Chapters 2 and 3.

Data independence is central to the approach adopted in this text for the construction of database systems. In the following subsections we describe this concept in greater detail, and go on to discuss the other important aims of database technology.

Data independence

Support for data independence is arguably the most important feature of a database system. The ability to separate the logical database definition from its physical storage organisation increases the capabilities to redefine and restructure the database. That is, the storage structures and access strategies may be altered in response to changing requirements, without having to alter existing applications. This property of database systems is consistent with the modern approach to software engineering whereby large software systems are constructed from modular units which serve to hide inessential details from the surrounding program environment.

There are, in fact, two distinct levels of data independence:

1. *Physical data independence* which, as described above, insulates applications from the underlying physical storage organisation of the data.
2. *Logical data independence* which insulates applications from changes made to the logical organisation of data, e.g. the addition of new record types or relationships.

Logical data independence may be effected by providing each application with its own *view* of the database. This view may simply be a subset of the overall logical data model, or it may be a derived structure which is tailored to the application. In the latter case for example, record or field types may have their names changed or may be omitted, or multiple fields in the global model may be combined into a single field in the view. The implementation of such a view requires that it be mapped to the global data model.

Integrity preservation

One of the primary functions of a database system is to maintain the *integrity* of the database, i.e. to preserve the consistency and correctness of the data. This is especially important in large multi-user environments in which the system must preserve integrity in the face of problems such as errors in updating programs, system software failures, hardware failures and the conflicting requirements of concurrently executing transactions.

The preservation of consistency and correctness is, of course, central to the software engineering approach to the construction and maintenance of large software systems. Thus many valuable concepts and techniques have been developed within the framework of software engineering which may be applied to the problem of maintaining integrity in database systems. These techniques will be discussed in depth in this and in the following chapters.

Access flexibility

Flexibility of access to data is an important requirement in modern data processing environments. It is commonly the case that database systems are implemented which support only pre-defined access paths, i.e. those paths which were foreseen as being necessary at the time of implementation. This is highly unsatisfactory for the user, particularly in an environment where the data requirements are varying continuously. Thus a user may find that though the data that he requires is stored or can be derived from the stored data, the restrictive nature of the query processing software makes it difficult for him to retrieve it.

A great advantage of the relational model of data is that at the logical level it places no restrictions on the access paths that may be followed. Thus in a system which offers a high-level relational interface, complex queries may be formulated with minimal effort. This of course places a great burden on the implementor to provide efficient query processing.

Optimisation of performance and efficiency

A database system must offer a high standard of performance and efficiency, especially for on-line query processing. Early relational systems were seriously deficient in this area, but great advances have been made in recent years. Improvements to performance may be effected at two levels: first by providing efficient data access structures at the physical storage level, and second by restructuring users' queries into a form which is more amenable to efficient implementation. These two approaches are very closely interrelated, since clearly high-level optimisation techniques for evaluating queries must take account of the existing access paths and their properties. Both forms of optimisation are discussed in detail in subsequent chapters.

Security preservation

A database system must provide mechanisms for the protection of data from unauthorised intrusion, whether accidental or malicious. This is especially important if the database contains sensitive information, and for such systems the techniques which may be employed to ensure confidentiality and security are quite complex (Date, 1983). However, there are some aspects of security which are relevant even in simple, single-user database systems. For example, protecting the database against accidental erasure or corruption, and using passwords to inhibit unauthorised access to database files.

Many powerful techniques for security preservation lie within the realm of the software engineer, and the most important of these are described in Chapter 8.

Administration and control

Database systems, in common with most software products, are not generally used by their designers or implementors, but rather by people who were not involved in the development of the system and who may have little or no knowledge of database technology. Also, a database system must respond to changes in its operating environment and to changing user requirements. Thus, the operation and maintenance of a large, multi-user database system requires *centralised* administration and control, and extensive *documentation*.

The person or group responsible for supervising the day-to-day management of a large multi-user database system is often referred to as the *Database Administrator*. The primary duties of this administrator involve co-ordinating conflicting access requirements, monitoring performance, and supervising back-up and recovery services. For both user and administrator, many commercial database management systems now provide extensive *Data Dictionary* facilities. These are among the most essential data management tools, providing intelligence on data resources and database usage, and supporting data administration, systems development, documentation and maintenance.

1.3 ARCHITECTURE OF A DATABASE SYSTEM

The requirements of a database system as described above has led to the identification of three distinct levels of abstraction in such a system (see Figure 1.1), namely the *physical level*, the global or *conceptual schema level* and the *user view level*. This three level architecture was proposed by the Standards and Planning Requirements Committee of the American National Standards Committee on Computers and Information Processing (ANSI/SPARC Report, Tsichritis and Klug, 1978). Although the architecture proposed by this group was rather detailed, the essence was to divide the database structure in such a way that the distinct layers could be described at different levels of abstraction, with clearly defined interfaces between them.

The merits of this three-level architecture have long been recognised, and most modern DBMSs support, to some extent, the separation of the physical database, the schema and the user views. The architecture is also consistent with the principles of software engineering, which advocate a separation of levels of concern and a modular approach to software development.

The physical level

The physical level refers to the physical representation and layout of the data on the storage devices. It is an aspect of the database seen only by system programmers concerned with efficient positioning and indexing, and with performance optimisation. We may view the physical level itself at different levels of abstraction, ranging from the concepts of files and records found in many programming languages, down to the level of tracks and cylinders on storage devices. The *storage schema*, which provides a mapping of the conceptual schema to the physical storage devices, should be device independent, dealing with storage space in terms of logical pages rather than physical units. It should be possible to modify the storage schema periodically to improve database performance, without affecting the conceptual schema. The details of physical storage organisation, at various levels of abstraction, are discussed in Chapters 6 and 7.

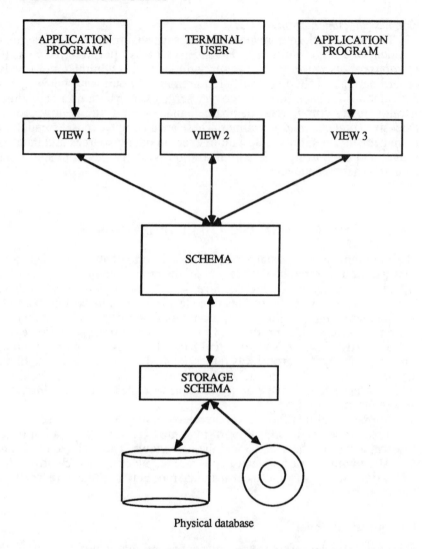

Figure 1.1   Architecture of a database system

The conceptual schema level

The conceptual schema level is the global level, i.e. the logical description of the entire database. It is the overall logical view of the data and their interrelationships as seen by the database modellers, by the systems analysts and programmers who are concerned with implementation, and by terminal users and application programs which require access to the entire database. The conceptual schema also contains the logical description of the *usage constraints* which are designed to preserve the integrity and privacy of the data against invalid modification or unauthorised access. The principal techniques of conceptual schema design are covered in Chapter 2, but aspects of this important and complex subject dominate many other chapters as well.

The user view

The user view level (sometimes called the *subschema* level in network and hierarchical systems) is concerned with individual user views of the database. Views are provided to satisfy the needs of applications which require access to only a subset of the data. As described earlier, a view may present to the user or application program, an aspect of the data model which is very different from that in the schema, and which has been tailored specifically to the application.

1.4   DATABASE SOFTWARE

Database software may be divided into three distinct categories:

1. Languages (or notations) to create, use and maintain the database.
2. Utilities to provide support facilities such as report generation, graphical output, and statistical operations.
3. Operational routines for run-time management, including routines for back-up and recovery, and for concurrency control.

We shall study operational routines for recovery and concurrency control in Chapter 8, but for the most part we shall concern ourselves in this book with database languages. In the commercial environment, database languages have traditionally been divided into several different categories, namely data description languages, data manipulation languages and query languages. These may be described as follows.

The schema data description language (DDL)

The schema DDL is a high level notation for describing the record types and relationships existing in the database in terms of an underlying data model. Commercial DBMSs typically provide their own unique schema DDL. With network and hierarchical systems the schema DDL may be quite complex and resemble a programming language (typically COBOL) in style and form. For relational systems the schema DDL is usually quite simple (reflecting the simpler structures of the relational model), and may even be interactive.

Subschema data description languages

Subschema DDLs are notations for describing a view of the database, often in a manner compatible with a standard programming language. Most network and hierarchical DBMSs support several subschema DDLs, interfacing typically to popular languages such as COBOL, FORTRAN, PL/I and

Pascal. Relational DBMSs typically provide a *view definition facility* which permits the description of logical relational views derived from the permanent structures present in the schema. Such views may then be accessed and manipulated using the same techniques as are used for the complete database.

The data manipulation language (DML)

The DML is a language used by the applications programmer or 'knowledgeable' terminal user to communicate with the database. It provides facilities for insertion, deletion, modification and retrieval of data. Commercial DBMSs usually provide data manipulation languages of various types, both procedural and non-procedural, for end-users as well as for system programmers. Thus a DML may take one of several possible forms:

1. An interactive command language.
2. A library of pre-defined procedures which may be called by application programs written in standard programming languages. This approach to data manipulation is valuable when complex computation is to be performed on the data.
3. A procedural programming language, unique to the particular DBMS, but which may be based on a standard programming language with added facilities for data manipulation within a database environment.

The data manipulation language SQL (Chamberlin et al., 1976), is rapidly emerging as an industry-wide standard interface to commercial relational systems. It is often provided both as a stand-alone command language as well as embedded in a variety of programming languages. The principal features of SQL are described in Chapter 4.

Some relational database management systems do not make any distinction between data description languages and data manipulation languages. Rather, the approach that they adopt is to combine data description, view definition, and data manipulation within the framework of a well-structured programming language. This approach is consistent, not only with the principles of software engineering, as outlined later in this chapter, but also with recent developments in database technology. For example, there have been a number of attempts in recent years, to integrate the relational model of data with languages such as Pascal, Modula-2 and ADA. Some of these languages are described in Chapter 5.

Query languages

A query language is a very high level, non-procedural language (often 'English-like') provided by most DBMSs to facilitate retrieval or simple updates when communicating with the database from a terminal. The user is not required to specify the detailed logical procedures, as is the case with a DML, but only a 'structured' statement of the information required or the action to be carried out. The query language processor must then determine the correct access paths required to resolve a query. Query languages range in power and sophistication from semi-procedural interactive programming languages to very high level 'natural' languages. While being extremely convenient for naive end-users, most query languages lack the power of conventional programming languages to perform complex computation or operating system functions.

1.5 THE DATABASE LIFE CYCLE

Any large software project may be divided up into several *project phases* (see for example the book by Pomberger, 1984). The five phases of the database life cycle are: *requirements analysis, data modelling, implementation, testing* and *maintenance*. These are examined in detail below. However database development is an *iterative* process. Often the data modelling phase will highlight ambiguities or inconsistencies in the requirements analysis, while the implementation and test phases may indicate that errors were made in constructing the data model. A common scenario is for the user to place additional demands on the system following the implementation and testing phases. If the original design and implementation is poorly structured this iterative process can easily lead to a system which is of poor quality and which is difficult to maintain.

1.5.1 Requirements analysis

The objective of the requirements analysis phase is to describe precisely the information content of the proposed database system and to determine the transaction demands that will be placed on the system. This analysis should lead to the production of a *requirements specification*, which is a detailed and precise description of the database system, its functions and its user interfaces. This requirements specification must be accepted by both users and database designer as complete and consistent and must therefore be clearly understood by everyone involved. For this reason, natural languages tend to be widely used for drafting requirements specifications. However, the imprecision and ambiguity of such languages tend to make it very difficult to test specifications for completeness and consistency. The discipline of software engineering has attempted to provide some methodical aids for constructing specifications, ranging from elementary aids such as flowcharts and decision tables to more elaborate techniques such as *SADT* (Structured Analysis and Design Technique) as described by Schoman and Ross (1977). However most of these special techniques are rather inflexible and not well-suited to database design. Thus requirements specification remains, like data modelling and programming, a creative task for which a precise and comprehensive methodology has not yet been developed. We shall continue our discussion therefore with a (somewhat informal) description of the requirements analysis phase.

The first step in the requirements analysis phase is to identify the data objects present in the real-world situation to be modelled, the properties of those objects, and the associations among them. Functionally different applications (user views) must be identified, not only so that such views may be incorporated in the overall system design, but also to identify access rights for the purposes of security and privacy. Thus the database designer must discuss the requirements in depth with every possible class of user and study the manner in which data is currently processed. In the existing environment, data may be processed manually or possibly in a computerised system using files and application programs. In the former case the data processing needs may not be well defined, and decisions must be made as to what can and should be automated. Where a file-based computerised system exists, the various application programs may be rather loosely related. Some may be grossly inefficient, while others may be redundant or of historical interest only.

The objectives of the database designer at the requirements analysis stage are:

1. To obtain a clear and concise description of the infrastructure of the enterprise to be modelled.
2. To derive information about the nature and volume of data to be stored and processed. In particular, the properties (or attributes) of the data objects must be ascertained together with their domains, ordering requirements, sort criteria, units of measurement, etc. The frequency with which the data objects are accessed or updated and the expected growth in the volume of the data are also important factors which may influence the implementation phase, as are the requirements for data protection.
3. To compile information on the nature and volume of the transactions (functions) occurring in the enterprise and the relationships between the various transactions. Important factors which must be determined include the exact purpose of the transaction, the frequency with which it is performed, the data requirements of the transaction, and the data and information which it produces. It is also important to ascertain the nature of any interactions which may take place between the various transactions. In particular, information is required on the data flow between transactions and the sequence in which they must be performed.

1.5.2   Data modelling

The quality of a database system is significantly influenced by the quality of the data model, and thus data modelling occupies an important position in the database life cycle. For that reason, a large portion of this book is devoted to the subject. The purpose of data modelling is to develop a global design for the database with the ultimate objective of achieving an efficient implementation which satisfies the requirements. As with any design process, data modelling requires a certain amount of ingenuity and creativity, but meaningful and effective guidelines can still be laid down.

In Chapter 2 we present a detailed methodology for relational database design which uses the *entity-relationship model* (Chen, 1976) as a first step in the design process. This model has been very successful as a tool for communication between the designer and the end-users during the requirements analysis and design phases because of its ease of understanding and clarity of representation. One of the main reasons for its effectiveness is that it is a *top-down* approach which makes use of the *principle of abstraction*. (These factors will be discussed in greater detail later in the chapter.) Our database design methodology benefits from the simplicity of the entity-relationship model coupled with the structure and mathematical formalism of the relational data model.

1.5.3   Implementation

By implementation we mean the transformation of our design into a database system which operates on a particular machine, usually under the control of a database management system. The design of the system should ideally be independent of any particular DBMS, but not all such systems are equally well suited to the task of transforming the design into an efficient and easily-maintainable implementation.

In order to provide for the phases of the database life cycle which follow implementation (testing and maintenance), a good implementation should be able to reflect good design decisions. In particular, the level of abstraction employed in the design should also be realised in the implementation. The DBMS used for implementation should provide high-level structures for the representation of complex data objects and their interrelationships. It should also provide a range of software tools (languages and utilities) which enable users to interact with the database at a level suited to their requirements, but in a manner which preserves the consistency and correctness of the database.

The criteria for choosing a DBMS will emerge as we progress in this book through the various subject areas of database technology and a summary of these criteria are presented in Chapter 9.

1.5.4   Testing

The quality of a database system is measured first by its correctness and reliability, and second by the degree to which it satisfies the demands of the initial requirements analysis. The purpose of the testing phase therefore is twofold:

1. To discover any errors that may have arisen during the modelling and implementation phases.
2. To ascertain, in conjunction with the user community, whether the system satisfies the information demands of users and the requirements of application programs.

By error we mean any deviation from the behaviour stipulated by the requirements analysis. Such errors may be caused by a faulty or inadequate requirements analysis, incorrect data modelling, or programming errors made during the implementation phase. Testing therefore is an activity which relates to the entire project and rather than be treated as an isolated phase, it should be distributed over all phases of the database life cycle, including the maintenance phase. For a complex database with a large number of different user groups, it may be necessary to develop *prototype* database systems in a number of iterations. At each stage of the iteration these prototypes can be discussed with the users to ensure that the needs of all applications are satisfied.

At the current level of sophistication in software engineering there is no universal recipe for testing software systems. The scope and number of tests will vary considerably from system to system. The effort put into this phase will depend on the complexity of the enterprise and the level of expertise available for the data modelling and implementation phases.

Note that it is also important to test the *robustness* of the system against incorrect user interaction and against errors in application programs. Protecting the database against such errors is an important aspect of database technology and, in Chapters 5 and 8, we shall consider various aspects of this problem in detail.

1.5.5   Maintenance

As described above it is almost impossible to devise an exhaustive test phase for a large database system, and in practice many errors and inadequacies in the system first come to light during actual use. These must be monitored and eliminated within the framework of the maintenance phase of the database life cycle. An exact requirements analysis is also very difficult in many cases and so new user demands are often added during the operation of a database system which require system modifications.

The maintenance phase involves:

1. The correction of errors which arise during operation.
2. The implementation of system modifications which arise due to new user requests or changes in the original user requirements.
3. The implementation of performance enhancements and improvements to user interfaces.

As described in Section 1.2, the responsibility for maintaining a multi-user database system must reside centrally with the database administrator through whom all user requests and complaints are channelled. Database usage and performance must be constantly monitored with the assistance of DBMS utilities (such as a data dictionary) which provide statistics on important factors such as access times, storage utilisation and transaction throughput. Corrections, modifications and enhancements to the system, whether at the logical or physical levels, must be carried out with the minimum of disruption to the user community.

Maintenance can be a very expensive part of any database project and it is therefore prudent to pay particular attention to the *maintainability* of the system. Designing and implementing a database system which is easily maintained means ensuring a good *modular* structure with good supporting documentation. The techniques presented in this book for database design and development are designed to improve the maintainability of database systems.

1.6   SOFTWARE ENGINEERING AND DATABASES

The term 'software engineering' implies the application of scientific knowledge and discipline to the construction of computer software systems. In practice, this involves the production of a specification, a problem solution, and a program design prior to the inception of actual coding. Ideally therefore, software development should be like mathematics or any other branch of science or engineering, where one adopts a methodical approach to solving a problem and, most importantly, one is required to show that the solution is correct, i.e. that it solves the given problem. The following sections outline some of the most important issues in software engineering and show how they relate to the subject of database technology.

1.6.1   Data abstraction

One of the most important techniques for dealing with complexity in software systems is the *principle of abstraction*. Abstraction is used to construct solutions to problems without having to take account of the intricate details of the various component subproblems. The program design phase of any software project involves abstraction as a means for developing representations of the complex data objects and concepts inherent in the application. Abstraction allows the programmer to apply the principles of *stepwise refinement* by which at each stage of the program design unnecessary details associated with representation or implementation may be hidden from the surrounding program. This ability to decompose a large problem into a number of smaller ones, and to specify unambiguously the interactions among the components, is a vital tool in the construction of large software systems.

Database systems are typically large software systems, which are distinguished by the fact that they involve the processing of data with three important characteristics:

1.   There is a large amount of data, which must be held in external storage.
2.   The data objects have complex interrelationships.
3.   The data must be shared among many different users.

Very few of the popular programming languages provide adequate constructs for the efficient processing of large volumes of interrelated data. The simple sequential and random file structures found in most languages offer only minimal facilities in this area. However many modern languages do offer very powerful algorithmic constructs for the representation of complex data objects. The ability to define such abstract objects, together with

appropriate operations, is invaluable for database applications.
Database management systems on the other hand, in general provide
highly efficient facilities for organising and accessing data on external storage devices, but rather primitive constructs for logical data structuring. For
example, most commercial database management systems offer only very
simple data types such as integer, character, string, etc., and the database
designer and applications programmer is limited to these types even when
communicating with the database from within a sophisticated programming
language.

Special purpose *database programming languages*, which are discussed
in Chapter 5, have tried to bridge the gap between the programming language and DBMS approaches to the management of data. These languages
typically provide database constructs (usually the *relation* data type) within
the framework of a modern well-structured language. Unfortunately
implementations of these languages have, for the most part, been confined
to specific machines and operating systems and are not widely available.

However, any language which supports abstraction allows the programmer to build more sophisticated file management structures which may
provide a range of high-level operations for the manipulation of external
data, while at the same time absolving the user of the mundane responsibility for reading from and writing to actual physical storage devices. In addition, abstraction facilities allow one to create complex data objects within a
program which model closely those used in the problem solution. Thus the
process of transforming the problem solution into a program is greatly
eased.

1.6.2   Concurrency

When several application programs or terminal users are interacting with a
shared database simultaneously, their operations on the database must be
carefully controlled. Specifically, the effect of a database procedure (often
called a *transaction*) must be that which would be obtained if no other
transaction were executing concurrently. The effect of executing several
transactions concurrently, therefore, must be the same as if they had been
executed serially in some order. By 'effect' here, we mean the final state of
the database together with any results produced by the transactions.

To prevent any transaction from reading or updating data that are being
updated by another transaction we could provide a *locking* mechanism
which guarantees exclusive access to an item of data while a lock is in
force. Although most operating systems provide for file locking, few support locks on pages or records. Such smaller locks are essential in many
database environments and must therefore be provided by the database
management system. A programming language which offers high-level
facilities for concurrency control gives the database programmer great
flexibility in scheduling transactions while preserving the integrity of the
database.

Concurrency control in database management systems, including alternatives to locking, is discussed in detail in Chapter 8. This discussion also

includes a description of some of the abstractions for concurrency found in high-level programming languages and their applicability to concurrency control in database systems.

1.6.3 Program correctness

Program correctness has been a strong motivation for much of the work in software engineering and programming language design. Ideally correctness should be determined by a formal mathematical proof that a program conforms to its specification. However the current widespread practice of using natural language for specifications and machine-oriented languages for implementation is not conducive to presenting mathematical proofs of programs, and this obligation is normally discharged by testing, i.e. by showing that the solution solves *some* instances of the problem.

The construction of formal proofs of correctness of programs is beyond the scope of this text and is adequately covered by other authors (Brady, 1977; McGetterick, 1982). However, we shall in this book be intimately concerned with those aspects of programming language design and programming style which influence the ease of program verification. It has long been recognised that both the characteristics of a given programming language and the practices used to write programs in the language have a significant influence on program correctness. Support in a language for concepts such as data abstraction and strong type-checking greatly ease program testing and verification. Also highly desirable is the ability to break a large program down into modules which may be separately compiled, and tested in isolation.

For a database system, correctness implies not only that it conforms to its specification, but also that the values and relationships maintained in the system obey the consistency constraints inherent in the data model, and *at all times* are an appropriate representation of the state of the enterprise. The preservation of the consistency and integrity of the data in a large multi-user database environment is a major problem. A relatively minor update to the database may require multiple changes to be propagated throughout the storage structures which represent the database at the physical level. An update which is only partially carried out may result in the database being inconsistent with the underlying data model, and incorrect with respect to its representation of the enterprise. The application of the techniques of software engineering to the preservation of consistency and correctness in database systems will be discussed in detail in Chapter 5 and also in Chapter 8.

1.7 THE PROGRAMMING LANGUAGE MODULA-2

The developments in software engineering, as described above, have led to the emergence of a new class of programming languages over the past decade, which provide sophisticated facilities for data abstraction, modularity and concurrency. Two of the most important of these languages are *Ada* (Ichbiah et al., 1979) and *Modula-2* (Wirth, 1977 and 1982). A comparison of these languages highlights striking similarities, particularly in the constructs they provide for modular programming and data abstraction. Concurrency is also provided by both languages, though at a rather lower level in Modula-2. Thus the two languages are very comparable, if one is primarily concerned with the extent to which the principles of modern software engineering may be applied (Pomberger, 1984).

A great advantage of Modula-2 over Ada is that it is a *small* language. This small size has led to the development of efficient Modula-2 compilers for a wide variety of computers ranging from desk-top microcomputers to mainframes. Also, in addition to its support for modularisation and data abstraction, the language contains a range of low-level programming features which make it suitable for systems programming as well as applications programming. As described in Section 1.3, implementing database systems requires a multilevel approach, ranging from the organisation of physical storage at the low level to providing high-level user views. Modula-2 supports such a multilayered approach to software development by providing separate compilation of modules and strong type and interface checking. These facilities offer great advantages for maintaining integrity and security in database systems.

Thus Modula-2 is a language which is suitable both for the implementation of database management systems, and for the development of application programs. It is also an ideal language for interacting with an existing DBMS, where a suitable module interface has been provided.

2

Relational Data Modelling

R.T.C. LIBRARY, LETTERKENNY

2.1 INTRODUCTION

Logical database design is a two-stage process, involving:

1. The design of a conceptual schema which is an abstraction of the real-world situation under consideration.
2. The design of a logical data structure, representing this schema, which may be mapped onto an actual implementation.

As described in Chapter 1, the first step is concerned with analysing the information requirements of the application, preparing an informal requirements specification, and from this constructing a high-level *data model*. A data model may be defined as a pattern according to which data are logically organised. It consists of named logical units of data and expresses the relationships among the data as determined by some interpretation of the real world. Data modelling therefore is concerned with abstracting the objects and concepts involved in some real-world situation.

In this chapter we discuss a methodology for database design, concentrating initially on conceptual schema design and then on relational data modelling. Network and hierarchical modelling are described in the following chapter. We introduce an informal model called the *entity-relationship model* (Chen, 1976) which provides us with a natural means for representing entities and their interrelationships. Due to its expressiveness and ease of use, this model has attracted considerable attention during the last decade in both industry and the research community. Modified and extended by others (see for example the review paper of Teorey et al., 1986), it still remains the premier model for conceptual schema design. One of the main reasons for this popularity is that it provides a top-down approach to database design, employing the concepts of abstraction. In this respect it is compatible with the modern principles of software engineering. We shall use the entity-relationship

17

model in our first-level design strategy and study the translation between entity-relationship models of data and the implementable models which form the basis of modern database management systems.

2.2   ENTITY-RELATIONSHIP MODELLING

In the entity-relationship model information is represented by means of three primitive concepts:

1. *Entities*, which represent the objects being modelled.
2. *Attributes*, which represent the properties of those objects.
3. *Relationships*, which represent the associations among entities.

Each of these concepts are described in detail in the following sections.

2.2.1   Entities and attributes

A dictionary definition of an entity is: 'Being, existence, as opposed to non-existence; the existence as distinct from the qualities or relations of anything', (Shorter Oxford English Dictionary). For database applications an entity therefore is a thing about which descriptive information is to be stored, which is capable of independent existence and can be uniquely identified. The thing may be an *object* such as a house, a student or a car; or an *event* or activity such as a football match, a holiday or the servicing of a car.

An entity is meaningfully described by its attributes. For example, a house might be described by the attributes address, style, and colour; a car might be described by the attributes registration number, make, model and year of registration; a football match might be described by attributes such as home team, away team, date, home team score, away team score. If an attribute has itself descriptive information then it should be classified as an entity. For example, if we wish to record additional information on the model of a car (other than the name of the model) then we should introduce the entity type MODEL which will have a relationship with the entity type CAR.

The name of an entity together with its attributes define an *entity type* of which there may be many *instances*. The distinction between entity types and instances is directly analogous to that between data types and their instances in programming languages. An instance of an entity type is an occurrence of that type for which actual values of the attributes have been specified. For example the attribute values (18 Main Street, semi-detached, blue) define an instance of the entity type HOUSE - a semi-detached house, painted blue on 18 Main Street. The attribute values (Everton, Liverpool, 18/11/87, 2, 1) define an instance of the entity type FOOTBALL_MATCH - a match between the teams Everton and Liverpool on the 18 November 1987 in which Everton was the home team and won the match by two goals to one.

An attribute or set of attributes whose values uniquely identify each instance of an entity type is called a *candidate key* for that entity type. For example, the attribute ADDRESS is a key for the entity type HOUSE; REGISTRATION# is a key for the entity type CAR. Since we defined an entity as a thing which is capable of unique existence, a key must always exist. However, an entity type may have more than one candidate key. For example, a student may be identified by a unique identification number (student number), or by the combined values of his or her name and address. It is useful to choose a *primary key* from among the candidates. The primary key will play an important role when we come to look at the mapping of entity-relationship models onto implementations. When possible we should try to avoid composite primary keys for entities, i.e. keys involving several attributes.

2.2.2   Relationships

A relationship is a named association between two or more entity types. For example, the relationship PLAYS-FOR between the entity types PLAYER and TEAM; the relationship CITIZEN-OF between the entity types PERSON and COUNTRY.

The *functionality* of a relationship may be one-to-one (1:1), one-to-many (1:N) or many-to-many (N:M). As an example, consider a possible college database which might contain the following relationships:

1:1   The relationship HEAD-OF between the entity types LECTURER and DEPARTMENT is 1:1. This means that a department has *at most one* head and that a lecturer is head of *at most one* department.

1:N   The relationship TEACHES between the entity types LECTURER and COURSE is 1:N. This assumes that a lecturer may teach *any number* of different courses but a given course is taught by *at most one* lecturer.

N:M   The relationship ENROLS between the entity types STUDENT and COURSE is N:M. Thus a student may enrol for *many* different courses and each course may have *many* students enrolled.

Some relationships can have properties which may be represented by attributes. For example the relationship ENROLS between the STUDENT and COURSE entity types could have attributes such as DATE (date of enrolment), PRACTICAL-MARKS and EXAM-MARKS. These attributes cannot be associated solely with the entity type STUDENT or with the entity type COURSE. Rather they are properties of each student-course pair connected via the relationship ENROLS. Thus if we state that student John Smith enrolled on 15 October 1987 and achieved practical marks of 70% and exam marks of 65%, we must identify which course these values relate to in order for the statement to have full meaning. A student will in general have a different set of values of these attributes for each course on which he/she is enrolled. Thus such properties are best considered as attributes of the relationship.

R.T.C. LIBRARY, LETTERKENNY
COS · 74

4 — 5 539.

Membership class

If the semantics of a relationship are such that every instance of an entity type must participate in the relationship, then the membership class of the entity type is said to be *mandatory* in that relationship. Otherwise, the membership class is *optional*.

For example, suppose that in our college database we have an entity type EXAMINATION which has an N:1 relationship HOLDS with the entity type COURSE. That is, each course may hold many examinations but a given examination relates to exactly one course. The membership class of EXAMINATION in the relationship HOLDS is mandatory, since every examination must be related to a course. However the membership class of COURSE in the relationship is optional, since a course may not have any examinations.

The decision as to whether the membership class of an entity type in some relationship is mandatory or optional, may sometimes be at the discretion of the data modeller. For example, consider once again the 1:N relationship TEACHES between the entity types LECTURER and COURSE. If we wish to enforce the rule that every course *must* have a lecturer, then the membership class of COURSE in the relationship TEACHES is said to be mandatory. However, if we wish to allow a situation in which a course may exist without a lecturer being assigned to teach it, then the membership class of COURSE in the relationship TEACHES is said to be optional.

As we shall see later in this chapter, the membership classes of the entity types in a relationship may influence the way in which the relationship is implemented. If an entity type is a mandatory member of some relationship then the implementation should enforce the integrity constraint that no instance of that entity type which does not participate in the relationship may exist in the database.

2.2.3   Schematic entity-relationship models

Schematic entity-relationship models use diagrams to depict the natural structure of the data. In these diagrams rectangles represent entity types and diamonds represent relationships. Relationships are linked to their constituent entity types by arcs, and the degree of the relationship is indicated on the arc.

The complete ER model also includes a list of attributes for each entity type and relationship. These are sometimes included on the diagram, but in this text in the interests of clarity the attributes will be listed separately.

Example. An ER model for a small college database comprising the entity types DEPARTMENT, COURSE, STUDENT and LECTURER might be represented schematically as shown in Figure 2.1. Each department has many lecturers, one of whom is the head of department. A lecturer belongs to only one department. Each department offers many different courses, each of which is taught by a single lecturer. A student may enrol for many courses offered by different departments.

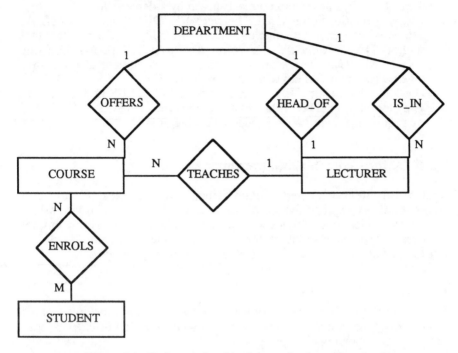

Figure 2.1   Entity-relationship diagram for the college database

The entity types (with primary key attributes underlined) are:

1. Entity type DEPARTMENT with attributes DNAME (a unique departmental name), LOCATION, FACULTY, . . .
2. Entity type COURSE with attributes C# (a course number which is unique within the college), TITLE, TERM (the term in which the course is given), . . .
3. Entity type STUDENT with attributes S# (a unique student number), SNAME, ADDRESS, SEX, . . .
4. Entity type LECTURER with attributes LNAME (the name of a lecturer is assumed to be unique within the college), ROOM#, . . .

The relationships are:

1. The 1:1 relationship HEAD_OF between LECTURER and DEPARTMENT. The membership class of this relationship is optional for LECTURER (i.e. a lecturer may or may not be head of a department), but mandatory for DEPARTMENT (if we wish to insist that every department must have a head).
2. The N:1 relationship IS_IN between LECTURER and DEPARTMENT. The membership class of this relationship is mandatory for LECTURER. That is, a lecturer must belong to a department.
3. The 1:N relationship OFFERS between entity types DEPARTMENT

and COURSE. The membership class of this relationship is mandatory for COURSE, since every course is given by a department.
4. The M:N relationship ENROLS between STUDENT and COURSE. As described earlier in this chapter, this relationship may have attributes such as DATE (the date of enrolment), PRACTICAL-MARKS and EXAM-MARKS, which are associated with a student *and* a course together as a pair and not with either individually.
5. The 1:N relationship TEACHES between LECTURER and COURSE. The membership class of this relationship is mandatory for COURSE if we require that every course must have a lecturer.

2.2.4 More complex relationships

Real-world situations often contain rather more complex relationships among entity types than the simple binary 1:1, 1:N or N:M relationships considered so far. For example we may have relationships among entities of the same type or relationships involving more than two entity types. The most important of these are described in the following sections.

Involuted relationships

Involuted relationships are relationships among different instances of the same entity type. Such relationships may also be 1:1, 1:N or N:M as illustrated by the following examples:

Example 1: A 1:1 involuted relationship
An instance of the entity type PERSON may be related to another member through the relationship MARRY. This relationship, shown in Figure 2.2, is a 1:1 involuted relationship if we assume that a person may be married to at most one other, i.e. past marriages are ignored and polygamy is forbidden!

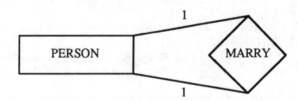

Figure 2.2 A 1:1 involuted relationship

The membership class of PERSON in this relationship is clearly optional. That is, a person may or may not be married.

Example 2: A 1:N involuted relationship
An instance of the entity type EMPLOYEE may supervise other instances. If we assume that a given employee may have at most one supervisor then we have a 1:N involuted relationship SUPERVISES, as shown in Figure

2.3. The arrow in this diagram is necessary to indicate the direction of the relationship, namely that one employee supervises many others and not that many employees supervise one other.

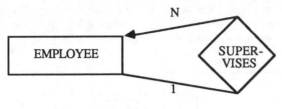

Figure 2.3

The membership class of the entity type EMPLOYEE in this relationship could be optional or mandatory depending on the enterprise being modelled. That is, if every employee has a supervisor then the membership class is mandatory. Otherwise it is optional.

Example 3: An N:M involuted relationship
An instance of the entity type PART might be composed of other parts, while a given part may be a component of many other parts. This situation could be represented by an N:M involuted relationship COMPRISES as shown in Figure 2.4.

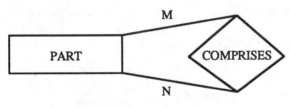

Figure 2.4

Subtypes

A particular weakness of the original entity-relationship model as proposed by Chen was the absence of the concept of a *subtype* and *generalisations* of such subtypes. An entity type E_1 is a subtype of an entity type E_2 if every instance of E_1 is also an instance of E_2. An entity type E is a generalisation of the entity types $E_1, E_2 \ldots E_n$, if each occurrence of E is also an occurrence of one and only one of the entities $E_1, E_2 \ldots E_n$. Smith and Smith (1977) introduced the term generalisation in their semantic hierarchy model and thereby provided a formal basis for subtypes within an abstract data model. These ideas have been extended by others specifically with regard to the entity-relationship model (e.g. Scheuermann et al., 1980; Navathe and Cheng, 1983; Sakai, 1983).

As an example of subtypes, consider that in the college database it may be more appropriate to represent heads of departments as *professors*, a special category of lecturer. Also, it should be clear that the entity types LECTURER and STUDENT share some properties by virtue of the fact that they may both be considered as different categories of an entity type PERSON. In fact, the entity types LECTURER and STUDENT are subtypes of the entity type PERSON, while the entity type PROFESSOR is a subtype of the entity type LECTURER. Also, the entity type PERSON is a generalisation of the entity types STUDENT and LECTURER if every instance of PERSON in the database is either an instance of STUDENT or an instance of LECTURER.

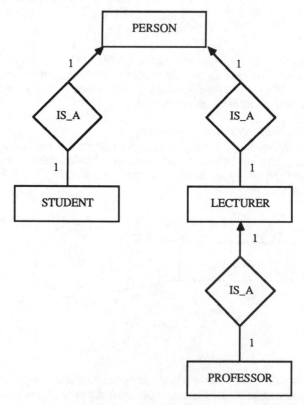

Figure 2.5   A type hierarchy

The *type hierarchy* relating the entity types PERSON, LECTURER, STUDENT and PROFESSOR is illustrated in Figure 2.5. The relationship between a subtype and its parent type is represented by a special kind of 1:1 relationship *IS_A*. Subtypes share some, but not necessarily all, of the attributes and relationships of the parent type. Also, a subtype may have additional attributes and relationships which are specific to the subtype. Thus for example, in the college database we may wish to enforce the rule that only instances of the subtype PROFESSOR may participate in the relationship HEAD-OF. In this case the relationship would be defined between the entity types PROFESSOR and DEPARTMENT. A professor shares all the attributes of a lecturer but may have additional attributes such as CHAIR-TITLE which is relevant only to professors.

It is advantageous to recognise subtypes when they arise since their inclusion adds clarity and precision to the schema and can improve the efficiency of any subsequent implementation. Subtypes arise particularly if there are many different user views in the enterprise being modelled, and it is important that the data modeller recognise generalisations and type hierarchies when constructing the global data model.

Ternary relationships

Relationships may involve more than two entity types. As an example, consider the database illustrated in Figure 2.6, which is to hold information on companies, the products that they manufacture, and the countries to which they export these products. The set of countries to which a product is exported varies from product to product and also from company to company. The relationship SELLS is *ternary*, i.e. it involves three entity types.

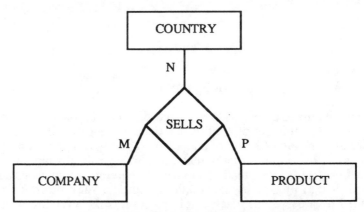

Figure 2.6 A ternary relationship

The functionality of the ternary relationship SELLS is shown in Figure 2.6 to be 'many-to-many-to-many' (N:M:P). This reflects the following facts about the relationship:

For a given (company, product) pair there are in general many countries to which that product is sold. For a given (country, product) pair there may be several companies exporting that product to that country. For a given (company, country) pair there may be many products exported by that company to that country.

The functionality of a ternary relationship could also be 'one-to-many-to-many', 'one-to-one-to-many' or even 'one-to-one-to-one', and the semantics of the relationship must be carefully examined to determine its functionality. We shall return to this problem later in the chapter when we consider the representation of ternary relationships in the relational model.

Ternary relationships must be defined carefully and should be introduced only when the relationship cannot be represented by several binary relationships among the participating entity types. For example, if a company manufactures many products and exports *all* of these products to a number of different countries, then the two independent binary relationships shown in Figure 2.7 should be defined instead of the ternary relationship. We shall return to this point later in the chapter when we discuss a concept known as *multivalued dependency*.

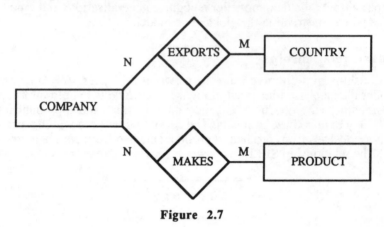

Figure 2.7

2.2.5   Mapping to an implementation

A great advantage of ER models is that they can be understood by non-specialists. The number of entities in a database is generally considerably smaller than the total number of data items. Thus by using the concept of an entity as an abstraction for those real-world objects about which we wish to collect information, we greatly simplify the requirements analysis and conceptual design phases. A schematic ER model may be modified and extended by a user until it accurately represents the structure of the data being modelled. In this regard ER models are independent of any particular database management system. These systems generally impose restrictions on the way in which the data may be represented, whereas the ER model, being at a higher level, can more accurately reflect the natural structure of the data. Also, unlike many implementations, ER models are flexible and extendible, and so adapt easily to new developments.

The translation of an ER model into an implementation is reasonably straightforward. Every database management system provides some mechanism for representing entities and the connections between them (relationships), but of course compromises have to be made depending on the facilities available. Network database management systems, for example, often impose restrictions on the types of relationship that can be directly represented. With such systems it may be necessary to decompose N:M relationships and involuted relationships into more primitive structures to facilitate implementation.

The relational model on the other hand can, despite its relative simplicity, capture much of the semantic information of ER models and represent that information by a collection of two-dimensional tables. These tables, or *relations*, may be thought of as an abstraction of a restricted form of the well known data-processing concept of a file. Thus the relational model is a convenient model to choose for the implementation of database systems via high-level modular programming languages, such as Modula-2, which provide built-in facilities for constructing sophisticated file abstractions.

2.3   THE RELATIONAL DATA MODEL

The relational data model was conceived by Codd (1970, 1972a, 1972b). The model has a sound theoretical foundation, based on the mathematical theory of relations and the first-order logic, but presents the user with a simple view of the data in the form of two-dimensional tables. The strong theoretical foundation of the model permits the application of systematic methods, based on high-level abstractions, to the design and manipulation of relational databases. This greatly reduces the complexities faced by the data modeller and by the end-user.

We shall begin this section by examining the formal definition of a relation, and we shall study the concepts of attribute and key as applied to relations. We shall then present a methodology for translating ER models into relational form.

Definitions

A mathematical definition of a relation may be stated as follows:

Given a collection of sets $D_1, D_2, \ldots, D_n$ (not necessarily distinct), R is a *relation* on those n sets if it is a set of ordered n-tuples $(d_1, d_2, \ldots, d_n)$ such that d_1 belongs to D_1, d_2 to D_2, $\ldots$, d_n to D_n. The sets D_i are the called the *domains* of R. The value of n is called the *degree* of R.

It is convenient to represent a relation as a table. The columns of the tabular relation represent *attributes*. Each attribute A has a distinct name, and is always referenced by that name, never by its position. Attribute names have no underlying ordering, and so if the columns of a tabular relation are permuted, the attribute values in each row must be permuted accordingly.

Each attribute A has an associated domain which consists of all the allowable values of A. The relational notion of a domain is closely related to the concept of a *data type* in programming languages and we shall discuss the significance of domains in greater depth in Chapter 5. Attribute values in a relation must be single, non-decomposable data items. That is, an attribute value may not represent a group of data items which are distinguishable by the underlying database management system.

Each row (often called a *tuple*) of a tabular relation is distinct. That is, no two tuples may agree on all their attribute values. Also, the ordering of tuples is immaterial. These properies follow from the fact that a relation, as defined above, is a *set* of tuples.The *cardinality* of a relation is the number of tuples which it contains at any instant in time.

As an example, consider the relation CAR defined by the following scheme (a *relation scheme* is simply the name of the relation followed by its attribute names in parentheses).

CAR (REG#, MAKE, MODEL, YEAR)

In tabular format an instance of this relation might appear as shown in Figure 2.8.

REG#	MAKE	MODEL	YEAR
ZID654	Ford	Fiesta	1987
BXI930	VW	Golf	1986
COI453	Nissan	Sunny	1987
ZXI675	Ford	Escort	1985
RST786	Fiat	Uno	1983
TXI521	Ford	Orion	1985
HCY675	VW	Jetta	1986

Figure 2.8   An instance of the relation CAR in tabular format

The degree of this relation is 4, since it has 4 attributes, and the cardinality of this instance is 7, since there are 7 tuples.

As the reader may have already appreciated, a tuple in a relation corresponds closely to the familiar data processing concept of a record, while attributes correspond with fields. As with attributes, each field has a name and denotes the smallest item of data which has meaning in the real world. Also, each field has a specific data type. A record, like a tuple, has a specific format since its fields have specific data types.

Keys

A key K of a relation R is a subset of the attributes of R which have the following time-independent properties:

1. *Unique identification*: The value of K uniquely identifies each tuple in R.
2. *Non-redundancy*: No attribute in K can be discarded without destroying property 1.

Since each tuple in a relation is distinct, a key always exists. That is, a key consisting of *all* the attributes of R will always have property 1. It then remains to find a subset with property 2. A relation may have more than one candidate key. That is, it may have more than one set of attributes which satisfy properties 1 and 2 above. In this case we must choose one as the *primary key*. An attribute which participates in the primary key is called a *prime attribute*. The value of a prime attribute in any tuple may not be null. In specifying relation schemes we shall underline the prime attributes.

2.3.1 Transforming an ER model into a relational schema

The following is a set of guidelines for converting an ER model into a relational schema. They are not hard and fast rules and the database designer must use them in conjunction with common sense and an intimate knowledge of the application. However, used wisely, they should lead to a good first approximation to the optimal relational schema.

Transformation of entity types

Each entity type is represented by a relation scheme in which the attributes of the entity type become attributes of the relation. For example, the entity type STUDENT defined in our description of the college database in Section 2.2 may be represented by a relation scheme of the form:

STUDENT (S#, SNAME, ADDRESS, SEX, . . .)

The primary key of the entity type will serve as the primary key of the relation provided it satisfies the properties of unique identification and non-redundancy defined above.

However, an entity relation such as that defined above may contain additional attributes arising from its participation in relationships. The representation of relationships in the relational model is described in the following sections.

Transformation of binary relationships

The techniques for transforming a relationship depend on the functionality of the relationship and on the membership classes of the participating entity types. The following guidelines are appropriate:

Mandatory membership classes
If entity type E_2 is a *mandatory* member of an N:1 relationship with entity type E_1, then the relation scheme for E_2 contains the prime attributes of E_1. For example, if we insist that every course must be offered by a department then the entity type COURSE is a mandatory member of the relationship OFFERS. The relation scheme for COURSE should therefore contain the prime attributes of DEPARTMENT, i.e.:

COURSE (C#, DNAME, TITLE, TERM, ...)

A key posted into another relation in this way is often called a *foreign key*. In this example the foreign key DNAME represents the relationship OFFERS between DEPARTMENT and COURSE.

Optional membership classes
If entity type E_2 is an *optional* member of an N:1 relationship with entity

type E_1 then the relationship is usually represented by a separate relation scheme containing the prime attributes of E_1 and E_2, together with any attributes of the relationship.

For example, consider the relationship, shown in Figure 2.9, between the entity types BORROWER and BOOK in a library database. At any given time a book may or may not be on loan (assume that only current loans are recorded in the database).

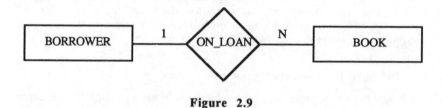

Figure 2.9

We might represent the above ER model by the relational schema:

BORROWER (B#, NAME, ADDRESS, ...)

BOOK (ISBN, B#, TITLE, ...)

where we have included in the BOOK relation the foreign key B#, to hold the identification number of the borrower who currently has a particular book on loan. However, the value of the B# attribute will be *null* in many of the tuples in the BOOK relation, i.e. for all those books which are not currently on loan. The term *null value* in this context means that a value for the attribute is unavailable due to the fact that an instance of the entity type BOOK does not participate in the relationship at present.

The semantics of null values in relations are discussed by Codd (1979) and the topic has aroused considerable discussion in the literature in recent years. In particular the presence of null values can add significant complications to the manipulation of a relational database. It should be pointed out that null values do not only arise due to the optionality of relationships as in the above example. For example, their presence may be due to the fact that an attribute value is simply *unknown* at the present time, or it may be that the value of a particular attribute is *undefined* for some instance of an entity type.

In the above example we can avoid the problem of null values by introducing a separate relation to represent the relationship ON_LOAN:

BORROWER (B#, NAME, ADDRESS, ...)

BOOK (ISBN, TITLE, ...)

ON_LOAN (ISBN, B#)

Thus only those books which are currently on loan appear in the ON_LOAN relation. A separate relation for an optional relationship is particularly advisable if the relationship has attributes. For example, we could associate attributes such as DATE-OF-LOAN and DATE-DUE with the ON_LOAN relationship and these are readily incorporated into the

ON_LOAN relation. Posting these attributes in the BOOK relation would compound the problem of null values.

Note, however, that there may be cases where the membership class of an entity type in a relationship is 'almost mandatory' i.e. a large percentage of tuples participate in the relationship. In such cases it may be better to tolerate a small number of null values rather than introduce a separate relation.

N:M binary relationships
An N:M relationship is always represented by a separate relation scheme which consists of the prime attributes of each of the participating entity types together with any attributes of the relationship. This transformation applies irrespective of the membership classes of the participating entity types. For example the relationship ENROLS between the entity types STUDENT and COURSE would be represented by the following scheme:

ENROLS (S#, C#, DATE, PRACTICAL-MARKS, EXAM-MARKS)

Example: Relational schema for the college database.
Applying the above guidelines to our entity-relationship model for the college database, we obtain the following relational schema:

DEPARTMENT (DNAME, LNAME, LOCATION, FACULTY)

COURSE (C#, DNAME, LNAME, TITLE, TERM)

STUDENT (S#, SNAME, ADDRESS, SEX)

LECTURER (LNAME, DNAME, ROOM#)

ENROLS (S#, C#, DATE, PRACTICAL-MARKS, EXAM-MARKS)

In this schema the foreign key LNAME in the DEPARTMENT relation represents the relationship HEAD_OF, indicating that the membership class of this relationship is mandatory for DEPARTMENT. The foreign keys LNAME and DNAME in the COURSE relation represent respectively the relationships TEACHES and OFFERS, the entity type COURSE being a mandatory member of each of these relationships. The foreign key DNAME in the LECTURER relation represents the relationship IS_IN between DEPARTMENT and LECTURER, of which LECTURER a mandatory member. Finally the relation ENROLS arises from the M:N relationship as described above.

Transformation of involuted relationships

The transformation of involuted relationships follows, to a large extent, the guidelines given above for binary relationships. The techniques involved are best illustrated by a number of examples.

Example 1: A 1:1 involuted relationship
A common example of a 1:1 involuted relationship is the relationship of marriage between instances of the entity type PERSON (shown in earlier

Figure 2.2). This is clearly an optional relationship since there will generally be many persons who do not participate in the relationship. Therefore we represent the relationship by a separate relation scheme as follows:

PERSON (ID#, NAME, ADDRESS, . . .)

MARRIAGE (HUSBAND-ID#, WIFE-ID#, DATE-OF-MARRIAGE)

Note that we must resolve the attribute name clash in the relation MARRIAGE by distinguishing between the ID# of the husband and of the wife. Assuming that each person has only one spouse, either HUSBAND-ID# or WIFE-ID# may serve as the primary key of the relation MARRIAGE. If we wish to store details of remarriages then the functionality of the relationship becomes N:M and both HUSBAND-ID# and WIFE-ID# form the key attributes.

Example 2: A 1:N involuted relationship
An example of an involuted 1:N relationship is that between employees and supervisors, where supervisors are also employees (shown previously in Figure 2.3). If every (or almost every) employee has a supervisor, then we have a mandatory relationship and this may be represented by posting the key of the supervisor into the relation scheme for EMPLOYEE in the following manner:

EMPLOYEE (ID#, SUPERVISOR-ID#, ENAME, . . .)

If only some employees are supervised then we should have a separate relation to represent the relationship as in the following schema:

EMPLOYEE (ID#, ENAME, . . .)

SUPERVISES (ID#, SUPERVISOR-ID#, . . .)

Example 3: An N:M involuted relationship
An example of an N:M involuted relationship is given by the situation where we have parts which form the components of other parts (shown previously in Figure 2.4). This translates to the following relational schema:

PART (P#, PNAME, DESCRIPTION, . . .)

COMPRISE (MAJOR-P#, MINOR-P#, QUANTITY)

The relational schema in this case contains a separate relation for the relationship COMPRISES which, according to our guidelines, should contain the key attributes of the participating entity types. For an involuted relationship however these key attributes come from the same entity type and we must distinguish between them. Thus MAJOR-P# and MINOR-P# both denote part numbers (P#) from the PART relation. The semantics of this relation are that the part represented by MAJOR-P# contains a fixed number (represented by the attribute QUANTITY) of the parts whose identification number in the PART relation is MINOR-P#.

Transformation of subtypes

The relational representation of a subtype simply contains the key attributes of the parent type, together with any additional attributes specific to the subtype. For example, suppose that we introduce the subtype PROFESSOR of the entity type LECTURER into our college schema. Then the relational schema will require a separate relation for PROFESSOR of the form:

PROFESSOR (LNAME, CHAIR-TITLE)

In this relation the key attribute LNAME is a foreign key from the LECTURER relation which represents the IS_A relationship between the subtype and its parent type. Through this foreign key we have access to the additional attributes of a professor which he shares with other lecturers.

In general the transformation of a type hierarchy results in a separate relation for the root entity type and for each subtype. The key of each relation is the key of the root entity relation, which also contains attributes which are common to all the subtypes. The relation for each subtype contains, together with the key, attributes which are specific to that subtype.

Thus the type hierarchy illustrated in Figure 2.5, involving the entity type PERSON with subtypes STUDENT and LECTURER, and the entity type PROFESSOR which is a subtype of LECTURER, would be represented by a relational schema of the following form:

PERSON (ID#, attributes common to all persons)

STUDENT (ID#, attributes specific to students)

LECTURER (ID#, attributes specific to lecturers)

PROFESSOR (ID#, attributes specific to professors)

where the attribute ID# is a key attribute whose value uniquely identifies one instance of the entity type PERSON. The PERSON relation will contain a tuple for every student, lecturer and professor. The LECTURER relation will have a tuple for every professor.

Transformation of ternary relationships

Every ternary relationship is transformed into a separate relation scheme containing the key attributes of the three participating entity types together with any attributes of the relationship. For example the ternary relationship SELLS illustrated in Figure 2.6 would be represented by the following relations:

COMPANY (COMP-NAME, ...)

PRODUCT (PROD-NAME, ...)

COUNTRY (COUNTRY-NAME, ...)

SELLS (COMP-NAME, PROD-NAME, COUNTRY-NAME)

A possible additional attribute of the relation SELLS could be the

QUANTITY of the product sold each year by the company to the country. The key attributes of the relation representing the ternary relationship are determined by the functionality of the relationship. If SELLS is M:N:P then all three foreign keys make up the key for SELLS. However, if every company exports each of its products to only one country (but that country varies with product and company) then clearly only COMP-NAME and PROD-NAME are required to form the key for SELLS.

To illustrate this point further, consider a situation in which trainees work on a variety of projects under the supervision of instructors. No instructor can supervise any given trainee on more than one project and no trainee can work on any given project under the supervision of more than one instructor. As shown Figure 2.10 this situation may be represented by a ternary relationship SUPERVISES involving the entity types TRAINEE, INSTRUCTOR and PROJECT.

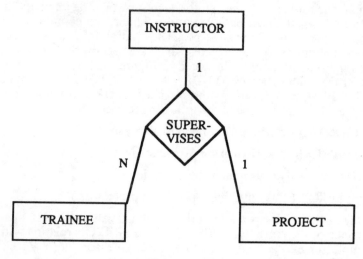

Figure 2.10

The relationship SUPERVISES is 1:1:N and, applying our guidelines, a relational schema for this database is given by:

TRAINEE (EMP#, . . .)

INSTRUCTOR (EMP#, . . .)

PROJECT (PROJ#, . . .)

SUPERVISES (INSTRUCTOR-EMP#, TRAINEE-EMP#, PROJ#)

Note that the SUPERVISES relation has another candidate key, i.e. we could have:

SUPERVISES (TRAINEE-EMP#, PROJ#, INSTRUCTOR-EMP#)

As an example of a 1:1:1 ternary relationship, consider the following relationship between teachers, textbooks and subjects. A teacher uses one textbook for a given subject. Different teachers use different textbooks for the same subject. No teacher will use the same textbook for different subjects, but different teachers can use the same textbook for different subjects (e.g. *Macbeth* is used by one teacher for English Literature and by another for Drama). Figure 2.11 illustrates the ternary relationship USES between the entity types TEACHER, TEXTBOOK and SUBJECT.

The relationship USES is 1:1:1 and a relational schema for this database is:

TEACHER (<u>STAFF#</u>, ...)

TEXTBOOK (<u>BOOK-NAME</u>, ...)

SUBJECT (<u>SUBJECT-NAME</u>, ...)

USES (<u>STAFF#, BOOK-NAME</u>, SUBJECT-NAME)

The relation USES actually has three candidate keys. Any combination of two attributes chosen from the three forms a key for the relation.

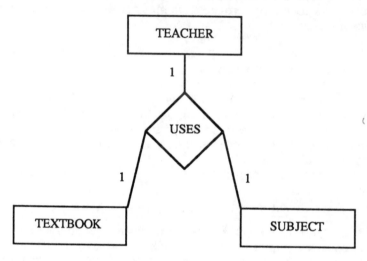

Figure 2.11

2.4   NORMALISATION OF RELATION SCHEMES

A relational schema designed according to the guidelines of the previous section may still contain ambiguities or inconsistencies which must be resolved before implementation. This process of refinement is known as *normalisation.*

Normalisation theory is built around the concept of *normal forms.* Relation schemes designed according to the guidelines of Section 2.3 should, at the very least, be in *first normal form* (1NF). A first normal form relation is a relation in which every attribute value is an atomic, non-decomposable data item. This property was inherent in our definition of a relation. In his seminal paper on the relational model Codd (1970) defined two further normal forms, *second normal form* (2NF) and *third normal form* (3NF). Later, third normal form was shown to have certain inadequacies and a stronger form was introduced called *Boyce-Codd normal form* (BCNF), (Codd, 1974). Subsequently Fagin introduced *fourth normal form* (4NF), (Fagin, 1977) and also *fifth normal form* (5NF), (Fagin, 1979).

Before we consider these normal forms in some detail, it must be stressed that normalisation theory is nothing more than a formalisation of good database design principles. The derivation of appropriate entities, attributes and relationships from the initial requirements analysis will have a crucial influence on the level of normalisation present in the resultant relational schema. Any ambiguities or inconsistencies present in this schema will most likely have arisen due to an inadequate or incorrect entity-relationship model. Entity normalisation will be preserved under the transformations described in Section 2.3.

Further discussion of normalisation requires firstly a definition of the term *functional dependence.*

2.4.1 Functional dependence

Given a relation R, attribute B of R is functionally dependent on attribute A of R (written as A → B) if and only if, whenever two tuples of R agree on their A-value they also agree on their B-value. That is, at any instant in time each value of A has exactly one value of B associated with it. (Attributes A and B may be composite.)

As an example, consider the following (badly designed) relation scheme:

REPORT (S#, C#, TITLE, LNAME, ROOM#, MARKS)

A tuple <s, c, t, l, r, m> in this relation indicates that student *s* obtained marks *m* on course number *c* which has title *t* and is given by lecturer *l* who has room number *r*. Assume that each course has only one lecturer and each lecturer has one room. Some of the functional dependencies existing in this relation are as follows:

S#, C# → MARKS

This implies that for a given pair of (S#, C#) values occurring in the relation REPORT there is exactly one value of MARKS.

C# → TITLE

C# → LNAME

C# → ROOM#

For a given value of C# there is exactly one value of TITLE, LNAME, and ROOM#.

LNAME → ROOM#

Each lecturer has exactly one associated value of ROOM#.

The attribute MARKS is said to be *fully* functionally dependent on the key since it is dependent on the key attributes S# and C# as a composite pair, but not on either individually. In general, an attribute B of relation R is fully functionally dependent on attribute A of R if it is functionally dependent on A and not functionally dependent on any proper subset of A.

The attributes TITLE, LNAME and ROOM# are said to be *partially* dependent on the key since they are dependent only on C# and not on S#. The attribute ROOM# is said to be *transitively* dependent on C# since it is dependent on LNAME which in turn is dependent on C#. Such partial and transitive dependencies in relation schemes can give rise to serious problems when manipulating the database, and so they must be removed before implementation.

R.T.C. LIBRARY
LETTERKENNY

2.4.2   Second normal form

A relation is said to be in second normal form (2NF) if it is in 1NF and every non-prime attribute is fully functionally dependent on the key.

The relation REPORT defined above is not in 2NF and this can give rise to the following anomalies:

1. If we wish to insert details of a new course into the database we cannot do so until at least one student has registered for the course (we cannot have a null value in the prime attribute S#). Similarly, if we wish to insert details of a new lecturer and his room number we cannot do so until he is assigned to a course and at least one student has registered for that course.
2. If we wish to change the title of course 361 from Database Technology to Database Systems then we must search for every tuple containing this value of C# and update all of them. There will be as many tuples as there are students enrolled for course 361.
3. If every student enrolled for course 361 drops out of that course and we delete the corresponding tuples, then all details of the course will disappear from the database.

To convert to 2NF and overcome these anomalies we split the relation into two, bringing together into a separate relation scheme those attributes which are partially dependent on the key.

REPORT (S#, C#, MARKS)

COURSE (C#, TITLE, LNAME, ROOM#)

These relations are in 2NF since in each of them the non-prime attributes are fully dependent on the key. However the relation COURSE requires further normalisation due to the existence of the transitive dependency:

C# → LNAME → ROOM#

2.4.3   Third normal form

A relation is said to be in third normal form (3NF) if it is in 2NF and contains no transitive dependencies.

More precisely, *a relation is in 3NF if whenever X → A holds in R and A is not in X then either X contains a key for R, or A is prime.*

The relation COURSE defined above is not in 3NF since we have the dependency LNAME → ROOM# and LNAME is not a key and ROOM# is non-prime. This transitive dependency can also give rise to anomalies:

1. We cannot insert details of a new lecturer and his room# until he is assigned to a course.
2. To change the room# for a lecturer we must change it in every tuple corresponding to a course given by that lecturer.
3. If a lecturer ceases to give any course then all details of that lecturer and his room# are deleted from the database.

To convert to 3NF we split the relation COURSE into two relations, separating out the transitive dependency. This gives a final relational schema defined by the following:

REPORT (S#, C#, MARKS)

COURSE (C#, TITLE, LNAME)

LECTURER (LNAME, ROOM#)

These relations are now fully normalised. Note however, that had we started with a good design (i.e. an ER model in which students, courses and lecturers were represented by entity types) and applied our transformation guidelines, we would have obtained the above schema directly.

The reduction of the original REPORT relation into the three relations above constitutes what is known as a *non-loss decomposition.* In general, a relation R(A, B, C) in which we have the functional dependency, A → B, can always be non-loss decomposed into its 'projections' $R_1(A,B)$ and $R_2(A,C)$. This result is known as Heath's theorem (Heath, 1971). No information is lost in such a decomposition since the original relation can always be reconstructed by 'joining' the projections. (The operations of projection and join will be described in detail in Chapter 4.) Thus, any information that can be derived from the original structure can also be derived from the new structure. As we have seen from the anomalies described above, the converse is not necessarily true. Thus a non-loss decomposition may be regarded as a more precise representation of the real world.

2.4.4   Boyce-Codd normal form

Third normal form does not deal satisfactorily with relations which have multiple candidate keys, where those keys are composite and overlap (i.e.

have at least one attribute in common).

In order to define a further normal form, called Boyce-Codd normal form (BCNF) it is convenient to introduce the concept of a *determinant*. A determinant is an attribute, or group of attributes, on which some other attribute is fully functionally dependent. Then we have that,

A relation R is in BCNF if and only if every determinant is a candidate key.

As an example, consider a college in which each subject is taught by several teachers but each teacher teaches only one subject. Each student takes several subjects and has only one teacher for a given subject. This might be represented by the following relation scheme:

ENROLS (S#, TEACHER-NAME, SUBJECT-NAME)

However, this relation is not even in 2NF since we have the partial dependency,

TEACHER-NAME → SUBJECT-NAME

Alternatively, we could have

ENROLS (S#, SUBJECT-NAME, TEACHER-NAME)

This relation is in 3NF but not in BCNF since we have the dependency,

TEACHER-NAME → SUBJECT-NAME

and TEACHER-NAME is not a candidate key. Thus we cannot insert the fact that a teacher teaches a certain subject until at least one student enrols for that subject. Also, the fact that a teacher teaches a certain subject is recorded, with great redundancy, for every student to whom he teaches that subject. The solution, once again, is a non-loss decomposition given by:

CLASS (S#, TEACHER-NAME)

TEACHES (TEACHER-NAME, SUBJECT-NAME)

These relations are fully normalised. The fact that a teacher teaches a certain subject is recorded only once in the TEACHES relation and the problems described above are avoided.

In entity-relationship modelling, the relation ENROLS would arise from an incorrect representation of the interrelationships between the entity types STUDENT, TEACHER and SUBJECT, as a single ternary relationship. The problems with this relation would have been avoided if we had realised at the data analysis stage that we actually have two independent binary relationships in this situation - an N:M relationship between STUDENT and TEACHER, and a 1:N relationship between SUBJECT and TEACHER. A transformation of these two binary relationships would have led to the relations CLASS and TEACHES.

2.4.5   Multivalued dependency and fourth normal form

Fourth normal form is best described by an example. Thus, consider the following relation representing the relationship between companies, products and countries:

SELLS (<u>COMPANY</u>, <u>PRODUCT</u>, <u>COUNTRY</u>)

A tuple $<x, y, z>$ in this relation indicates that company x sells product y in country z. An instance of this relation might have the form shown in Figure 2.11.

It is straightforward to check that this relation is in BCNF. However, if we know that each manufacturer sells *all* its products in *every* country to which it exports, then it is clear that this relation contains a great deal of redundancy.

COMPANY	PRODUCT	COUNTRY
IBM	PC	France
IBM	PC	Italy
IBM	PC	UK
IBM	Mainframe	France
IBM	Mainframe	Italy
IBM	Mainframe	UK
DEC	PC	France
DEC	PC	Spain
DEC	PC	Ireland
DEC	Mini	France
DEC	Mini	Spain
DEC	Mini	Ireland
ICL	Mainframe	Italy
ICL	Mainframe	France
. . .	. . .	. . .

Figure 2.11 An instance of the relation SELLS

For example, to add a new product for IBM we must add a tuple for every country to which IBM exports. In a properly normalised relational schema this information should only have to be added once. Similarly, if DEC starts exporting all it products to China, then a separate tuple must be inserted for each product.

It is clear that the redundancy is eliminated if we replace SELLS by a non-loss decomposition consisting of two relations, MAKES and EXPORTS, whose schemes are given by:

MAKES (<u>COMPANY</u>, <u>PRODUCT</u>)

EXPORTS (<u>COMPANY</u>, <u>COUNTRY</u>)

The information that is held in the instance of SELLS shown in Figure 2.11 can then be represented by the instances of the MAKES and EXPORTS relations shown in Figure 2.12.

MAKES   EXPORTS

COMPANY	PRODUCT
IBM	PC
IBM	Mainframe
DEC	PC
DEC	Mini
ICL	Mainframe

COMPANY	COUNTRY
IBM	France
IBM	Italy
IBM	UK
DEC	France
DEC	Spain
DEC	Ireland
ICL	Italy
ICL	France

Figure 2.12   Instances of the relations MAKES and EXPORTS

The normalisation rules that we have studied so far do not help us to eliminate the redundancy in the relation SELLS. This is because the redundancy
is not caused by partial or transitive functional dependencies. Rather, the
problem arises in the relation SELLS because we have two *multivalued
dependencies*:

COMPANY →→ PRODUCT

COMPANY →→ COUNTRY

Given a relation R (A, B, C), the multivalued dependency, A →→ B holds
in R if and only if the *set* of B-values matching a given (A-value, C-value)
pair in R depends only on the A-value and is independent of the C-value
(A, B, and C may of course be composite.) Thus in the above example the
set of countries to which a company exports a product is determined by the
company name and is independent of the product name. Similarly the set of
products exported to a country by a company is independent of the country
name.

It is possible of course that in the real-world situation the multivalued
dependencies described above do not hold. For example, the set of countries to which a company exports a product may vary from product to
product. In this case the relation SELLS would be in fully normalised
form.

We are now in a position to define fourth normal form:

*A relation R is said to be in fourth normal form (4NF) if and only if,
whenever there exists a multivalued dependency in R, say A →→ B, then
all attributes of R are functionally dependent on A.*

Equivalently, R is in 4NF if it is in BCNF and all multivalued dependencies
in R are in fact functional dependencies. In the relation SELLS, neither of
the multivalued dependencies are functional dependencies. That is, neither
PRODUCT nor COUNTRY is functionally dependent on COMPANY.

It is important to realise that violations of fourth normal form arise from errors made at the data analysis stage. In the above example, the relation SELLS results from a ternary relationship involving the three entity types COMPANY, PRODUCT and COUNTRY. A proper data analysis however, should have revealed (at the entity-relationship modelling stage) that the relationships between the entity types COMPANY and PRODUCT, and COMPANY and COUNTRY were independent.

2.4.6   Limitations of normalisation

As we have seen, normalisation to a large extent removes the anomalies present in some 1NF and 2NF relations which may arise due to incorrect entity-relationship modelling. For most practical applications reduction to 3NF is adequate, but sometimes further refinement to BCNF or 4NF is warranted. There is in fact a fifth normal form (5NF), which is designed to cope with a type of dependency called 'join dependency' which is not covered by the other normal forms. However such dependencies are rare and 5NF is of little practical significance. For a comprehensive description of 5NF see Fagin (1979) or Date (1986), or the more informal description given by Kent (1983).

It should be borne in mind however, that full normalisation may not always be desirable and the database designer may take advantage of his intimate knowledge of the real world and choose not to normalise in some particular instance. For example, consider the following relation:

CUSTOMER (NAME, STREET, CITY, POSTCODE)

Strictly speaking, the attribute POSTCODE uniquely identifies STREET and CITY so that we have the transitive dependencies:

POSTCODE → STREET

POSTCODE → CITY

Thus CUSTOMER is not in 3NF. However, in practice the attributes STREET, CITY and POSTCODE are always used together as a unit and decomposing the relation would not be advisable in this case. This rather contrived example is given to illustrate the point that, as in many other aspects of database design, the data modeller must use common sense when normalising and should not consider the rules given above as absolute.

It is also important to bear in mind that from a practical point of view normalisation, while often facilitating update, tends to have an adverse effect on retrieval. Related data which may have been retrievable from one relation in an unnormalised schema may have to be retrieved from several relations in the normalised form. The database designer may therefore be tempted to take account of performance requirements when deciding whether to fully normalise all relations. A 'pragmatic' approach such as this is valid provided the integrity of the database is not compromised for the sake of efficiency.

2.5 RELATIONAL DATABASE DESIGN METHODOLOGY

We are now in a position to define a methodology for relational database design (adapted from Teorey et al., 1986) which leads us from the initial requirements analysis to a set of normalised relations which are an accurate representation of the real-world situation. The steps involved in this methodology, as illustrated in Figure 2.13, are described below.

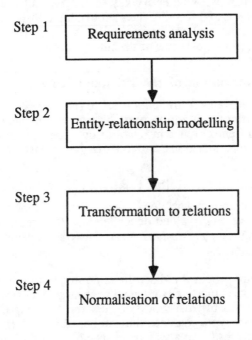

Step 1	Requirements analysis
Step 2	Entity-relationship modelling
Step 3	Transformation to relations
Step 4	Normalisation of relations

Figure 2.13   A methodology for relational database design

Step 1. Requirements analysis

As outlined in Chapter 1, the objectives of the requirements analysis stage are to identify the data requirements of the enterprise and to describe informally the information to be recorded about the data objects and their inter-relationships. For a large enterprise with many different classes of users, *multiple views* of data and relationships occur. These views must be amalgamated into a single global view, eliminating redundancy and inconsistency from the model in the process. For example, the modeller must be able to recognise among the differing views, *synonyms* (words of different forms having the same meaning), and *homonyms* (words of the same form having different meanings). In addition, it is important to identify data objects which may belong to the same type hierarchy.

The requirements analysis stage should also involve an analysis of the types of transactions (operations) to be performed on the database since these may have a significant influence on the information content of the database. Requirements analysis is a crucial step in the design process since we must ensure that we incorporate all the necessary information for the particular application.

Step 2. ER modelling of requirements

At this stage we construct an ER model to describe the data objects and their interrelationships. We identify key attributes, decide on the functionality of relationships and whether the membership classes of the participating entity sets are optional or mandatory. We then construct a schematic ER model which gives a global view of the entire database.

Step 3. Transformation of the ER model to a relational schema

We apply the guidelines from Section 2.3 to map the ER model onto a set of relations. Particular attention must be paid at this stage to the membership classes of entity types in relationships, to involuted relationships, to subtypes and generalisations, and to ternary relationships.

Step 4. Normalisation of the relational schema

For each relation produced at Step 3, derive a list of functional dependencies and, if present, multivalued dependencies. If necessary, reduce each relation to the highest stage of normalisation required using the techniques described in Section 2.4.

This methodology provides a disciplined approach to relational database design which is particularly advantageous for large databases. Using entity types as abstractions for real-world objects and focusing on the relationships among entity types, reduces the number of data elements to be considered and simplifies the analysis stage. The reduction of the ER model to a set of normalised relations is to a large extent a mechanical process, though the designer may wish to use his intimate knowledge of the application to refine the resultant schema in order to improve processing efficiency.

2.6   CASE STUDY: A HOSPITAL DATABASE

In this section we shall apply the methodology described in the previous section to design a relational database for a hospital. The hospital wishes to maintain a database to assist with the administration of its wards and operating theatres, and to maintain information relating to its patients, surgeons and nurses.

Step 1: Requirements analysis

A requirements analysis yields the following informal description of the information to be recorded:

The patients occupying each ward.
Most patients are assigned to a ward on admittance and each ward may contain many patients. However, consultants (senior surgeons) at the hospital may have private patients who are assigned to private rooms. The information to be recorded about a patient includes a unique medical number, name, address, etc.

The nurses assigned to each ward.
A nurse may or may not be assigned to a ward and he/she cannot be assigned to more than one ward. A ward may have many nurses assigned to it. Nurses are identified by their staff number and each ward has a unique number.

The operations undergone by patients.
A patient may have a number of operations. The information to be recorded about an operation includes the type of operation, the patient, the surgeons, date, time and location.

The surgeons who perform operations.
Only one surgeon may perform an operation, any other surgeons present being considered as assisting at the operation. Surgeons come under the direction of senior surgeons, called consultants, who may also perform or assist at operations. Information recorded about a surgeon includes name (assumed unique), address, phone number, etc. Each consultant has a speciality.

The theatres in which operations are performed.
An operation can be performed in only one theatre but a given theatre may be the location of many operations. Each theatre has an identifying number and some may be specially equipped for certain classes of operation.

The nurses assigned to each theatre.
A nurse may or may not be assigned to a theatre and he/she cannot be assigned to more than one theatre. A theatre may have many nurses assigned to it.

Step 2: Entity-relationship modelling

The following is a list of entities, attributes and relationships which represent the informal description of the database outlined above:

1. Entity type SURGEON, with attributes SNAME, SADDRESS, and PHONE-NO. Since there are relatively few surgeons in any hospital it is reasonable to assume that their names are distinct, so SNAME should serve as a key for this entity type.
2. Entity type CONSULTANT which is a subtype of the entity type SURGEON. Every consultant is a specialist in a particular branch of

surgery and this is recorded as an additional attribute SPECIALITY.
3. Entity type PATIENT, with attributes MED-NO (a unique medical number), PNAME, PADDRESS, DATE-OF-BIRTH, SEX, . . .
4. Entity type PRIVATE-PATIENT which is a subtype of the entity type PATIENT. The number of the private room to which such a patient is assigned is recorded as an additional attribute, ROOM#.
5. Entity type NURSE, with attributes N# (a unique staff number), NNAME, GRADE, . . .
6. Entity type WARD, with attributes WARD# (a unique ward number), WARD-TYPE, NO-OF-BEDS, . . .
7. Entity type THEATRE, with attributes THEATRE# (a unique theatre number), THEATRE-TYPE, . . .
8. Entity type OPERATION, with attributes OP# (a unique identification number), OP-TYPE, DATE, TIME, . . .

The attribute lists are by no means complete since this information depends to a large extent on the specific application. Also, a number of the attributes listed may be composite, i.e. it may be necessary to break them down into smaller components.

Appropriate relationships, as extracted from the requirements analysis, are as given in the following list:

1. PERFORMS, a 1:N relationship between entity types SURGEON and OPERATION, with the entity type OPERATION being a mandatory member of this relationship, i.e. every operation must be performed by a surgeon.
2. ASSISTS, an N:M relationship between entity types SURGEON and OPERATION. A possible attribute for this relationship is the ROLE played by the surgeon at the operation.
3. SUPERVISES, a 1:N relationship between the entity types CONSULTANT and SURGEON. The membership class of SURGEON in this relationship is optional since there may be surgeons (e.g. consultants) that are not supervised.
4. TREATS, a 1:N relationship between the entity type CONSULTANT and the subtype PRIVATE-PATIENT. The membership class of PRIVATE-PATIENT in this relationship is mandatory. That is, every private patient is assigned to a consultant for treatment.
5. UNDERGOES, a 1:N relationship between entity types PATIENT and OPERATION. The entity type OPERATION is a mandatory member of this relationship since an operation must always have an associated patient.
6. OCCUPIES, a 1:N relationship between entity types WARD and PATIENT, where the membership class of PATIENT is 'almost' mandatory since most patients are assigned to a ward on entry to the hospital.
7. LOCATED, a 1:N relationship between entity types THEATRE and OPERATION. The entity type OPERATION is a mandatory member of this relationship since clearly every operation must be located in a theatre.
8. WARD-ASSIGN, a 1:N relationship between entity types WARD and

NURSE. A possible attribute for this re;ationship is DATE-ASSIGNED giving the date on which a particular nurse was assigned to a ward. The NURSE entity type is an optional member of this relationship since a nurse may or may not be assigned to a ward.

9. THEATRE-ASSIGN, a 1:N optional relationship between THEATRE and NURSE, with attribute DATE-ASSIGNED.

In addition to the above relationships, we have an IS_A relationship between the subtype CONSULTANT and the entity type SURGEON, and another between the subtype PRIVATE-PATIENT and the entity type PATIENT.

A schematic ER model is illustrated in Figure 2.14.

Step 3: Transformation to relations

We are now ready to apply the guidelines of Section 2.3 to transform our ER model into a set of relations. Recall that each entity type is represented by a separate relation, but that the representation of a relationship depends on its semantics and its functionality. In applying our guidelines we might obtain the following relational schema:

SURGEON (SNAME, SADDRESS, PHONE-NO)

CONSULTANT (SNAME, SPECIALITY)

PATIENT (MED-NO, WARD#, PNAME, DATE-OF-BIRTH, SEX)

PRIVATE-PATIENT (MED-NO, SNAME, ROOM#)

NURSE (N#, NNAME, GRADE)

THEATRE (THEATRE#, TH-TYPE)

OPERATION (OP#, SNAME, THEATRE#, MED-NO, OP-TYPE,
            DATE, TIME)

SUPERVISES (SURGEON-SNAME, CONSULTANT-SNAME)

ASSISTS (OP#, SNAME, ROLE)

WARD-ASSIGN (N#, WARD#, DATE-ASSIGNED)

THEATRE-ASSIGN (N#, THEATRE#, DATE-ASSIGNED)

In this schema the relationship OCCUPIES is represented by the foreign key WARD# in the PATIENT relation since this relationship is 'almost mandatory' for PATIENT. That is, most patients are assigned to wards. The relationship TREATS is represented by the foreign key SNAME (the name of the consultant) in the PRIVATE-PATIENT relation. Also, the foreign keys SNAME, MED-NO and THEATRE# in the OPERATION relation represent respectively the PERFORMS, UNDERGOES and LOCATED relationships of which OPERATION is a mandatory member.

The M:N relationship ASSISTS is represented by a separate relation scheme containing the key attributes of SURGEON and OPERATION, together with the attribute ROLE.

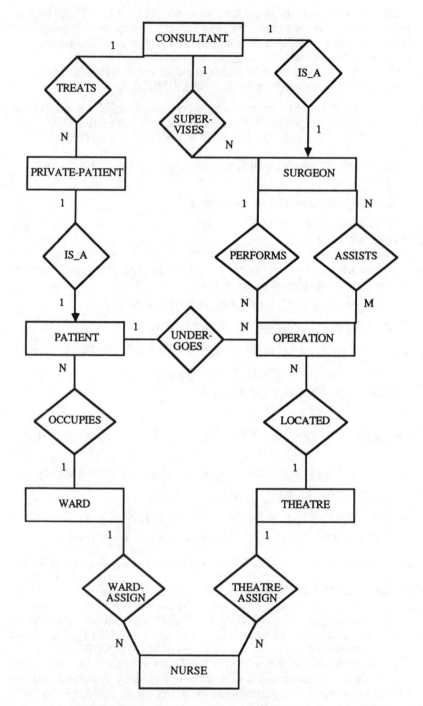

Figure 2.14 ER model for the hospital database

The optional 1:N relationships WARD-ASSIGN and THEATRE-ASSIGN are each represented by a separate relation scheme containing the key attributes of the participating entity sets together with the additional attribute DATE-ASSIGNED. If the majority of nurses were assigned to wards we might choose to represent the WARD-ASSIGN relationship by posting the foreign key WARD# into the NURSES relation (together with the attribute DATE-ASSIGNED).

The optional 1:N relationship SUPERVISES is represented by a separate relation, but could be represented by posting the name of the supervising consultant (C-SNAME) into the SURGEON relation:

SURGEON (SNAME, SADDRESS, PHONE-NO, C-SNAME)

The attribute C-SNAME in this case will be null for all those surgeons who do not come under the direction of a consultant.

Step 4: Normalisation of relation schemes

The schema above is in fact in 4NF, the highest stage of normalisation required. (Verification of this is left as an exercise.) This is a reflection of the fact that our initial entity-relationship model was sound.

EXERCISES

In each of the following exercises, give a design for the database in the form of:

(i)   An entity-relationship diagram.
(ii) A set of fully normalised relations.

2.1 You are required to design a database to hold information on the countries of the world and their reserves of precious minerals. For each mineral the database records the name of the mineral and its current price per ounce. For each country, the information recorded includes the name of the country, its gross national product (GNP), and for each mineral found in that country, the yearly production and the estimated reserves (both measured in tonnes). A country may have reserves of many minerals and each mineral may be found in many countries.

2.2 An electronics firm maintains a database concerning the devices it manufactures and the components that each device requires. For each component, the database contains an identification number (unique), name, descriptive details, the name and address of the supplier, and the quantity in stock. Each component has only one supplier but a given supplier may supply many different components. For each device, the database records a unique identification number and name, together with the current price of the device and the quantity in stock. The database also records the quantity of each component required for the manufacture of each device.

2.3 A car hire firm maintains a database to record details of its fleets of cars and vans, and its hire transactions. For each car or van, the details recorded include the registration number (unique), make, model, engine capacity and date of registration, together with the date of each service. The record for a car also includes the style of the car (saloon/hatchback), and the number of doors. Additional information recorded for each van is its carrying capacity (in cubic metres) and its maximum load (in tonnes). Each time a vehicle is hired, the name, address, telephone number and driving licence number of the customer are entered into the database together with an identification of the vehicle which has been hired. The dates and times of the beginning and end of the hire period are also recorded, as are the number of miles covered by the customer and the total cost of the hire. For each model of vehicle the daily, weekly and monthly hire rates are stored. These hire rates vary from model to model.

2.4 Design a database for a major sporting event, e.g. the Olympics, or the World Cup finals, which maintains details of competitors, events, venues and results.

2.5 Design a database for a small library holding details of members, books, reservations and loans.

2.6 Design a database for a travel agency which will maintain details of customers, package holidays, resorts, hotels and flights to and from resorts.

3

Network and Hierarchical Data Modelling

3.1 INTRODUCTION

During the past decade the relational data model has replaced the network model as the dominant influence in database management systems. During the seventies the majority of commercial database management systems were based on the network model, while IBM's hierarchical system, IMS, also had a large share of the market. Until around 1980, relational systems remained largely experimental and the few commercial products which were available at that time could not compete with network or hierarchical systems in the areas of performance and efficiency. Fortunately that situation has now changed. Most new database management systems are relational and many of these can perform at least as well as the best network systems, even in transaction-intensive application areas.

However, a large number (probably the majority) of existing databases have been implemented using hierarchical or network systems, and so these models continue to be of interest. In this chapter therefore, we give a brief overview of the main concepts underlying the network and hierarchical models, and compare and contrast these with the relational approach.

3.2 THE NETWORK DATA MODEL

In the network data model we have record types representing entity sets and *links* representing relationships between entity sets. To facilitate implementation, links are normally restricted to be binary (i.e. involving only two record types) and either 1:1 or 1:N. However, as we shall see, more complex relationships can be decomposed into combinations of simpler relationships.

A network database may be represented by a directed graph, called a network data structure diagram (or Bachman diagram), which is really just a more restrictive form of the entity-relationship diagram. The nodes of a network data structure diagram represent the record types in the database and the directed arcs represent 1:N relationships (1:1 relationships are represented by undirected arcs). All nodes and links must be explicitly named. More than one link may be defined between the same two record types, but self-referencing links (representing involuted relationships) are not permitted in general.

Example. A Network Representation of the Hospital Database

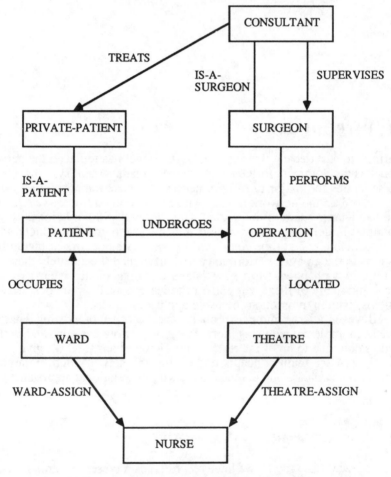

Figure 3.1   Network data structure diagram for the hospital database

Figure 3.1 illustrates a network data structure diagram for the hospital database designed in the case study of Chapter 2. The M:N relationship

ASSISTS between the entity types SURGEON and OPERATION has been omitted for the moment. In the next section we shall study the representation of M:N relationships in the network model

R.T.C. LIBRARY
LETTERKENNY

3.2.1 Decomposition of N:M relationships

Arbitrary N:M relationships may be reduced to binary 1:N relationships by introducing intermediate record types (sometimes called link record types). To illustrate this decomposition, consider the N:M relationship ASSISTS, shown in Figure 3.2, between the entity types SURGEON and OPERATION. A surgeon assists at many operations and each operation has many surgeons assisting.

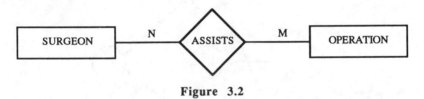

Figure 3.2

Introducing an intermediate record type, ASSISTANT, we may reduce this N:M relationship to two binary 1:N relationships as shown in Figure 3.3.

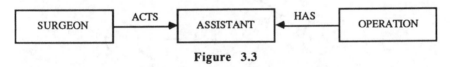

Figure 3.3

Each instance of the ASSISTANT record type is linked to exactly one SURGEON record and exactly one OPERATION record. In practice the link record type might not always be a recognisable entity and may simply be a 'dummy' record with a single identifying attribute. In the above case, ASSISTANT may have other attributes, such as the role played by a surgeon at a particular operation.

Ternary relationships also cannot be directly represented in the network model and must be decomposed in a similar manner to binary 1:N relationships involving link record types.

3.2.2   Implementation of a network

Data description and data manipulation in network database management systems both tend to be heavily influenced by factors relating to the physical storage organisation of the network. Thus, before proceeding further, it is instructive to examine some of the techniques used for implementing links in network databases.

We may represent the records of a given record type by a file in the obvious manner, but there are a number of ways we can represent links so that we can travel efficiently from one record to another. For example, consider the network data structure diagram illustrated in Figure 3.4.

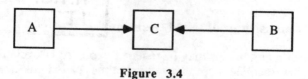

Figure 3.4

Consider the *instance* of this data structure diagram shown in Figure 3.5.

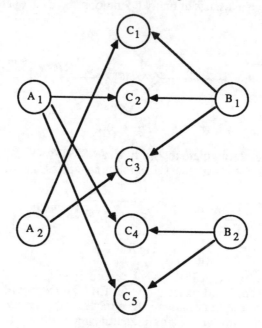

Figure 3.5

In an implementation the A —> C link might be represented by pointers and the B —> C link by physical contiguity (reserved space). That is, each C record is stored in close proximity to the B record to which it is related, and each A record contains a pointer to each of its related C records. There are of course, many possible variations on such structures. It is more useful however to implement links by linked-list or *ring* structures as shown in Figure 3.6.

In such a structure the A-record is often referred to as the *owner* and the C-records as the members. Note that we can visit any of the records of type C that are related to A_1, starting at A_1. Also we can travel from any of C_2, C_4, or C_5 back to A_1. Traversing the ring may be made more flexible and efficient by including backward (or *prior*) pointers and/or a direct pointer to the owner in each member record.

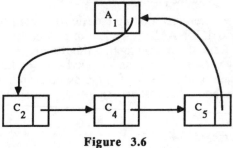

Figure 3.6

If we implement all relationships as rings the network then takes the form of a *multilist* (or multiring) structure as illustrated in Figure 3.7.

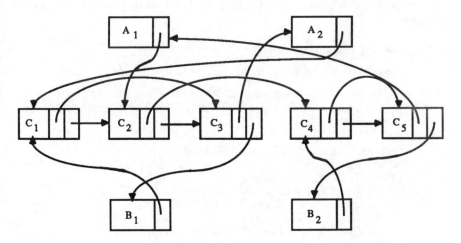

Figure 3.7

In this structure each record has as many pointers as it has links. Thus the pointers may occupy fixed field positions in the records and in traversing the database there is little danger of following the wrong chain.

Consider the difficulties of representing N:M links with multilists: each record could be on many chains for the same relationship; we would not know in advance how many pointers were required in a record for each link; in traversing the database we would have difficulty determining which pointer was for which chain.

3.2.3   Answering queries in a network database

Consider the network implementation of the hospital database and the following queries:

Simple query

'What is Dr Smith's phone number?'

To answer this query we must look up the file for record type SURGEONS using the NAME field. If NAME is the key or part of the key then the look-up may be done efficiently, assuming that the file may be directly accessed on the basis of key values. Otherwise we need a 'secondary index' or some other fast access path on the NAME field to avoid searching the whole file. (Secondary indexes and other fast access methods are described in Chapter 6.)

Query involving a single link

'List the names of the patients on ward 10.'

To answer this query we must first find the record for ward 10 in the WARD file. We then follow the chain corresponding to the OCCUPIES link and print the NAME field of each PATIENT record we encounter on the chain.

Query involving two links

'List the names of patients that have had operations in theatre B.'

To answer this query we must start at the appropriate theatre record and traverse two links, LOCATED and UNDERGOES. The algorithm may be written informally as follows:

```
FIND record for theatre B in the THEATRE file;
Follow the chain corresponding to the LOCATED link to the first
OPERATION record in the chain;
WHILE (not at end of LOCATED chain) DO
    Follow UNDERGOES chain to PATIENT record;
    PRINT PATIENT.PNAME;
    GET next OPERATION record in LOCATED chain;
END;
```

3.3 THE CODASYL DBTG PROPOSALS

The dominant influence in the development of the network data model and database systems using that model has been a series of proposals put forward by the Data Base Task Group (DBTG) of the Conference on Data Systems and Languages (CODASYL, 1971). This group proposed a formal notation for defining network databases, i.e. a network data definition language (CODASYL DDLC, 1973, 1978, 1981) and also a procedural data manipulation language which may be used for writing application programs to access network databases (CODASYL COBOL, 1978). This section gives a brief overview of some of these proposals, which have formed the basis for a number of popular database management systems.

3.3.1 The set type

The concept of a link, that is a named 1:N relationship between record types, is known as a *set* type in CODASYL terminology. A set type consists of one *owner* record type and one *member* record type. A *set occurrence* then is a group of one owner record occurrence and one or more member record occurrences.

As an example, consider the small section of the hospital database illustrated in Figure 3.8.

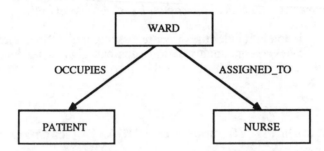

Figure 3.8   Set types OCCUPIES and ASSIGNED_TO

The network data structure diagram in Figure 3.8 contains two set types:

1. Set type OCCUPIES with owner record type WARD and member record type PATIENT.
2. Set type ASSIGNED_TO with owner record type WARD and member record type NURSE.

Figure 3.9 shows an *instance* of this network.

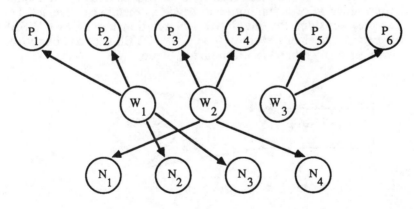

Figure 3.9   Set occurrences

Figure 3.9 shows three occurrences of the OCCUPIES set consisting of the record occurrences (W_1, P_1, P_2), (W_2, P_3, P_4), and (W_3, P_5, P_6) respectively. There are also three occurrences of the ASSIGNED_TO set consisting of the record occurrences (W_1, N_2, N_3), (W_2, N_1, N_4) and (W_3). Note that the occurrence of ASSIGNED_TO with W_3 as owner has no members.

CODASYL systems often place two restrictions on sets in order to simplify navigation in the database and facilitate implementation. These are:

1. *'The same record type cannot be both an owner record type and a member record type in the same set.'*
   This means that involuted relationships cannot be directly represented in CODASYL systems.

2. *'The same record occurrence cannot be in more than one occurrence of a given set.'*
   This restriction precludes the direct representation of N:M relationships but as we have seen, such relationships can always be decomposed into two 1:N relationships with the introduction of an intermediate record type.

3.3.2   Translating ER models to CODASYL schemata

In mapping an ER model to a CODASYL implementation, the following guidelines may be applied:

1. Entity types translate directly to record types.
2. Attributes translate to data items (fields) in those record types.
3. 1:1 and 1:N relationships that are not involuted translate directly to set types.
4. N:M relationships translate to *two* set types whose members are of an intermediate record type.
5. Involuted relationships cannot usually be translated directly and require the introduction of a dummy record type as member of the set. For example, consider the involuted 1:N relationship SUPERVISES between instances of the entity type EMPLOYEE (i.e. one employee supervises many others) as illustrated in Figure 3.10.

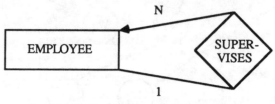

Figure 3.10

This must often be reduced to the structure illustrated in Figure 3.11, containing a set SUPERVISES with owner record type EMPLOYEE and member record type DUMMY. Each DUMMY record is a pointer to (or the key value of) an EMPLOYEE record.

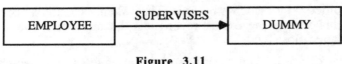

Figure 3.11

6. Ternary relationships (and those of higher degrees) must be reduced to binary 1:N relationships through the introduction of intermediate record types.

3.3.3 The CODASYL schema DDL

A CODASYL schema has three main sections, an identification section, a record declaration section and a set declaration section. The identification section names the schema and the associated physical files and defines access rights, passwords, etc. A typical syntax might be:

```
SCHEMA NAME IS <Schema Name>
FILE NAME IS <File Name> {,<File Name>}
USER NAME IS '<User Name>' {, '<User Name>'}
PASSWORD IS <Password>
AREA NAME IS <Area Name> {,<Area Name>}
```

The AREA clause defines the names of areas into which the physical database may be partitioned. All occurrences of a given record type may be stored within one area. This may enhance the efficiency of a large database and may facilitate dumping and recovery from software or hardware failures.

Record declarations

The record declaration section names each record type in the database and defines its associated fields (data items). The manner in which occurrences of each record type are to be accessed (location mode) must also be specified. Three location modes are commonly available:

1. DIRECT <database key>

   Each record occurrence is assigned a database key that determines its placement within a defined area. The database key permits rapid direct access to the record.

2. CALC <Procedure Name> USING <Attribute List>

   Record placement is determined by hashing the attributes specified using a hashing procedure which may be supplied by the user or by the system.

3. VIA <Set Name> SET

   Record placement is determined with regard to the record's membership of the specified set. That is, record occurrences are positioned physically close to the owner of the occurrence of the specified set to which it belongs. Thus when accessing an occurrence of this set via the owner record, all the member records will be clustered close by.

A WITHIN clause in each record entry specifies the area in which occurrences of the record are to be stored.

As an example, a record entry for PATIENT in the hospital database might take the following form:

```
RECORD NAME IS PATIENT
LOCATION MODE  IS CALC USING MED-NO
WITHIN PATIENT-AREA
ITEM  MED-NO           INT(6)
ITEM  PNAME            CHAR(30)
ITEM  SEX              CHAR(1)
```

Set declarations

The set declaration section contains one entry for each set type in the schema. The owner and member record types are defined and an ORDER clause is used to specify the logical position of the members records in each set occurrence. For example, member records may be sorted on some field, or they may be linked together as a queue (first in, first out) or as a stack (first in, last out). The order of member records may also be maintained manually by allowing the user to insert a new member before or after a specified existing member.

Set membership may be defined as OPTIONAL or MANDATORY. If mandatory membership is specified then the system will enforce the rule that every occurrence of the member record type must belong to an occurrence of the set. An *insertion mode* must also be specified for set members. A MANUAL insertion mode implies that application programs must explicitly insert member records into the appropriate set occurrence. If an AUTOMATIC insertion mode is specified, then at the time of creation a member record is automatically inserted into the *current* set occurrence. (The idea of currency is discussed in greater detail below in Section 3.3.4.)

An example of a set declaration, for the OCCUPIES set in the hospital database, is as follows:

```
SET NAME IS OCCUPIES
OWNER  IS  WARD
MEMBER IS  PATIENT
ORDER IS SORTED BY  MED-NO  DESCENDING
INSERTION IS OPTIONAL, AUTOMATIC
```

We may also have what are known as *singular sets*, which effectively link together all the occurrences of a given record type. The owner is a built-in record type called SYSTEM and there is exactly one occurrence of the set whose members are all the records of the member type. For example, the following is a declaration of a singular set for PATIENT records, logically linked in alphabetical order.

```
SET  NAME IS ALL-PATIENTS
OWNER IS  SYSTEM
MEMBER IS  PATIENT
ORDER IS SORTED BY  PNAME  ASCENDING
INSERTION IS MANDATORY, AUTOMATIC
```

This set would enable application programs to scan PATIENT records alphabetically. Singular sets generally have very little system overheads and it is possible to have more than one singular set for a record type (e.g. sorted on different data items).

Other DDL facilities

Other CODASYL DDL facilities include the following:

1. Access rights may be specified for each record and set type, thereby providing additional security. Also, sensitive data items may be encrypted (i.e. coded before storage).
2. Integrity preservation may be enhanced by specifying ranges for data items or by incorporating into the schema procedural checks which must be performed before insertion or deletion of data.

3.3.4   The CODASYL DML

An important concept in CODASYL data manipulation is the idea of 'currency'. In conventional file processing, the current record of a file may be defined as the last record read from that file by the program (cf. the file buffer f^ in Pascal). In CODASYL systems this idea is extended and a collection of 'currency indicators' is maintained which includes the following:

1. CURRENT OF RUN-UNIT

   The most recently accessed record of any type in the run-unit. (A run-unit is a CODASYL term for a program or a terminal session.)

2. CURRENT OF <record type identifier>

   For each record type R, the most recently accessed record of this type is pointed to by CURRENT OF R.

3. CURRENT OF <set type identifier>

   For each set type S, the most recently accessed record in any occurrence of S (whether owner or member) is pointed to by the variable CURRENT OF S. We may also have the pointers, CURRENT OWNER OF S and CURRENT MEMBER OF S.

These currency indicators may be regarded as pointers to (or key values of) the appropriate records.

Reading a record from the database to the workspace is a two-stage process. First, using a sequence of FIND statements, we locate the desired record (i.e. the desired record becomes the CURRENT OF RUN-UNIT). Then, to copy this record into the workspace, we execute the command,

GET <record type>

Thus the FIND command is used to *navigate* in the database and this important command has a wide variety of formats. For example, we can perform the following operations using the FIND command:

1. Find a record given its database key:

    FIND <record name> USING <database key>

    In this case the location mode for the record type must be CALC or DIRECT.

2. Scan all the members of a set occurrence by virtue of their logical position in the occurrence:

    FIND [FIRST | LAST | NEXT | PRIOR] MEMBER IN CURRENT
    <set name> SET

3. Scan all the members of a set occurrence to find those with particular values in specified fields:

    FIND [DUPLICATE] <record name> RECORD IN CURRENT
    <set name> SET USING <field list>

    The field values being searched for must be assigned to the attributes in the field list prior to issuing this command.

4. Find the owner record in the current occurrence of a given set:

    FIND OWNER OF CURRENT <set name> SET

Examples
The following examples use a simplified pseudo-CODASYL DML (loosely based on Modula-2) which is similar in principal, but not in syntax, to those found in actual systems. (The syntax of actual CODASYL DMLs tends to be heavily influenced by COBOL.) The examples are given to illustrate the principal ideas of navigation and data retrieval in a CODASYL system.

1. Find all the female patients.

```
PATIENT.SEX := F;
FIND PATIENT RECORD IN CURRENT ALL-PATIENTS
        SET USING SEX;
WHILE NOT FAIL DO
    GET PATIENT;
    PRINT PATIENT.PNAME;
    FIND DUPLICATE PATIENT RECORD IN
        CURRENT ALL-PATIENTS SET USING SEX;
END;
```

In this example we set the SEX field of PATIENT to F (for female) and scan the singular set ALL-PATIENTS to find those members that match this field value. FAIL is a Boolean variable whose value indicates the success or failure of the previously executed FIND command.

2. Find all the patients on ward #10.

```
WARD.WARD# := 10;
FIND WARD RECORD USING WARD#;
FIND FIRST MEMBER IN CURRENT OCCUPIES SET;
WHILE NOT FAIL DO
     GET PATIENT;
     PRINT PATIENT.PNAME;
     FIND NEXT MEMBER IN CURRENT OCCUPIES SET;
END;
```

Here we first of all find the appropriate WARD record using its database key (WARD#). We then scan the occurrence of the set OCCUPIES which is owned by this WARD record, printing out the name of each patient record encountered.

3. Find the names of patients that have had operations in Theatre 'B'.

```
THEATRE.THEATRE# := B;
FIND THEATRE RECORD USING THEATRE#;
FIND FIRST MEMBER IN CURRENT LOCATED SET;
WHILE NOT FAIL DO
     FIND OWNER OF CURRENT UNDERGOES SET;
     GET PATIENT;
     PRINT PATIENT.PNAME;
     FIND NEXT MEMBER IN CURRENT LOCATED SET;
END ;
```

In this example, we must first find the correct THEATRE record using its database key (THEATRE#). We then scan the occurrence of the LOCATED set which is owned by this THEATRE record. For each OPERATION member record found, we find the owner of the occurrence of the UNDERGOES set of which this OPERATION record is a member. This yields a patient record that satisfies the query.

3.4   THE HIERARCHICAL DATA MODEL

The hierarchical data model is based on tree structures with record types as nodes. It is a more restrictive model than the network model and in fact may be considered as a subset of that model. The IMS database management system from IBM is based on the hierarchical model, but nowadays the model is largely only of historical interest. For that reason we shall outline only the principal features of the model.

Tree structures

A tree may be defined as a finite set of one or more nodes such that:

1. There is one specially designated node called the *root* of the tree.
2. The remaining nodes are partitioned into m ($m \geq 0$) disjoint sets T_1, T_2 ,...T_m and each of these sets is in turn a tree.

The trees T_1, T_2 ,...T_m are called the subtrees of the root.

Hierarchical databases

A hierarchical database is a collection of disjoint trees with record occurrences as nodes. Each tree has one root record node and all trees are constructed according to the connections between record types permitted by the *hierarchical definition tree* for the database. A link between a parent record type and a child record type on the hierarchical definition tree indicates that a 1:N relationship exists between those record types.

Example. A hierarchical definition tree for a university department
Consider a university consisting of a number of departments. Each department contains a number of research staff and lecturers, each of whom belongs to only one department. Each lecturer teaches a number of courses and each course has only one lecturer. Each research student is assigned to a single lecturer and a lecturer may have many such students. A hierarchical definition tree representing these associations might take the form shown in Figure 3.12.

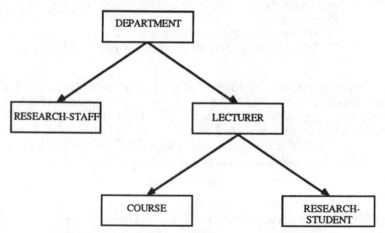

Figure 3.12   A hierarchical data definition tree

Note that there is *at most one* link between any two record types so that links need not be named. No record type may be linked to itself (no involuted relationships), and each record type has only one parent (except the root which has no parent). All links represent 1:N relationships (which of course include 1:1 relationships as special cases). Many-to-many relationships cannot be directly represented.

3.4.1   Conversion of a network to a hierarchy

Any network data structure diagram can be converted to a series of hierarchical definition trees by introducing multiple 'copies' of record types into the schema. Only one of these copies is the actual record type, the others being dummy or *virtual*. Virtual record types simply represent pointers or references to records of a given type.

The technique for conversion may be described as follows:

Step 1. Select a node R with no arcs entering (preferably one with many arcs leaving). Make R the root of a tree, and add to this tree all possible nodes, connected according to the rules for a hierarchical definition tree as described above. Any node which has already appeared in a tree is replaced by a virtual node.

Step 2. Remove R from the network, together with its arcs, and remove any node which as a result of the removal of R has no arcs entering or leaving.

Step 3. Go to step 1, and continue until no nodes remain in the network.

Example. Conversion of the hospital network database to a hierarchy.

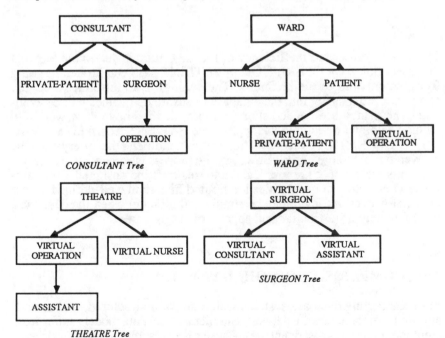

Figure 3.13 A hierarchical version of the hospital database

In converting the network version of the hospital database to a hierarchy we may choose WARD, THEATRE or CONSULTANT as the root of our first tree. Whichever one we choose, we end up with the same set of trees, the only difference being the position of virtual records on the trees. The resulting set of trees is shown in Figure 3.13.

3.4.2   Answering queries in the hierarchical model

Consider again the following query, which was solved in Section 3.3.4 for the network case:

'List the names of all patients that have had operations in Theatre B.'

To answer this query using the access paths provided by the above hierarchical data definition trees, we require an algorithm of the following form:

```
FIND the record for Theatre B in the THEATRE file;
FOR (each virtual operations record connected to Theatre B) DO
    FOR (each ward) DO
        FOR (each patient in that ward) DO
            FOR (each operation of that patient) DO
                IF virtual-operation = operation
                THEN print patient-name END
            END
        END
    END
END;
```

The awkwardness and inefficiency of this algorithm is due to the fact that the direct link *from* OPERATION *to* PATIENT has been broken in going from the network to the hierarchy. The solution is to introduce a certain amount of redundancy into the database to ensure that values will be available where they are needed. For example, in the above case we could include a pointer directly to the appropriate PATIENT record in each VIRTUAL OPERATION record. With this amendment the query may be answered much more easily. However, the process is somewhat arbitrary.

Thus we see that hierarchical databases must be designed very carefully. Their retrieval capabilities are limited to certain well-defined access paths. However, retrieval may be simple and efficient when the data has a natural hierarchical structure and appears on a single tree.

3.5   COMPARISON OF THE DATA MODELS

For constructing database systems which are well-structured, understandable and maintainable, the network and hierarchical data models suffer from a number of serious disadvantages. These may be summarised as follows:

1.   The models impose restrictions on the types of relationships that can be

directly represented. N:M and involuted relationships are awkward to represent in both models, often requiring the introduction of meaningless record types. Also, the hierarchical model cannot directly represent multiple relationships between the same record types.

2. For a large database the logical data model may be very complex. The necessity to introduce dummy or virtual record types in order to represent the natural relationships among the data, imposes a considerable burden on the database designer.

3. The data manipulation languages are highly procedural and access-path dependent. The database applications programmer is responsible for correctly navigating through the maze of record types and links in order to retrieve the desired information. Application programs written for network and hierarchical databases tend to be complex and therefore difficult to maintain.

4. Physical and logical data independence are difficult to achieve. This is highlighted by the fact that the data description and data manipulation languages of network and hierarchical database systems typically contain a wide variety of features which are directly related to physical storage organisation.

By comparison, with the relational model we have that:

1. The logical model is a simple collection of two-dimensional tables. These tables may represent entity types and a wide range of both simple and complex relationships.

2. The model involves no explicit positional, pointer or access-path considerations and a high degree of both logical and physical data independence can be achieved.

3. As we shall see in Chapter 4, relational data manipulation languages are succinct, powerful and relatively non-procedural.

EXERCISES

3.1 The entity relationship diagram for a genealogical database contains the entity set PERSONS and the involuted relationships FATHER-OF, MOTHER-OF and SPOUSE-OF which relate members of this entity set. Many CODASYL database management systems require that the owner and member record types in a set type be distinct. Show how this genealogical ER diagram may be mapped onto such a CODASYL implementation.

3.2 A wholesale distribution company maintains a database concerning its customers and the items it supplies to those customers. For each customer the database records details such as name, address, telephone number and credit limit. For each item it contains information such as the item's current price and the quantity in stock. At a particular time the customers and the items supplied represented in the database are as indicated in the following table:

CUSTOMER	ITEMS SUPPLIED
Smith	flour, yeast
Jones	flour, sugar
Adams	flour, yeast, sugar
Brown	sugar

(a) Draw a network data structure diagram which represents the relationship between items and customers. Sketch the *actual* network database, as defined by the above table, using the multilist structure to represent the links between records. With reference to this multilist structure outline algorithms for the following operations:

    (i) List the names of all the items supplied to a specified customer.

    (ii) List the names of all customers supplied with sugar.

    (iii) List the names of all customers supplied with at least one item in common with customer Smith.

(b) Convert the network data structure diagram from part (a) into hierarchical data definition trees and with reference to these structures outline algorithms for the operations (i) to (iii) above.

3.3   A college runs many evening courses (e.g. metalwork, car mechanics, pottery, art, etc). Each course may be taught by several lecturers and each lecturer may teach several courses. Each course always uses the same room but a room may be used by many different courses at different times. At enrolment time a student may enrol for any number of courses by paying the appropriate fee, which varies from course to course. Each student enrolling is given a card which records an identity number unique to that student together with his or her name, address, and telephone number.

    The college wishes to set up a database to maintain details of courses, lecturers, room bookings, timetabling of courses, students and enrolments. The system available is a network database management system.

    (i) Construct a suitable entity-relationship diagram to represent the above information.

    (ii) Reduce this ER diagram to an equivalent network data structure diagram, converting any many-to-many relationships into one-to-many relationships.

    (iii) Write out declarations for the record types and set types which would be required to define this database in a CODASYL environment.

4

Relational Database
Languages

4.1 INTRODUCTION

Relational database languages provide notations for deriving information
from the permanent relations in the database. There are many such languages available but most of them are based on one of two fundamental
approaches, namely,

1. *Relational algebra*, in which specialised operators are applied to relations.
2. *Relational calculus*, which is based on predicate calculus, and in which
   queries are expressed by specifying a predicate that tuples must satisfy.

In this chapter we shall study the algebra and calculus in some detail, and
also the correspondence between the two formalisms.

However, the algebra and calculus provide facilities only for retrieval
of information. In a practical language we must also have the capability of
updating the database, of applying aggregrate functions to derived data, and
of formatting output. Thus, we shall also study the principal features of one
of the most commonly used commercial languages, called SQL, whose
retrieval operations are based primarily on the calculus but also have some
algebraic features.

Finally in this chapter the very important subject of high-level query
optimisation is discussed. We shall not concern ourselves directly with
physical storage organisation at this stage (this is discussed in Chapters 6
and 7) but rather with techniques for *rewriting* relational queries in order to
minimise computation time. Of course, such optimisation cannot be
considered in isolation from physical storage since we must be aware of
which operations are most difficult to perform. However, a great deal of
optimisation can be performed at this high level and for very large database
systems, such optimisation may reduce the number of accesses to

secondary storage by orders of magnitude thereby improving significantly on response time.

4.2 RELATIONAL ALGEBRA

Relational algebra, first proposed by Codd (1970), is based on function application and the evaluation of algebraic expressions. Each operator of the relational algebra takes either one or two relations as its operands and produces a new relation as its result. The algebra was never intended as a stand-alone relational query language and perhaps for that reason, a standard syntax has not emerged. However it has been used as the basis for some database programming languages (described in Chapter 5) and the syntax we adopt here is similar to that used in these languages. We shall not however, define a precise syntax for the algebra, but rather rely on examples to illustrate its principal features.

We shall use as an example a simplified version of the college database schema from Chapter 2, which describes the relationships between students, courses and lecturers and consists of the following relations:

STUDENT (S#, SNAME, LEVEL)

COURSE (C#, TITLE, LNAME)

REPORT (S#, C#, MARKS)

LECTURER (LNAME, ROOM#)

In the following examples we shall assume that the relations contain the tuples as shown in Figure 4.1.

4.2.1   Set operators

As we saw in Chapter 2, relations may be considered as *sets* of tuples. Thus we may apply set operations such as union, intersection and difference to pairs of compatible relations, as follows:

Set union
The set of tuples that are in relation R, or in relation S, or in both is denoted by:

R *union* S

In accordance with the rule that all tuples in a relation must be distinct, duplicate tuples are eliminated from the result of the union.

Set intersection
The intersection of relations R and S is the set of tuples that are in R and also in S, and is denoted by:

R *intersect* S

STUDENT

S#	SNAME	LEVEL
876543	Jones	2
864532	Burns	1
856434	Cairns	3
876421	Hughes	2

COURSE

C#	TITLE	LNAME
216	Databases	Black
312	Software	Welsh
251	Numerical	Quinn
121	Compilers	Holt

REPORT

S#	C#	MARKS
876543	216	82
864532	216	75
864532	312	71
856434	121	49
876421	312	39
876543	251	70
864532	251	69
864532	121	78

LECTURER

LNAME	ROOM#
Black	1017
Welsh	1024
Holt	2014
Quinn	1010

Figure 4.1   An instance of the college database

Set difference
The set of tuples that are in R but not in S is denoted by:

   R *minus* S

For these expressions to be valid, the relations R and S must be *union compatible*, i.e. they must have the same degree and the same attribute names and types. Strictly speaking the attributes need not be in the same order, since in the relational model the ordering of attributes is immaterial. However, for simplicity we will assume that the ordering of attributes is the same in each relation.

   Note that the intersection operator is not strictly necessary, since we have that:

   R *intersect* S = R *minus* (R *minus* S)

However, for convenience intersection is often provided as a separate operator.

Examples
To illustrate the use of the set operators, suppose we have another instance of the STUDENT relation, called NEW_STUDENT as illustrated in Figure 4.2. This relation is clearly union-compatible with the relation STUDENT

and therefore may be combined with STUDENT in set operations. The relations which result from taking the union, intersection and difference of STUDENT and NEW_STUDENT are illustrated in Figure 4.3.

NEW_STUDENT

S#	SNAME	LEVEL
876342	Smith	3
865698	Turner	2
875923	Murphy	2
856434	Cairns	3
871290	Noble	1

Figure 4.2   Another instance of the STUDENT relation

STUDENT *union* NEW_STUDENT

S#	SNAME	LEVEL
876543	Jones	2
864532	Burns	1
856434	Cairns	3
876421	Hughes	2
876342	Smith	3
865698	Turner	2
875923	Murphy	2
871290	Noble	1

STUDENT *intersect* NEW_STUDENT

S#	SNAME	LEVEL
856434	Cairns	3

STUDENT *minus* NEW_STUDENT

S#	SNAME	LEVEL
876543	Jones	2
864532	Burns	1
876421	Hughes	2

Figure 4.3   The results of set operations

Note that the tuple for the student named Cairns appears only once in the relation (STUDENT *union* NEW_STUDENT) even though it is present in both the STUDENT and NEW_STUDENT relations.

4.2.2   Selection

Selection is a unary operator which selects from a relation those tuples that satisfy a given Boolean condition. We shall denote a selection on a relation R according to the Boolean condition B by:

R *where* B

The condition B is a formula involving,

(i)   Operands that are either constants or attributes.
(ii)   The comparison operators =, <, >, ≤, ≥, ≠.
(iii)   The logical operators *and*, *or*, and *not*.

For example, consider the following queries.

Query 1: 'Retrieve from the STUDENT relation the tuples for those students in level 1.'
In relational algebra, this may be written,

RESULT := STUDENT *where* LEVEL = 1 ;

Given the previously defined instance of the STUDENT relation, the RESULT relation would have the following form:

S#	SNAME	LEVEL
864532	Burns	1

Query 2: 'Retrieve from the COURSE relation the tuple(s) for the course(s) entitled "Databases".'

RESULT := COURSE *where* TITLE = 'Databases' ;

In this case the RESULT relation would contain the following:

C#	TITLE	LNAME
216	Databases	Black

Query 3: 'Retrieve from the REPORT relation details of those students taking course 216 who achieved a mark greater than 70 on that course.'

RESULT := REPORT *where* (C# = 216) *and* (MARK > 70) ;

As this example illustrates, the Boolean condition may involve any number of separate conditions. The RESULT relation would contain the following two tuples:

S#	C#	MARKS
876543 864532	216 216	82 75

4.2.3   Projection

Projection is a unary operator which projects out a vertical subset of a given relation, i.e. a subset obtained by selecting only specified attributes and eliminating duplicate tuples in the resultant relation. We shall denote the projection of a relation R on its attributes A_1, A_2, ... A_n by

$$R [A_1, A_2, ... A_n]$$

Consider the following examples.

Query 1: 'Retrieve the room numbers of all lecturers.'

RESULT := LECTURER [ROOM#] ;

Here the RESULT relation will contain the following tuples:

ROOM#
1017 1024 2014 1010

Note that since duplicates are eliminated, if two or more lecturers shared the same room, that room number would appear only once in the resultant relation.

Query 2: 'Retrieve the name of the lecturer who teaches course 312.'
To answer this query in relational algebra we must first select the appropriate tuple from the COURSE relation and then project it on the attribute LNAME.

RESULT := (COURSE *where* C# = 312) [LNAME] ;

This yields a RESULT relation containing just one tuple of the following form:

LNAME
Welsh

4.2.4   Cartesian product

Let R and S be relations of degree n_1 and n_2 respectively. Then the algebraic expression,

R *times* S

yields the Cartesian product of R and S, which is the set of all $(n_1+ n_2)$-tuples whose first n_1 components form a tuple in R and whose last n_2 components form a tuple in S.

For example, the Cartesian product of STUDENT and LECTURER, contains the tuples in the following table:

S#	SNAME	LEVEL	LNAME	ROOM#
876543	Jones	2	Black	1017
864532	Burns	1	Black	1017
856434	Cairns	3	Black	1017
876421	Hughes	2	Black	1017
876543	Jones	2	Welsh	1024
864532	Burns	1	Welsh	1024
856434	Cairns	3	Welsh	1024
876421	Hughes	2	Welsh	1024
876543	Jones	2	Holt	2014
864532	Burns	1	Holt	2014
856434	Cairns	3	Holt	2014
876421	Hughes	2	Holt	2014
876543	Jones	2	Quinn	1010
864532	Burns	1	Quinn	1010
856434	Cairns	3	Quinn	1010
876421	Hughes	2	Quinn	1010

Note that since two attributes of any relation may not have the same name, the names of any attributes common to the operand relations must be qualified in the result relation by the appropriate operand relation name.

As an example of the use of the *times* operator, suppose we wished to find all possible combinations of S# with C#. This could be done with the statement:

ALL_COMB := (STUDENT [S#]) *times* (COURSE [C#]) ;

That is, we project STUDENT on S# to obtain all S#s, COURSE on C# to obtain all C#s, and take the Cartesian product to obtain all possible combinations of the two. We could then use this result to find, for each student, those courses which he or she does not take. This could be achieved with the statement:

DO_NOT_TAKE := ALL_COMB *minus* (REPORT [S#, C#]) ;

That is, we subtract out all those (S#, C#) pairs which appear in the REPORT relation. This leaves us with a relation which contains each S# paired with those C#s which he/she does not take.

As another example, consider the query: 'Find all pairs of students who are at the same level'. To answer this query we need to take the Cartesian product of the STUDENT relation with itself. Many relational data languages permit such an operation by allowing one to introduce an *alias* for a given relation in a manner similar to the following:

TEMP *aliases* STUDENT
RESULT := ((TEMP *times* STUDENT)
        where ((TEMP.LEVEL = STUDENT.LEVEL)
        and (TEMP.S# < STUDENT.S#)))
        [TEMP.SNAME,STUDENT.SNAME]

This would give a RESULT relation of the following form:

TEMP.SNAME	STUDENT.SNAME
Hughes	Jones

The *aliases* operator takes a copy of the second operand relation and places it in the first relation. Of course in an actual implementation the system would not take an actual physical copy of the relation as this would be wasteful of time and storage space. Rather, TEMP would be recognised as a logical copy of the relation STUDENT.

4.2.5   Natural join

The natural join is a binary operator which takes two relations which have at least one common attribute and joins them such that each tuple of the resultant relation consists of a tuple from the first relation concatenated with each tuple from the second relation which has the same values of the common attributes. (Attributes which have the same names in the two relations are assumed to represent the same property.) In forming the result of the join duplicate columns are eliminated. For example, consider the instances, illustrated in Figure 4.4, of the relations R (A,B,C) and S (B,C,D), which have the attributes B and C in common.

| | R | |
A	B	C
a_1	b_1	c_1
a_2	b_1	c_1
a_3	b_2	c_2
a_4	b_2	c_3

| | S | |
B	C	D
b_1	c_1	d_1
b_1	c_1	d_2
b_2	c_3	d_3

Figure 4.4

In computing the join of R and S, we take each tuple of R and compare its B- and C-values with each tuple of S. Thus the first tuple of R which consists of the values $<a_1, b_1, c_1>$ will be concatenated only with the first two tuples of S, which also contain the values b_1 and c_1 for the B and C attributes respectively. Unlike the Cartesian product where, in the resultant relation, we had to qualify the names of common attributes, the result of a natural join contains only one copy of such attributes. The result of the join is shown in Figure 4.5.

R *join* S

A	B	C	D
a_1	b_1	c_1	d_1
a_1	b_1	c_1	d_2
a_2	b_1	c_1	d_1
a_2	b_1	c_1	d_2
a_4	b_2	c_3	d_3

Figure 4.5   The natural join of R and S

Returning to the college database the following examples show how we may use the natural join to answer rather more complex queries than we have considered so far.

Query 1: 'Retrieve the names of all students taking course 251.'

RESULT := ((REPORT *where* C# = 251) *join* STUDENT)
[SNAME] ;

Query 2: 'Retrieve the room number of the lecturer who takes course 351.'

RESULT := ((COURSE *where* C# = 351) *join* LECTURER)
[ROOM#] ;

Query 3: 'Retrieve the names of the lecturers who teach courses attended by at least one student at level 2.'

RESULT := (((STUDENT *where* LEVEL = 2) *join* REPORT) *join* COURSE) [LNAME] ;

We shall now look at the evaluation of Query 3 in detail, in order to see clearly the steps involved in evaluating a complex algebraic expression. The operation

STUDENT *where* LEVEL = 2

yields the following relation:

S#	SNAME	LEVEL
876543	Jones	2
876421	Hughes	2

Joining this relation with REPORT, where the common attribute is S#, we obtain the following relation:

S#	SNAME	LEVEL	C#	MARKS
876543	Jones	2	216	82
876543	Jones	2	251	70
876421	Hughes	2	312	39

The next step is to join this relation with COURSE, where this time the common attribute is C#. This gives the relation:

S#	SNAME	LEVEL	C#	MARKS	TITLE	LNAME
876543	Jones	2	216	82	Databases	Black
876543	Jones	2	251	70	Numerical	Quinn
876421	Hughes	2	312	39	Software	Welsh

Finally we project out LNAME, giving Black, Quinn and Welsh as the answers to the query.

Note that the natural join can be expressed in terms of other operators. Thus, given two relations R(A,B,C) and S(C,D), with common attribute C, we have that,

R $join$ S = ((R $times$ S) $where$ R.C = S.C) [A, B, R.C, D]

That is the natural join of two relations is equivalent to taking the Cartesian product of the relations, selecting those tuples which agree on the common attributes, and using the project operator to remove duplicate columns. However, the natural join is such a common and useful operator that it is almost always provided for in implementations of algebraic languages.

Theta-join

The natural join is only one of many possible join operators. The *theta-join* of R and S, written

R $join$ (A $\ominus$ B) S

is defined as those tuples in the Cartesian product of R and S in which the value of the predicate (R.A $\ominus$ S.B) evaluates to true. The symbol $\ominus$ represents one of the comparative operators (=, >, <, $\neq$, $\leq$, $\geq$). In common with the natural join the theta-join can always be rewritten in terms of a Cartesian product and a selection. It is rarely implemented as a specialised operator.

4.2.6   Division

The result of dividing a relation R by a relation S, denoted by,

R $divideby$ S

is the set of all tuples $<x>$ such that the tuples $<x, y>$ appear in R for *all* tuples $<y>$ in S. Here x and y each represent a group of one or more attribute values. Thus if R is of degree n and S is of degree m, then the result of R $divideby$ S will be of degree $n - m$. The division operator provides a means for implementing universal quantification in the algebra.

Consider the instances of the relations R_1(S#, C#), R_2(C#) and R_3(C#) illustrated in Figure 4.6.

R_1		R_2	R_3
S#	C#	C#	C#
S_1	C_1	C_1	C_1
S_1	C_2		C_2
S_1	C_3		C_3
S_2	C_1		
S_2	C_2		
S_3	C_1		
S_4	C_4		

Figure 4.6   Instances of the relations R_1, R_2, and R_3.

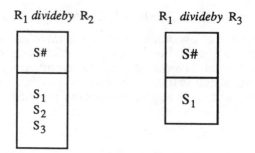

R_1 *divideby* R_2 R_1 *divideby* R_3

Figure 4.7   The results of division operations

Then the results of R_1 *divideby* R_2, and R_1 *divideby* R_3 are given in Figure 4.7. That is, the attribute values S_1, S_2, and S_3 appear in R_1 with *every* C# value in R_2. Only the attribute value S_1 appears in R_1 with every C# value in R_3.

Examples.
Query 1: *'Retrieve the names of the students who take all the courses.'*

RESULT := ((REPORT *divideby* (COURSE [C#]))
            join STUDENT) [SNAME] ;

In this query, projecting the COURSE relation on C# gives us a relation containing all the course numbers. Dividing this into REPORT will yield a relation, with attributes S# and MARKS, containing only those student numbers in the REPORT relation which appear with every C#. Finally, to obtain the student names we must join with the STUDENT relation and project out the attribute SNAME. Performing these operations on our instance of the college database, we find that only the student named Burns satisfies the query.

Query 2: *'Retrieve the numbers of those students taking at least those courses taken by the student with number 856434.'*

RESULT := (REPORT *divideby* ((REPORT *where* S# = 856434)
            [C#])) [S#] ;

To answer this query, we must first obtain the set of courses taken by the student with S# = 856434. This is performed by the expression:

(REPORT *where* S# = 856434)[C#]

Dividing this relation into REPORT and projecting on S#, we obtain the numbers of those students who appear in the REPORT relation with all the course numbers in the above relation.

Note that division, like join, is not a necessary algebraic operation in that it can be expressed in terms of other operations. For example, if we have relations R(A,B,C,D) and S(C,D), then we have that,

R *divideby* S ≡ R[A,B] *minus* ((R[A,B] *times* S) *minus* R)[A,B]

The division operator is rarely provided in implementations of algebraic query languages.

Thus, from the preceding sections we see that only a subset of five operators, comprising set union, set difference, Cartesian product, selection and projection are necessary to define the relational algebra. The others may be provided for convenience, but only the natural join is commonly implemented in algebraic query languages.

4.3 RELATIONAL CALCULUS

There are two different kinds of relational calculus: tuple-oriented calculus, in which the primitive objects are tuples, and domain-oriented calculus in which the primitive objects are elements of the attribute domains. Tuple-oriented calculus has formed the basis for several commercially available relational data languages, notably SQL (Chamberlin et al., 1976) and QUEL (Stonebraker et al., 1976). Domain-oriented calculus underlies IBM's relational database system Query-by-Example (or QBE), (Zloof, 1975).

4.3.1 Tuple relational calculus

The expressions of the tuple calculus are constructed from the following elements:

1. *Tuple variables* which are constrained to range over a named relation. If t is a tuple variable ranging over relation R, then $t.A$ represents the A-component of t where A is an attribute of R.

2. *Conditions* of the form $x \ominus y$, where $\ominus$ is a comparative operator (=, <, >, ≠, ≤, ≥). At least one of x and y must be of the form $t.A$. The other may be a constant. Conditions may also take the form, R(t), representing the assertion that t is a tuple in relation R.

3. *Well-formed formulas* (WFFs) constructed from the logical connectives (*and, or, not*) and the quantifiers ∃ (the existential quantifier meaning, *there exists*) and ∀ (the universal quantifier meaning, *for all*), constructed according to the following rules:
    (i)   Every condition is a WFF.
    (ii) If f_1 and f_2 are WFFs then so are f_1 *and* f_2 , f_1 *or* f_2, *not* f_1, and *not* f_2.
    (iii) If f is a WFF in which t occurs as a *free* variable, then ∃ t (f) and ∀t (f) are WFFs. (An occurrence of a variable in a WFF is *bound* if it has been introduced by a quantifier. Otherwise the variable is free.) The WFF ∃ t (f) asserts that *there exists* a value of t such that when we substitute this value for all free occurrences of t in f,

the formula f becomes true. The WFF ∀t (f) asserts that the formula f is true whatever value we substitute for *all* free occurrences of *t* in f;

(iv)   Nothing else is a WFF.

Tuple calculus expressions

A tuple calculus expression is of the form

{ *t*.A, *u*.B, *v*.C, . . . I f }

where *t*, *u*, *v*, . . . are tuple variables, A, B, C, . . . are attributes of the associated relations, and f is a WFF containing *t*, *u*, *v*, . . . as free variables.

Examples
The following examples refer to the college database introduced earlier. In these expressions the tuple variables *s*, *r*, *c* and *l* range over the relations STUDENT, REPORT, COURSE and LECTURER respectively.

Query 1: 'Retrieve all course numbers.'

{ *c*.C# I COURSE(*c*) }

In English, this tuple calculus expression reads, 'Retrieve the C# component of all tuples *c* such that *c* is a tuple in the COURSE relation'.

Query 2: 'Retrieve the numbers of all students at level 1.'

{ *s*.S# I STUDENT(*s*) *and* *s*.LEVEL = 1 }

We may read this expression as 'Retrieve the S# component of all tuples *s* where *s* is a tuple in the STUDENT relation and the LEVEL component of *s* is equal to 1'.

Query 3: 'Retrieve the numbers and names of students taking course 121.'

{ *s*.S#, *s*.SNAME I STUDENT(*s*) *and* ∃ *r* (REPORT(*r*)
    and r.S# = *s*.S# *and r*.C# = 121)}

This may be read as 'Retrieve the S# and SNAME components of all tuples *s* where *s* is a tuple in the STUDENT relation, and there exists a tuple, *r*, in the REPORT relation with the same S# value as *s* and a C# value equal to 121'.

Query 4: 'Retrieve the numbers of those courses which are taken by at least one student in level 1.'

{ *c*.C# I COURSE(*c*) *and* ∃ *r* (REPORT(*r*) *and r*.C# = *c*.C#
    and ∃ *s* (STUDENT(*s*) *and s*.S# = *r*.S#
    and s.LEVEL = 1))}

In this example we see that quantified WFFs may be nested to arbitrary depths.

Query 5: 'Retrieve the names of those students who take all courses.'

{ s.SNAME | STUDENT(s) *and* $\forall$ c $\exists$ r (COURSE(c) *and*
REPORT(r) *and* c.C# = r.C# *and* r.S# = s.S#)}

This example shows the use of both the universal and existential quantifiers. Note the ease with which this query may be expressed in the calculus, in comparison with the algebra, because of the availability of the universal quantifier.

4.3.2   Domain relational calculus

In domain relational calculus the variables range over domains rather than relations. Also, we have *membership conditions* of the form:

R (A:v_1, B:v_2, C:v_3, ...)

where A, B, C, ... are attributes of R and v_1, v_2, v_3, ... are either domain variables or constants. For example, the condition

STUDENT (S# : 872501, LEVEL : 1)

is true if and only if there exists a tuple in the STUDENT relation having S# = 872501 and LEVEL = 1.

The rules concerning WFFs etc. as given for the tuple calculus, apply also to the domain calculus.

Domain calculus expressions

To illustrate the domain calculus we shall give domain calculus expressions for each of the five queries considered above for the tuple calculus.

Query 1: 'Retrieve all course numbers.'

{ C | COURSE(C# : C) }

Query 2: 'Retrieve the numbers of all students in level 1.'

{ S | STUDENT (S# : S, LEVEL : 1) }

Query 3: 'Retrieve the numbers and names of the students taking course 121.'

{ S, N | STUDENT (S# : S, SNAME : N)
and REPORT (S# : S, C# : 121) }

Query 4: 'Retrieve the numbers and titles of courses taken by at least one student at level 1.'

{ C, T | COURSE (C# : C, TITLE : T)
and $\exists$ S (REPORT (C# : C, S# : S)
and STUDENT (S# : S, LEVEL : 1))}

Query 5: '*Retrieve the names of those students who take all courses.*'

  { N | ∃ S(STUDENT (S# : S, SNAME : N) *and*
        ∀C (*if* COURSE (C# : C) *then* REPORT (S# : S, C# : C)))}

4.4   THE SQL LANGUAGE

SQL (originally spelled SEQUEL and usually pronounced this way) was developed by IBM (Chamberlin et al., 1976) in the late seventies as part of their experimental relational database system called 'System R'. This system is now marketed as DB2 and, because of the overwhelming influence of IBM, SQL is rapidly becoming the internationally recognised standard relational database query language. Thus, most currently available relational database systems provide an SQL-like interface. SQL is based mainly on relational calculus, using English key words in place of the quantifiers and logical connectives. However, it also provides set operations which give it a flavour of relational algebra.

   Implementations of SQL contain sophisticated features for retrieval, insertion, deletion and update as well as built-in functions for tailoring output. In the following sections we shall examine, by way of examples, only at some of the principal features of the language. A complete description of the syntax is given in Appendix 2.

4.4.1   Retrieval operations

Query 1: '*Retrieve the numbers and names of all students at level 1.*'

      SELECT S#, SNAME
      FROM   STUDENT
      WHERE LEVEL = 1 ;

This example presents the simplest form of the SELECT statement in SQL, whereby specified attributes (S# and SNAME) are selected from tuples in a specified relation (STUDENT) for which some specified condition (LEVEL = 1) is satisfied. An important point to stress is that, as in relational algebra, the result of a query in SQL is another relation - a relation derived from the permanent relations in the relational schema for the database. Recall that the same query expressed in relational algebra takes the form:

      (STUDENT *where* LEVEL = 1) [S#, SNAME]

while in tuple calculus the same query takes the form:

      { *s*.S#, *s*.SNAME | STUDENT(*s*) *and s*.LEVEL = 1}

However, SQL being an end-user language also includes facilities for tailoring the output of a query. For example, we may order the resulting tuples according to some sort criterion, by including an ORDER BY clause:

```
SELECT S#, SNAME
FROM STUDENT
WHERE LEVEL = 1
ORDER BY SNAME ASC ;
```

The result of this query will be a relation containing the numbers and names of students at level 1, in ascending alphabetical order.

Query 2: 'Retrieve the numbers and names of students who take course 121.'

```
SELECT STUDENT.S#, STUDENT.SNAME
FROM STUDENT, REPORT
WHERE STUDENT.S# = REPORT.S#
AND REPORT.C# = 121 ;
```

In this example, unlike the first query, we must qualify the attribute names with the names of the relations in order to avoid ambiguity.

This example shows how the SQL SELECT statement handles queries which would require join operations in relational algebra. Also, since the condition in the WHERE clause may involve comparison operators other than equality, we may easily perform theta-joins in SQL. (See Query 5 below.) Note that the solution above is similar in form to the equivalent tuple relational calculus expression given in Section 4.3.1, namely:

$$\{ \ s.S\#, s.SNAME \mid STUDENT(s) \ and \ \exists \ r \ (\ REPORT(r) \\ and \ r.S\# = s.S\# \ and \ r.C\# = 121 \ )\}$$

An alternative solution to the above query in SQL is the following:

```
SELECT S#, SNAME
FROM STUDENT
WHERE S# IN
     (SELECT S#
      FROM REPORT
      WHERE C# = 121 ) ;
```

R.T.C. LIBRARY
LETTERKENNY

Note here the use of a *nested* SELECT clause in conjunction with the IN operator. A nested SELECT clause denotes a set of tuples, i.e. an unnamed intermediate relation. In this example the inner SELECT clause retrieves the set of student numbers, S#, from the REPORT relation, where each of those students takes course 121. The outer SELECT clause retrieves from the STUDENT relation the name, SNAME, corresponding to each S# value in that set.

SELECT clauses can be nested to any depth, subject to restrictions imposed by specific implementations. The next example has three such clauses.

Query 3: 'Retrieve the numbers and names of students who take at least one of the courses given by the lecturer named Quinn.'

```
SELECT S#, SNAME
FROM STUDENT
WHERE  S# IN
       (SELECT S#
        FROM REPORT
        WHERE  C# IN
               (SELECT C#
                FROM  COURSE
                WHERE  LNAME = 'Quinn' ) ) ;
```

Alternatively, we could write:

```
SELECT  STUDENT.S#, STUDENT.SNAME
FROM  STUDENT, REPORT, COURSE
WHERE  STUDENT.S# = REPORT.S#
AND  REPORT.C# = COURSE.C#
AND  COURSE.LNAME = 'Quinn' ;
```

Whether one uses this form or the nested query form above is largely a matter of personal choice. Both forms are equally valid and ideally both should be equally efficient in any given implementation.

Query 4: 'Find all pairs of student numbers such that the students are at the same level.'
In Section 4.2.4 we saw that in relational algebra this query required the use of the *aliases* operator and a Cartesian product. In SQL we may express this query in the following form:

```
SELECT  STUDENT.S#, TEMP.S#
FROM  STUDENT, STUDENT TEMP
WHERE  STUDENT.S# < TEMP.S#
AND  STUDENT.LEVEL = TEMP.LEVEL ;
```

Here again we have introduced an alias relation called TEMP in the FROM clause, which is a logical copy of the STUDENT relation. The first condition in the WHERE clause (STUDENT.S# < TEMP.S#) ensures that a student number does not appear in the result paired with itself, and that any given pair appears only once.

Query 5: 'Retrieve all details of those students who do not take course 121.'
In SQL this query may be expressed in the following way:

```
SELECT *
FROM  STUDENT
WHERE NOT EXISTS
        ( SELECT *
          FROM  REPORT
          WHERE  REPORT.S# = STUDENT.S#
          AND  REPORT.C# = 121 )  ;
```

This example firstly illustrates the use of the star symbol (*), which is a shorthand notation indicating that all the attributes of the relation (or relations) specified in the FROM clause are to be retrieved. Secondly we have used the SQL representation of the existential quantifier, EXISTS. In SQL the expression

EXISTS (SELECT . . .)

evaluates to true if the result of the enclosed SELECT expression is not empty. Thus the SQL solution to the above query is more easily understood if we reformulate the query as,

'Retrieve all details of those students such that there does not exist a tuple in the REPORT relation connecting them with course 121.'

Actually, as the careful reader may have already realised, this query could have been expressed in a simpler form, without the use of the existential quantifier, i.e.

```
SELECT *
FROM STUDENT
WHERE S# NOT IN
    ( SELECT S#
      FROM REPORT
      WHERE REPORT.C# = 121 ) ;
```

However there are certain classes of complex query which require the use of EXISTS, especially in its negated form. The next query illustrates such a situation.

Query 6: 'Retrieve the numbers of those students who take every course.'

As we saw in query 5 of section 4.2.1, to answer this query using relational calculus one may use the universal quantifier. SQL does not have an explicit equivalent to this quantifier but queries involving the universal quantifier can always be rewritten in terms of the existential quantifier in its negated form. Thus the above query may be re-expressed in the following form:

'Retrieve the numbers of those students such that there does not exist a course that they do not take.'

In SQL this may be expressed in the following form:

```
SELECT S#
FROM   STUDENT
WHERE  NOT EXISTS
    ( SELECT *
      FROM  COURSE
      WHERE NOT EXISTS
        ( SELECT *
          FROM  REPORT
          WHERE REPORT.S# = STUDENT.S#
          AND   REPORT.C# = COURSE.C# )) ;
```

Query 7: 'List the numbers of all those students who are at level 1 or who take course 121.'
The SQL answer to this query illustrates the use of a set operator, namely that of set union.

        (SELECT S#
        FROM STUDENT
        WHERE LEVEL = 1)
        UNION
        (SELECT S#
        FROM REPORT
        WHERE C# = 121) ;

The UNION operator in SQL performs exactly the same function as in relational algebra, merging the results of two subqueries and eliminating duplicate tuples.

Query 8: 'How many students take course 121 and what was the average mark obtained on this course?'
There are no explicit constructs in either relational algebra or relational calculus for answering this type of query. However, SQL being a practical end-user language, includes a variety of built-in functions to increase its retrieval capabilities. The most useful of these functions operate on the values of a single attribute of a relation (which may be a permanent relation or the result of a SELECT statement), and may be described as follows:

(i)   COUNT: counts the number of values in a specified column.
(ii) SUM: totals the values in a specified column containing numeric values.
(iii) AVG: calculates the average of the values in a specified column which contains numeric values.
(iv) MIN: returns the minimum value in a specified column.
(v)   MAX: returns the maximum value in a specified column.

Thus the above query may be expressed in SQL by the following statement

        SELECT COUNT(*), AVG(MARKS)
        FROM REPORT
        WHERE C# = 121 ;

4.4.2   Update operations

We shall merely illustrate update operations in SQL with three simple examples. For further details see Date (1986) and Appendix 2.

Example 1: Insert into the relation STUDENT a new tuple with the following field values: S# = 867520, SNAME = 'James Smith' and LEVEL = 2.

        INSERT
        INTO STUDENT
        VALUES (867520, 'James Smith', 2) ;

Example 2: Delete all students at level 3.

    DELETE
    FROM STUDENT
    WHERE LEVEL = 3 ;

All the tuples in the specified relation which satify the predicate in the WHERE clause are deleted.

Example 3: Change the lecturer on course 251 from Quinn to Black.

    UPDATE COURSE
    SET LNAME = 'Black'
    WHERE C# = 251 ;

All the tuples in the specified relation which satisfy the predicate in the WHERE clause are updated according to the assignments in the SET clause.

4.5   QUERY OPTIMISATION

As we have seen in this and the preceding chapters, the relational model provides users with a high-level view of the data in a database system, and hides from him the complexities of the physical organisation of the data. Data manipulation languages whether based on the algebra or calculus, allow users to formulate queries based on this abstract view of the data. This gives the user great power and flexibility, but imposes on the database management system almost the entire burden of ensuring efficient implementation of queries. Of course considerable optimisation can be performed at the level of physical storage by the use of efficient indexing and other fast data access techniques. We shall consider these in Chapters 6 and 7. In this section we shall be concerned with a higher level of optimisation involving the rearrangement of relational algebraic expressions to facilitate efficient implementation.

The calculus is often claimed to be higher-level than the algebra, since the algebra specifies the order of operations while the calculus leaves it to a compiler or interpreter to determine the most efficient order of evaluation. Our use of the algebra in considering query optimisation is justified by the fact that, as illustrated in the following section, there is a direct correspondence between the two formalisms.

4.5.1   Correspondence between the algebra and calculus

For every relational algebraic expression there is an equivalent 'safe' expression in tuple relational calculus. A safe calculus expression is one which denotes a subset of a finite domain formed from the Cartesian product of the stored relations. Thus a safe expression excludes conditions such as '*not* R(t)' (i.e. t is not a tuple in relation R), which has a potentially infinite domain. For a formal proof of this result see for example, Ullman (1982) or Yang (1986).

In the early days of the relational model, Codd (1972b) proved that the converse of this result, namely that the algebra is at least as powerful as the calculus. In doing so, he presented a *reduction algorithm* by which an arbitrary calculus expression can be reduced to an equivalent expression in the algebra. Codd coined the term *relationally complete* to describe a relational data language which is at least as powerful as the calculus - that is, a language whose expressive power is sufficient to define any relation definable via an expression in the relational calculus. Thus the algebra is relationally complete.

To illustrate this correspondence between the algebra and the calculus, we may write calculus equivalents for each of the five essential operators of relational algebra (i.e. set union, set difference, Cartesian product, selection, projection) as follows.

Set union

$$R_1 \ union \ R_2 \ = \ \{ \ t \ | \ R_1(t) \ or \ R_2(t) \ \}$$

Set difference

$$R_1 \ minus \ R_2 \ = \ \{ \ t \ | \ R_1(t) \ and \ not \ R_2(t) \ \}$$

Cartesian product

$$R_1 \ times \ R_2 \ = \ \{ \ <t, r> \ | \ R_1(t) \ and \ R_2(r) \ \}$$

(where $<t, r>$ means the concatenation of tuples t and r.)

Selection

$$R_1 \ where \ f(X) \ = \ \{ \ t \ | \ R_1(t) \ and \ f(t.X) \ \}$$

(where X represents a subset of the attributes of R_1.)

Projection

$$R_1[X] \ = \ \{ \ t.X \ | \ R_1(t) \ \}$$

(again where X represents a subset of the attributes of R_1.)

In view of the equivalence described above we are free to choose either the algebra or the calculus when we consider the subject of query optimisation. In this respect the algebra has a number of advantages. Firstly, it is *closed* under the algebraic operations, i.e. no operation produces an object outside the scope of the algebra. Secondly it has the property of *referential transparency*, i.e. a variable or expression always denotes the same value within a given scope (a property shared with functional programming languages). These properties mean that we may substitute equivalent algebraic expressions for existing expressions without altering the value of the result. This is very important in query optimisation.

4.5.2   Basic optimisation strategies

Expressions involving the *join* or *times* operators may, in particular, take a long time to evaluate when the relations involved are large. Projection operations, with the elimination of duplicates can also be somewhat time-consuming. (Strategies for implementing these operations at the level of physical storage are considered in detail in Chapter 7.) However, significant improvements can be made by re-ordering operations so as to minimise the size of relations involved in these operations. Basic strategies include:

(i)   Performing selections as early as possible.
(ii)   Combining multiple selections.
(iii)   Combining multiple selections and projections.

Combining multiple selections

The following equivalence obviously holds:

$$(R \ where \ B_1 \ ) \ where \ B_2 \ \equiv \ R \ where \ (B_1 \ and \ B_2 \ )$$

In a practical system some selections may be faster than others in that they are performed using a direct access technique (e.g. secondary indexing or hashing - see Chapters 6 and 7). Others may require a scan of the whole relation. Clearly, fast selections should not be combined with slow selections since the overall effect will be to make the entire selection slow. Thus it is clear that full optimisation requires a detailed knowledge of the physical storage organisation of the database and of the strategies for implementing operations. We shall return to such considerations in Chapters 6 and 7.

Commuting selections with joins and products

If condition B involves the attributes of R but not those of S, then we have:

$$(R \ join \ S) \ where \ B \ \equiv \ (R \ where \ B) \ join \ S$$

$$(R \ times \ S) \ where \ B \ \equiv \ (R \ where \ B) \ times \ S$$

This transformation can considerably reduce the number of tuples to be considered for the join. More generally, if we separate the condition B as follows:

$$B \ \equiv \ B_R \ and \ B_S \ and \ B_C \ and \ B'$$

where,

B_R involves only attributes of R;
B_S involves only attributes of S;
B_C involves the common attributes of R and S;
B' represents the remaining part of B;

then we have that:

$$(R \; join \; S) \; where \; B \; \equiv \; ((R \; where \; (B_R \; and \; B_C)) \; join$$
$$(S \; where \; (B_S \; and \; B_C))) $$
$$where \; B'$$

A similar equivalence holds for the *times* operator.

Example

Suppose we wish to find the numbers of all students at level 1 who take a course lectured by Quinn and have achieved a mark of over 70 on that course. This could be expressed as:

$$\text{RESULT} := (\text{STUDENT} \; join \; \text{REPORT} \; join \; \text{COURSE}) \; where$$
$$(\text{LEVEL} = 1 \; and \; \text{MARK} > 70 \; and$$
$$\text{LNAME} = \text{'Quinn'}) \; [\text{S\#}]$$

The condition LEVEL = 1 refers only to an attribute of STUDENT. The condition MARK > 70 refers only to an attribute of REPORT. The condition LNAME = 'Quinn' refers only to an attribute of COURSE. Thus, applying the above transformation, we obtain:

$$\text{RESULT} := (((\text{STUDENT} \; where \; \text{LEVEL} = 1) \; join$$
$$(\text{REPORT} \; where \; \text{MARK} > 70)) \; join$$
$$(\text{COURSE} \; where \; \text{LNAME} = \text{'Quinn'})) \; [\text{S\#}]$$

That is, the three selections are performed on their respective relations first, thereby significantly reducing the number of tuples which must be considered for the join operations.

Commuting selections and projections

If condition B involves only the projected attributes X, then we have that,

$$(R \, [X]) \; where \; B \; \equiv \; (R \; where \; B) \, [X]$$

This is a particularly useful transformation for a fast selection whose implementation might be inhibited by the projection.

Combining projections

If X, Y and Z are attributes of R, then the following equivalence holds:

$$((R \, [X,Y,Z]) \, [X,Y]) \, [X] \; \equiv \; R \, [X]$$

The equivalence is obvious for this simple case. However in a lengthy, complicated relational algebraic expression, detecting such redundant projections may not be so easy.

Moving projections before joins

In moving projections before joins we must be careful that we do not remove any of the common attributes from relations to be joined before the join has been carried out. If X denotes the common attributes of R and S, then we have that:

$$(R \, join \, S) \, [X] \; \equiv \; R \, [X] \, join \, S \, [X]$$

However this rule is not applicable to any set of attributes X. A more general equivalence may be constructed as follows (Gray, 1984):

Let A_R be the attributes of R, A_S be the attributes of S, and A_C be the set of attributes common to both R and S, i.e.

$$A_C = A_R \cap A_S$$

Then we have that,

$$(R \, join \, S) \, [X] \; \equiv \; ((R \, [(X \cap A_R) \cup A_C]) \, join$$
$$(S \, [\, (X \cap A_S) \cup A_C])) \, [X]$$

This is not always advantageous, since a projection may adversely affect the physical implementation of a join. For example, a projection to a temporary file may render existing indexes unusable for the join (see Chapter 7 on the use of index files for evaluating joins). However, projection does reduce the size of tuples and (with the removal of duplicates) the number of tuples to be considered for the join. Once again, the best strategy for optimisation requires a knowledge of the physical storage organisation and the techniques employed for evaluating algebraic operations at the physical level.

Optimising set operations

The following transformation rules may be useful, in certain circumstances, for optimising set operations:

1. $(R \, union \, S) \, where \, B \; \equiv \; (R \, where \, B) \, union \; (S \, where \, B)$

   With this transformation we reduce the number of tuples to be considered for the *union* operation.

2. $(R \, minus \, S) \, where \, B \; \equiv \; (R \, where \, B) \, minus \; (S \, where \, B)$

3. $(R \, union \, S) \, [X] \; \equiv \; (R \, [X]) \, union \; (S \, [X])$

4. $(R \, minus \, S) \, [X] \; \equiv \; (R \, [X]) \, minus \; (S \, [X])$

   provided X includes the key attributes of R (and hence of S).

5. $((R \, where \, B_1) \, [X]) \, union \, ((R \, where \, B_2) \, [X])$
   $$\equiv \; (R \, where \, (B_1 \, or \, B_2)) \, [X]$$

Note that the *intersect* operator is just a special case of *join*, so that rules for optimising joins apply also to intersections.

4.6   CASE STUDY

Consider a database which represents the relationships between gourmets, dishes and restaurants. Gourmets frequent many different restaurants each of which serves many different dishes. A given dish may be served by more than one restaurant and may be liked by more than one gourmet. Naturally each gourmet likes many dishes.

The entity-relationship diagram for this database is shown in Figure 4.8. It contains three entity types, GOURMET, RESTAURANT and DISH and three many-to-many binary relationships, FREQUENTS, LIKES and SERVES. (Note that if we had been required to represent a situation in which gourmets liked a given dish only at certain restaurants and not at others, then LIKES would have to be a ternary relationship.)

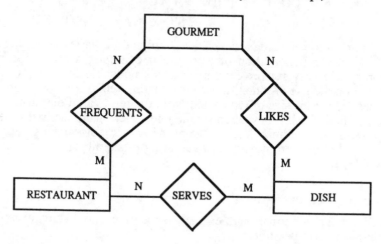

Figure 4.8

Assuming, for simplicity, that we do not wish to store any information on the entities other than an identifying name, this database may be represented by three relationship relations FREQUENTS, SERVES and LIKES which have the following schemes:

FREQUENTS (<u>GOURMET</u>, <u>RESTAURANT</u>)

SERVES (<u>RESTAURANT</u>, <u>DISH</u>)

LIKES (<u>GOURMET</u>, <u>DISH</u>)

For each of the following queries we shall give a solution in optimised relational algebra, tuple relational calculus, and SQL.

Query 1: 'List the restaurants that serve a dish that Joe likes.'

Algebra

JOES_DISHES := (LIKES *where* GOURMET = 'Joe') [DISH] ;

JOES_RESTS := (JOES_DISHES *join* SERVES)
[RESTAURANT] ;

Tuple-Calculus

{*s*.RESTAURANT | SERVES(*s*) *and* ∃ *l* (LIKES(*l*) *and*
l.DISH = *s*.DISH *and* *l*.GOURMET = 'Joe')}

SQL

```
SELECT  RESTAURANT
FROM   SERVES, LIKES
WHERE  SERVES.DISH = LIKES.DISH
AND  GOURMET = 'Joe'
```

Query 2: 'List the gourmets that frequent at least one restaurant that serves a dish they like.'

Algebra

TEMP := ((LIKES *join* SERVES) *join* FREQUENTS) [GOURMET] ;

Calculus

{ *f*.GOURMET | FREQUENTS(*f*) *and*
∃ *s* (SERVES(*s*) *and* *s*.RESTAURANT =*f*.RESTAURANT
and ∃ *l* (LIKES(*l*) *and* *l*.DISH = *s*.DISH
and *l*.GOURMET =*f*.GOURMET))}

SQL

```
SELECT GOURMET
FROM   FREQUENTS
WHERE  RESTAURANT IN
       (SELECT RESTAURANT
        FROM  SERVES
        WHERE  DISH IN
               (SELECT  DISH
                FROM  LIKES
                WHERE  GOURMET =
                       FREQUENTS.GOURMET ) ) ;
```

Query 3: 'List the restaurants that serve all the dishes liked by Joe.'

Algebra

(i)   In an algebra that does not include the *divideby* operator:

JOES_DISHES := (LIKES *where* GOURMET = 'Joe') [DISH] ;
ALL_RESTS := SERVES [RESTAURANT] ;
ALL_COMB := JOES_DISHES *times* ALL_RESTS ;
NOT_JOES := (ALL_COMB *minus* SERVES) [RESTAURANT] ;
JOES_RESTS := ALL_RESTS *minus* NOT_JOES ;

(ii) In an algebra that provides the *divideby* operator:

JOES_DISHES := (LIKES *where* GOURMET = 'Joe') [DISH] ;
JOES_RESTS := SERVES *divideby* JOES_DISHES ;

Calculus

{ *s*.RESTAURANTS | SERVES(*s*) *and* ∀ *l* (LIKES(*l*) *and*
l.GOURMET = 'Joe' *and* *l*.DISH = *s*.DISH)}

SQL

```
SELECT RESTAURANT
FROM SERVES
WHERE NOT EXISTS
    (SELECT DISH
     FROM LIKES
     WHERE GOURMET = 'Joe' AND  NOT EXISTS
        (SELECT RESTAURANT
         FROM SERVES TEMP
         WHERE  TEMP.DISH = LIKES.DISH
         AND  SERVES.RESTAURANT =
            TEMP.RESTAURANT ) ) ;
```

EXERCISES

4.1 Consider a simple library database holding details of books in stock, the library members and loans of books to members, consisting of the following relations:

BOOK (CAT#, TITLE, AUTHOR, PUBLISHER)

MEMBER (MEMBER#, NAME, ADDRESS)

LOAN (CAT#, MEMBER#, DATE-LOANED)

The attribute CAT# is a catalogue number unique to each book, and MEMBER# denotes a membership number unique to each member. The other attributes are self explanatory.

Give solutions in optimised relational algebra, tuple relational calculus and SQL to the following queries:

(a) Retrieve the titles and authors of all books published by 'Prentice Hall'.

(b) Retrieve the titles of all books which were loaned on 15 February 1987.

(c) Retrieve the name of the member to whom a book with the title *For whom the bell tolls* was loaned on 12 March 1987.

(d) Retrieve the title and author of any book, published by 'Prentice Hall', which which was on loan to a member with the name 'John Smith' before 21 June 1987.

(e) Retrieve the names and addresses of the members to whom all of the books written by the author 'E. Hemingway' have been loaned.

(f) Retrieve the titles and authors of all those books which have never been on loan.

(g) Retrieve all details of those books that have never been on loan to member number 34216.

(h) Retrieve the names of the members who have borrowed at least those books which have been borrowed by member number 167542.

4.2 Section 4.5.1 gives tuple relational calculus expressions for the five essential operators of relational algebra. Give similar calculus expressions for the natural *join* and *divideby* operators of the algebra.

4.3 Show that SQL is relationally complete by giving expressions in SQL for the five essential operators of relational algebra.

5

Programming Languages and Databases

5.1 INTRODUCTION

The development of database systems operating on large quantities of highly structured, interrelated data requires integrated programming environments. In particular, the integration of programming languages, database models, I/O interfaces and communication techniques. This chapter is particularly concerned with the integration of database models and programming languages, leading to the notion of database programming languages. Database programming languages combine the facilities for database definition and manipulation of a data model with the data structures and operators of a programming language. Most current database programming languages are an integration of Pascal- or Modula-like languages and versions of the relational database model.

Commercial database management systems typically provide interfaces to the common programming languages such as COBOL, FORTRAN, Pascal, and PL/1. These interfaces may take the form of a library of database access procedures which may be called from programs written in high-level languages. Such programs are then compiled and linked to the appropriate precompiled database procedures.

Alternatively, an applications programmer may be permitted to embed statements from a database language such as SQL in his programs, and a pre-compiler is used to translate the embedded statements into constructs of the programming language, typically into procedure calls to the database run-time system. Examples of systems using these techniques are ORACLE, INGRES and DB2. The advantage of such an approach is that the compiler of the programming language does not need to be modified to any significant extent. However, because the database constructs are not fully integrated into the programming language, facilities for type checking and the associated consistency constraints cannot always be effectively applied to the database constructs.

In recent years a number of database programming languages, including Pascal/R (Schmidt, 1977, Schmidt and Mall, 1980), Modula/R (Reimer, 1984), PLAIN (Wasserman et al., 1979, 1980), ASTRAL (Amble et al., 1976), RIGEL (Rowe and Shoens, 1979), Theseus (Shopiro, 1979), and RAPP (Hughes and Connolly, 1987), have been developed which integrate a complete set of relational database operations into a well-structured, strongly-typed language. Although the design goals vary among these languages, they are all united in their main objective, which is to provide an effective tool for the development of database application programs. In each of these languages a programmer can manipulate relations in much the same way as he can the more common language data structures such as arrays, sets or records. As the database constructs are fully integrated with the programming language, one can take full advantage of the type definition and type checking facilities of the language to help maintain database correctness and consistency. Also, the branching, iteration and input/output features of the programming language can be applied to objects of type relation.

The idea of extending programming languages to embrace database management concepts may be extended to allow *all* data objects (not just files or relations) to have *persistence*. That is, any data object may exist for an arbitrarily long time, beyond the lifetime of the program in which it is created. Now that virtual memory is commonplace, the distinction between primary and secondary memory should be less important. Thus the database applications programmer should be able to specify persistence as an orthogonal property of data, independent of type. The language PS-Algol (Atkinson et al., 1983) is designed to support persistence, and thereby offers a contrasting approach to database applications programming. Unlike the languages mentioned in the previous paragraph, PS-Algol does not involve the addition of new data structures to a language, but rather provides persistence as a property applicable to all existing data structures.

In this chapter we shall first of all use Modula-2 to illustrate the application of modern software engineering techniques to database applications programming. We shall then review the main features of some of the special purpose database programming languages mentioned above. Finally we look at the *functional data model* and at a programming language based on this model.

5.2   DATABASE INTEGRITY

The preservation of the integrity of a database system is concerned with the maintenance of the correctness and consistency of the data. In a multi-user database environment this is a major task, since integrity violations may arise from many different sources, such as typing errors by data entry clerks, logical errors in application programs, or errors in system software which result in data corruption. Many commercial database management systems have an integrity subsystem which is responsible for monitoring transactions which update the database and detecting integrity violations. In the event of an integrity violation, the system then takes appropriate action, which should involve rejecting the operation, reporting the violation, and if necessary returning the database to a consistent state. However, these integrity subsystems are in general rather primitive and the problems of maintaining the correctness of the database are left largely in the hands of the database implementor.

Integrity rules may be divided into three broad categories:

1. *Domain integrity rules*, which are concerned with maintaining the correctness of attribute values within relations. The rule, given in Chapter 2, by which the values of the primary key attributes in any tuple should not be null, also falls into this category.

2. *Intra-relation integrity rules*, which relate to the correctness of relationships among attributes of the same relation (e.g. functional dependencies), and to the preservation of key uniqueness.

3. *Referential integrity rules*, which are concerned with maintaining the correctness and consistency of relationships between relations.

In this chapter we firstly discuss each of these in more detail, and go on to describe those features of modern programming languages which are designed to assist software engineers in the construction of large, correct, and easily maintainable systems, and which may be applied very effectively to the problem of maintaining database integrity.

5.2.1   Domain integrity rules

As described in Chapter 2, a relation of degree n is defined to be a subset of the Cartesian product of n domains $D_1, D_2, ...D_n$, not necessarily distinct. That is, the values that appear in the relation in column i must belong to D_i. The columns are given names, called attributes, and it is these attribute names which are referenced in queries. Thus, every attribute of every relation, R, has an underlying domain, D_i, and any value submitted as a candidate value for R.A must belong to D_i. Entity integrity is equivalent to enforcing the rule that the domain for any primary key attribute must not include null.

A domain integrity rule therefore, is simply a definition of the *type* of the domain, and domain integrity is closely related to the familiar concept of type checking in programming languages. The definition of the type of a domain must be as precise as possible in order to avoid violations of domain integrity. Thus for example, if we have an attribute AGE, it is not sufficient to describe its type as INTEGER since this does not prevent unrealistic values for AGE (e.g. negative values) being entered into the database. At the very least we should be able to specify that the domain type for attribute AGE is POSITIVE_INTEGER, and ideally it should be possible to specify upper and lower bounds for values of AGE. Unfortunately, commercial database management systems typically provide only simple types for domains. For example, the ORACLE database management system provides the domain types: NUMBER, CHAR (variable length character strings), DATE, TIME, and MONEY. INGRES and DB2 provide similar restricted domain types. In this respect these systems are comparable with programming languages such as FORTRAN, COBOL and PL/1 which provide limited facilities for type definition and rather weak type checking. Modula-2 on the other hand is a programming language which provides strong type checking and abstract data types. The advantages of each of these for database applications are considered later in this chapter.

5.2.2   Intra-relational integrity rules

Intra-relational integrity rules are concerned with maintaining the correctness of relationships among the attributes of a relation. One of the most important of these is *key uniqueness*. As we saw in Chapter 2, the set property of a relation guarantees that no two tuples in a relation have the same values in all their components. A generalization of that property leads to a class of integrity rule that enforces the uniqueness of distinguished key components of tuples. Unfortunately, many relational database management systems do not enforce key uniqueness.

The implementation of key uniqueness requires that the system guarantees that no new tuple can be accepted for insertion into a relation if it has the same values in all its prime attributes as some existing tuple in the relation. In addition, we must also guarantee that no existing tuple in a relation is *updated* in such a way as to change its prime attribute values to be the same as those of some other tuple in the same relation. In fact, changing the values of prime attributes is an operation that should not be undertaken lightly, since as described in the next section, it may have significant consequences elsewhere in the database

5.2.3   Referential integrity rules

Whereas domain integrity is concerned with maintaining the correctness of attribute values, referential integrity is concerned with the correctness of relationships between relations, and may be defined as follows:

Let R_1 be a relation with an attribute, or group of attributes, A which forms the primary key of another relation R_2. Then, at any given time, $R_1.A$ must either be equal to the primary key value of some tuple in R_2, or it must be null (provided it is not prime). The attribute $R_1.A$ is said to be a *foreign key*.

As described in Chapter 2, foreign keys play an extremely important role in relational databases in that they serve to represent many different classes of relationship between entity types. As an example, consider that part of the simple college database from Chapter 2 which is concerned with the entity types STUDENT and COURSE and the relationship between them:

STUDENT (S#, SNAME, LEVEL)

REPORT (S#, C#, MARKS)

COURSE (C#, TITLE, LNAME)

The relation REPORT contains two foreign keys S# and C#. On updating this database we must adhere to the following rules in order to preserve referential integrity.

Rule 1

Before inserting or updating a tuple r in REPORT, check that a tuple s exists in STUDENT with s.S# = r.S#, and that a tuple c exists in COURSE with c.C# = r.C#.

Rule 2

Before deleting a tuple s from STUDENT, delete all tuples r in REPORT where r.S# = s.S#.

Rule 3

If changing the S# component of any tuple s in STUDENT, make the same change to the S# component of any tuple r in REPORT where r.S#=s.S#.

Rule 4

Before deleting a tuple c from COURSE, delete all tuples r in REPORT where r.C# = c.C#.

Rule 5

If changing the C# component of any tuple c in COURSE, make the same change to the C# component of any tuple r in REPORT where r.C# = c.C#.

Clearly in any database environment it is highly desirable that the users be absolved of the responsibility for maintaining referential integrity. This means that an update operation on any of the relations must automatically apply the appropriate referential integrity rules. The application of these rules may or may not be transparent to users. For example, a user who deletes a COURSES tuple from the database should be made aware of the fact that this will, by virtue of Rule 4 above, trigger the deletion of all tuples in the REPORT relation which reference the deleted course. However, in general the details of how these rules are implemented may be hidden from an end-user.

5.3   THE ADVANTAGES OF STRONG TYPE   CHECKING

The provision of a wide variety of data types, accompanied by strong type checking, are the central concepts of any programming language that aims to achieve a high degree of software integrity and maintainability. For database applications in particular, the programmer should be able to specify well-defined properties of data objects, and the rules of the language should guarantee that these properties are maintained throughout the program. Properties which are common to several objects should be separated out into a single type declaration, and referred to by name. If such a property is changed during system maintenance, only one declaration is affected, rather than the individual object declarations.

Modula-2 provides both *scalar* and *structured* data types. A data type is classified as scalar or structured depending on whether its set of associated values consists of indivisible data items or is made up of collections of such items.

5.3.1 Scalar types

The following five predefined scalar data types are provided in Modula-2:

CARDINAL: Non-negative integers in the range 0 to MaxCard (where MaxCard is implementation dependent).

INTEGER: Integers in the range -MaxInt to +MaxInt (where MaxInt is implementation dependent).

REAL: Numbers with a decimal point and an optional exponent. Implementations place restrictions on the number of significant figures and on the range of the exponent.

CHAR: Single characters from the ASCII character set

BOOLEAN: The values TRUE and FALSE.

In addition however, Modula-2 provides flexible facilities for programmer defined scalar types which may be enumerated types, subrange types, or set types.

Enumerated types

With an enumerated type the programmer chooses identifiers to represent the allowable values of the type. Thus an enumerated type has an explicitly declared set of constants each of which has a unique name.

Suppose for example that a relation has an attribute COLOUR and, in order to preserve domain integrity, the database programmer wishes to limit the values that this attribute may assume to the set {red, orange, green, yellow, blue}. In Modula-2 this could be easily done by declaring an enumerated type of the form:

```
TYPE
    colour = (red, orange, green, yellow, blue) ;
```

Any value submitted as a candidate for a variable of type colour must be from the given set. In most commercial database systems, and indeed in many other programming languages, the programmer would be forced to declare COLOUR as a string of characters and integrity preservation would be much more difficult to achieve. Other examples of enumerated type declarations are as follows:

```
TYPE
    WeekDay = ( Monday, Tuesday, Wednesday, Thursday, Friday) ;
    sex = ( Male, Female ) ;
    shape = ( Circle, Square, Rectangle, Triangle ) ;
    Planet = ( Mercury, Venus, Earth, Mars, Jupiter, Saturn, Neptune,
               Uranus, Pluto ) ;
```

Subrange types

A subrange type is a type whose set of allowable values is a range of values of some other type. Very often in database applications we wish to restrict the domain of an attribute to a specified range of values. For example, the marks obtained by a student should be in the range 0 to 100, and a letter of the alphabet must lie within a subset of the ASCII character set defined by the range 'A' to 'Z'. In Modula-2 such types may be declared as follows:

```
TYPE
    marks = [0..100] ;
    letter = ['A'..'Z'] ;
```

If an attempt is made to assign a value of say, 175 to a variable of type marks a run-time error will occur. This protects the database against violations of domain integrity.

Set types

A set is an unordered collection of values chosen from the same base type. The domain of a set type is therefore the set of all sets which may be constructed from the base type (the power set of the base type). In Modula-2 the base type must be a subrange type of the type CARDINAL, or an enumerated type.

For example, suppose that a travel agency maintains information on the facilities offered by various hotels. These facilities range from televisions to swimming pools, and each hotel offers a variable number of these. The property 'facilities offered' of the data object 'Hotel' could be represented by a set type in the following manner:

```
TYPE
    facilities = (television, telephone, restaurant, tennis, sauna, swimming) ;
    offered  = SET OF facilities ;
```

Variables of the same set type may be combined using set operators. The symbols +, -, *, and / denote respectively the union, difference, intersection, and symmetrical set difference. The operator IN may be used to determine if a value is contained in a set instance.

5.3.2   Structured types

Modula-2 offers four structured types: *array types, record types, pointer types and procedure types.* Instances of structured types are aggregates of component values.

Array types

For array types, components are of the same type and are indexed by values of a discrete type (i.e. INTEGER, CARDINAL, CHAR, BOOLEAN, an enumerated type, or subranges of these types). Multidimensional array types, containing more than one index type, may also be defined. Examples of array types are:

```
TYPE
    name = ARRAY [1..30] OF CHAR ;
    Rainfall = ARRAY WeekDay OF REAL ;
    Board = ARRAY [1..8],[1..8] OF BOOLEAN ;
```

Record types

With record types, components of differing types are collected together into a unit. Each component has its own identifier, but when used in a program a component identifier must be qualified by the record name. For database applications, record types are ideal for representing entity types, as defined in Chapter 2. For example, the entity type PERSON, with attributes NAME, ADDRESS, and SEX might be represented by the following type declaration:

```
TYPE
    person = RECORD
                name     : ARRAY [1..30] OF CHAR ;
                address  : ARRAY [1..50] OF CHAR ;
                sex      : (Male, Female)
             END ;
```

There are no restrictions placed on the type of a component, which may therefore be another structured type. Thus, if we wish to add the attribute DATEOFBIRTH to the entity type PERSON we may expand the above declaration as follows:

```
TYPE
    person = RECORD
                name     : ARRAY [1..30] OF CHAR ;
                address  : ARRAY [1..50] OF CHAR ;
                sex      : (Male, Female) ;
                dateofbirth : RECORD
                                day    : [1..31] ;
                                month  : [1..12] ;
                                year   : [1900..1987];
                              END ;
             END ;
```

Note that record types may also have *variant parts.* These are described in Appendix 1.

Pointer types

All of the data types discussed so far describe *static* data structures. A *dynamic* data structure is one that can change during the lifetime of a program. That is, both the number of components and the relationships among them may change during the course of its existence, under program control. Typical applications of dynamic data structures include stacks, queues, trees and lists, whose size and structure may change constantly during the lifetime of a program. Such dynamic data structures may be created and managed in Modula-2 by the use of *pointer types*. Objects of a pointer type may be used to 'point to' (or address) objects of other types in main memory.

For example, a family tree data type could be defined in Modula-2 as follows:

```
TYPE
    FamilyTree = POINTER TO PersonNode ;
    PersonNode = RECORD
                    name : ARRAY [1..30] OF CHAR ;
                    dateofbirth : datetype ;
                    father, mother : FamilyTree ;
                 END ;
```

Procedure types

In Modula-2 a variable may have a procedure type, and thereby may be assigned to actual procedure identifiers. Consider the following declarations:

```
TYPE
    TrigFunction = PROCEDURE (REAL) : REAL ;
VAR
    P : TrigFunction ;
```

The type TrigFunction represents all function procedures which have one formal REAL value parameter and which return a REAL result. Thus Trig-Function could be used in a program to represent the set of trigonometric functions, sine, cosine, etc., and the variable P could assume the role of any of these functions. For example, suppose we wished to write a procedure which would tabulate any trigonometric function over some range. Instead of writing a separate procedure for each function we may write a general procedure of the following form:

```
PROCEDURE Tabulate ( P : TrigFunction) ;

(* Tabulates the function defined by the value parameter P *)

BEGIN
    . . .

END Tabulate ;
```

5.3.3   Type checking in Modula-2

For each of the data types described above, there is a set of operations that may be performed on variables of that type. When an operator connects two operands, the operands must be expression compatible, and the operation must be admissible for the data types of the operands. Restricting our discussion to scalar types, two expressions with the data types T_1 and T_2 are expression compatible if one of the following conditions is true:

1. T_1 and T_2 are the same named data type.

2. T_1 is a subrange type of T_2, or T_2 is a subrange type of T_1, or both are subrange types of the same type.

3.   One expression has the data type INTEGER or CARDINAL and the other is a constant in the interval 0 to MaxInt.

Similar conditions also apply to the assignment statement, where the strong type checking feature of Modula-2 insists that the left and right hand sides of such a statement are assignment compatible. An object of type T_1 and an expression of type T_2 are assignment compatible if:

(a) T_1 and T_2 are expression compatible; or
(b)   either T_1 or T_2 is INTEGER (or a subrange of INTEGER) and the other is CARDINAL (or a subrange of CARDINAL).

These rules are checked by a Modula-2 compiler, and thus a common programming error, namely that of combining objects of different types, is trapped at the time of compilation. Strong type checking therefore encourages disciplined programming and helps to provide early recognition of possible sources of error.

Apart from the exceptions noted above, expressions or assignments involving variables or constants of different types are illegal. However, in database applications situations may arise in which it is desirable to compare values from different domains. For example we may wish to compare an integer value with a real value. To carry out such comparisons in Modula-2, the programmer is required to use an explicit conversion function such as TRUNC(x), which converts a real value x to an integer, or FLOAT(x) which converts an integer or cardinal argument x to a real (other type conversion functions are available). The advantage of this approach, as opposed to allowing a programmer to freely mix variables of different types, is that the type conversion is evident from the program text.

It should be noted that strong type checking does not by itself guarantee domain integrity and very often in database applications user-written procedural domain integrity rules are required. For example, suppose we have an attribute DATE which must lie in the range 01/01/1980 to 31/12/1986. Most commercial database management systems will check the validity of a date but the range check will be the responsibility of the programmer. In Modula-2 we might decide to split the type DATE into its three separate components DAY, MONTH and YEAR with ranges defined by the following type declaration:

```
TYPE
    DateType = RECORD
                    Day   : [1..31] ;
                    Month : [1..12] ;
                    Year  : [1980..1986] ;
              END ;
```

Note that this decomposition does not violate the requirement that in the relational model, attribute values should be non-decomposable data items. The decomposition of DATE illustrated here is performed at the *implementation* level and should be hidden from the user. To the user and to the data modeller, DATE is seen as scalar and non-decomposable. Techniques for 'hiding' the structure of objects or attributes will be considered in the next section.

However, the type definition for DATE above does not guard against entry of an invalid date such as 30/02/1986. Thus we require a procedure which will check the validity of a date and which will be called automatically before any date is entered into the database. Such a procedure might take the form:

```
PROCEDURE ValidDate ( d : DateType ) : BOOLEAN ;
VAR
    daysinmonth : [28..31] ;

BEGIN
    CASE d.month OF
    1,3,5,7,8,10,12 :  daysinmonth := 31 ;
    4,6,9,11        :  daysinmonth := 30 ;
    2               :  IF (d.year MOD 4 = 0)
                       THEN daysinmonth := 29
                       ELSE daysinmonth := 28
                       END
    END ;
    RETURN (d.day <= daysinmonth)
END ValidDate ;
```

5.4   ABSTRACT DATA TYPES

There are many database application areas where the data structures are of such complexity that the primitive typing facilities offered by commercial database management systems are found to be totally inadequate. In the design of large applications, data abstraction has long been recognised as a means to develop high-level representations of the concepts that relate closely to the application being programmed and to hide the inessential details of such representations at the various stages of program development. The historical roots of abstract data types lie in the work of Parnas (1972a, 1972b) on the need for information hiding, the systematic view of data structures presented by Hoare (1972a), and a formal treatment of data representations presented by Hoare (1972b) which separated abstract properties from implementation.

Thus many modern programming languages, such as Modula-2, offer a very general algorithmic facility for type definition. Module or 'information-hiding' mechanisms are provided so that arbitrary new types can be defined by both the necessary details for representation, which are hidden from the surrounding program, and the allowable operations to be maintained for objects of that type. Furthermore, since these mechanisms may be applied repeatedly, types may be mapped, step by step, from higher, user-oriented levels to lower levels, ending with the built-in language constructs. At each level, the view of the data may be abstracted from those details which are unnecessary for data usage, i.e. details with regard to representation, constraints, access rights, etc. This leads to a decoupling of the data structures, which define the database, and the application programs which operate on them.

This approach is consistent with the relational model of data in which, at the abstract level, attributes are viewed as atomic or non-decomposable objects. However, for a database management system to actually store and manipulate attribute values, the details of their machine representation must be incorporated into that part of the system which is normally hidden from a user's view.

In Modula-2 modules are collections of data types, data objects, procedures and statements. A main program is itself a module (a *program module*), and in accordance with the principles of abstraction outlined above, the data types, objects and procedures of a program module may be distributed among various *local modules*, each of which provides a solution to part of the overall problem. Modules of course must communicate with each other, and in Modula-2 all types, objects and operations which are provided by a module to the outside world must be explicitly declared in an *EXPORT clause*. Similarly, any type, object or procedure which is required by a module but is defined in some other module, must be declared in an *IMPORT clause*.

There are in fact four types of module in Modula-2, and these are described briefly below:

Program module
A program module is a separately compiled sequence of statements that is capable of execution. It has the following form:

```
MODULE name ;

    <Import list>

    <data declarations>

    <procedure declarations>

BEGIN
    . . .
END name ;
```

Thus a program module has no export list and imported objects are defined in other compilation units.

Local modules

Local modules may be declared within other modules or procedures. Unlike procedures, whose function is to perform some well-defined task, local modules serve to define and enclose data objects and procedures. Communication between a local module and its surrounding environment is via explicitly declared IMPORT and EXPORT lists.

Definition and implementation modules

A definition module serves to *describe* the data types, objects and operations (procedures) exported by an implementation module. An implementation module is always paired with a definition module with the same name. It contains the detailed data declarations and logic corresponding to the exports specified in the definition module.

The implementation of abstract data types in Modula-2 is by means of the definition module and implementation module constructs. A definition module contains the definitions of all exported objects (types, constants, variables and procedures), i.e. all objects that are to be visible to other modules. The implementation module contains the declarations of all non-exported objects together with all details of the implementation. This separation of definition and implementation has two significant advantages:

1. Definition modules are public whereas implementation modules are private. This coincides with the principles of abstract data types as outlined above.
2. Implementation modules may be separately compiled. This enables improvements to be made to the representation of data objects or to the implementation of operations without affecting the overall data structure defined in the interface (i.e. the definition module). Also, overheads are reduced since modules may be stored in compiled form and linked to other modules when required.

The general form of a definition module for an abstract data type is as follows:

```
DEFINITION MODULE ADTModule ;

TYPE
    ADT = . . . ; (* Abstract data type declaration *)

PROCEDURE Oper1 ( . . . ) ;

PROCEDURE Oper2 ( . . . ) ;


    . . .


END ADTModule.
```

The definition part acts like a prefix to the implementation part, and contains the list of all objects that are to be visible outside the module, and the declaration of all exported objects. Procedure declarations in the definition module consist of a heading only. The procedure body belongs to the corresponding implementation module. Variables declared in the definition module are visible and accessible only in those modules which import them. An importer of a module need only have available the definition module. Initialisation code is placed in the main body of the implementation module, and is executed when the procedure, to which the module is local, is called. If several modules are declared, then these bodies are executed in the sequence in which the modules occur.

A particularly powerful feature of the Modula-2 definition module for database applications, is the ability to define *opaque types*. An opaque type is a type exported by a definition module, the internal representation of which is given only in the corresponding implementation module. Opaque types are very useful in database applications in that they allow the programmer or database designer to define arbitrary, non-decomposable data objects, together with a set of operations which may be performed on those objects, while at the same time hiding details with regard to their representation.

As an example, let us return to the attribute DATE discussed earlier in this chapter. In most database applications we would wish to treat such an attribute as non-decomposable, but we may require to perform the following operations on variables of type DATE:

1. Read and validate a date.
2. Print out a date in the form *dd/mm/yyyy*.
3. Compute the number of days between two dates.
4. Given a date *d*, compute the date *n* days later.
5. Return the day of the week corresponding to a given date.

A definition module for the abstract data type DateType, with the above operations might take the following form:

```
DEFINITION MODULE DateModule ;

TYPE
    DateType ;
    (* DateType is not defined here - it is an opaque type *)

    DayType = (Sunday, Monday, Tuesday, Wednesday, Thursday, Friday,
            Saturday) ;

PROCEDURE ReadAndValidate ( VAR d : DateType;
                                VAR OK : BOOLEAN ) ;
    (* Reads and validates a date d, returning OK=TRUE if d is valid *)

PROCEDURE WriteDate ( d : DateType ) ;
    (* Writes out the date d in some suitable format *)

PROCEDURE NoOfDays ( d1, d2 : DateType ) : CARDINAL ;
    (* Computes the number of days between dates d1 and d2 *)
```

```
PROCEDURE NewDate ( d : DateType ; n : CARDINAL ) : DateType ;
    (* Given a date d, computes the date n days later *)

PROCEDURE DayOfWeek ( d : DateType ) : DayType ;
    (* Returns the day of the week corresponding to a given date d *)

END DateModule.
```

A user of the module DateModule may declare variables of type DateType in his program and apply the operations NoOfDays, NewDate, and DayOfWeek to these variables. He does not know, and does not need to know, how DateType is implemented. An outline of the implementation module is given below.

```
IMPLEMENTATION MODULE DateModule ;

FROM InOut IMPORT ReadInt, WriteInt, Write ;

TYPE
    DateType = RECORD
                    day : [1..31] ;
                    month : [1..12] ;
                    year : [1980..1986] ;
                END ;

PROCEDURE ReadAndValidate ( VAR d : DateType;
                                       VAR OK : BOOLEAN ) ;
VAR
    dayvalue, monthvalue, yearvalue : INTEGER ;

    PROCEDURE ValidDate ( d : DateType ) : BOOLEAN ;
    VAR
        daysinmonth : [28..31] ;
    BEGIN
        CASE d.month OF
        1,3,5,7,8,10,12      : daysinmonth := 31 ;
        4,6,9,11             : daysinmonth := 30 ;
        2                    : IF (d.year MOD 4 = 0)
                               THEN daysinmonth := 29
                               ELSE daysinmonth := 28
                               END
        END ;
        RETURN (d.day <= daysinmonth)
    END ValidDate ;

BEGIN
    ReadInt (dayvalue);
    ReadInt (monthvalue);
    ReadInt (yearvalue) ;
    OK := (dayvalue >= 1) AND (dayvalue <=31) AND (monthvalue >= 1)
            AND (monthvalue <=12) AND (yearvalue >=1980)
            AND (yearvalue <=1986) ;
```

```
IF OK THEN
    d.day :=dayvalue;
    d.month := monthvalue;
    d.year := yearvalue;
      OK := ValidDate (d) ;
  END ;
END ReadAndValidate ;

PROCEDURE WriteDate ( d : DateType ) ;
BEGIN
  WriteInt (d.day); Write ('/'); WriteInt (d.month); Write ('/'); WriteInt (d.year);
END WriteDate ;

PROCEDURE NoOfDays ( d1, d2 : DateType ) : CARDINAL ;
BEGIN
  (* Computes the number of days between dates d1 and d2 *)
END NoOfDays;

PROCEDURE NewDate ( d : DateType ; n : CARDINAL ) : DateType ;
BEGIN
  (* Given a date d, computes the date n days later *)
END NewDate;

PROCEDURE DayOfWeek ( d : DateType ) : DayType ;
BEGIN
  (* Returns the day of the week corresponding to a given date d *)
END DayOfWeek ;

BEGIN
  (* Initialisation code, if any, is placed here *)
END DateModule.
```

5.5   DATA ENCAPSULATION AND DATABASE VIEWS

A relational database system in general consists of a data structure and a collection of procedures and functions which operate on objects within that data structure. The data structure defines the permanent relations, corresponding to the relational schema, and includes the descriptions of attribute names and types. The program modules may consist of 'system procedures', which are responsible for performing management functions such as the production of statistical reports, and application procedures which retrieve and/or update data according to the requirements of a particular user or group of users. If the entire data structure is made global to all the procedures using the system, this leads to a number of serious disadvantages:

1. If we change the structure of the database we may have to alter every procedure which accesses the global data structure.
2. Since the access rights to the data structure are spread over many procedures it is extremely difficult to preserve the consistency and correctness of the database.

These disadvantages have long been recognised, not only in database systems but in all large programming environments, and in order to overcome them the principles of data encapsulation have emerged. With data encapsulation, the details of a data structure are kept secret from its surrounding environment by declaring it inside a module along with a number of access procedures which perform all necessary operations on objects within the data structure. Any procedure which requires access to the data structure can do so only via calls to the access procedures. In this way the data structure is decoupled from the system procedures and application procedures described above. Any changes to the data structure will normally require changes only to the access procedures.

In database applications data encapsulation provides a natural mechanism for defining the interface between a program and the database, i.e. an external subschema or user view. This interface is tailored to the particular application and its primary functions are to simplify access to the database, to preserve its consistency and integrity, and perhaps to protect parts of the database against accidental or malicious intrusion. Only those data types which are necessary for the application are exported by the module, together with appropriate high-level abstract operations which the user may apply to objects of those types. The exported operations will not usually be primitive operations on the stored relations. Rather, they will be at a much higher level, giving the user a simplified view of the database which is appropriate for his application.

In general, a database view may be realised in Modula-2 with definition and implementation modules of the following form:

DEFINITION MODULE ViewName;

    { Declarations of the exported data types.}

    { Declarations of the interfaces of exported procedures.}

END ViewName.

IMPLEMENTATION MODULE ViewName;

    { Declarations of the encapsulated data structure.}

    { Declarations of all procedures, both exported procedures and internal
                               procedures. }

BEGIN

    { initialisation section }

END ViewName.

For example, consider the following simple database for a small departmental library which records details of books, borrowers and loans:

BOOKS (<u>CAT#</u>, TITLE, AUTHOR)

BORROWERS (<u>CARD#</u>, NAME, ADDRESS, STATUS)

LOANS (<u>CAT#</u>, CARD#, DATEDUE)

In this database CAT# is a unique catalogue number which identifies each book. The attribute CARD# is a unique library card number assigned to each borrower. The LOANS relation records details of which book is currently on loan which borrower, and the date on which the book is due for return.

For this library database we can identify the need for two views:

1. A view for the librarian who will wish to perform operations such as:

    (a) record details of a new loan;
    (b) record the fact that a book has been returned;
    (c) print a list of overdue books.

2. A view for a library user, which provides read-only operations such as:

    (a) search for a book given the catalogue number;
    (b) list the books written by a given author.

Neither view requires that the actual structure of the database be revealed. That is, neither a librarian or a borrower need be aware that the database consists of three separate relations whose data structures are as defined above. The librarian's view is provided by a module of the following form:

```
DEFINITION MODULE LibrarianView ;

FROM DateModule IMPORT DateType ;

EXPORT QUALIFIED NewLoan, Return, OverdueList ;

(* Definition of access procedure interfaces *)

PROCEDURE NewLoan ( Catno : CARDINAL ; Cardno : CARDINAL ;
                    Datedue : Datetype ;
                    VAR successful : BOOLEAN ) ;
(* Inserts details of a new loan into the database *)

PROCEDURE Return ( Catno : CARDINAL; VAR successful : BOOLEAN) ;
(* Records in the database the fact that a specified book has been
     returned *)

PROCEDURE OverdueList ( CurrentDate : DateType ) ;
(* Given the current date, prints a list of books on loan which are overdue
     for return *)

END LibrarianView.
```

Note that the parameter names and types must be specified for each

116   PROGRAMMING LANGUAGES AND DATABASES

exported procedure since the librarian requires this information in order to call the procedures.

A module defining a view for a library user might take the following form:

```
DEFINITION MODULE UserView ;

EXPORT QUALIFIED CatSearch, AuthorSearch ;

PROCEDURE CatSearch ( Catno : CARDINAL ) ;

(* Searches the database for a book with the catalogue number given by
Catno, and if found, prints details of the book and an indication of whether it
is currently available for loan. *)

PROCEDURE AuthorSearch ( Author : ARRAY [0..30] OF CHAR ) ;

(* Searches the database for books by the given author and  prints details of
any such books found *)

END UserView.
```

5.6   DATABASE PROGRAMMING LANGUAGES

As mentioned in Section 5.1 the past decade has seen the emergence of a number of well-structured, strongly-typed relational database programming languages. The aim of each of these languages is to integrate the relation data type and existing data and control structures as closely as possible. Consequently most of these languages take advantage of the similarity in structure between the tuples of a relation and the record type, and use a syntax similar to that of their record structure for defining relations.

For example, the small library database defined in the previous section, consisting of the relations BOOKS, BORROWERS and LOANS might be declared in the database programming language Pascal/R in the following way:

```
TYPE
    NumberType = 1..9999 ;
    BookRecord = RECORD
                    catno  : NumberType ;
                    title  : string ;
                    author : string
                 END ;
    BorrowerRecord = RECORD
                    cardno  : NumberType ;
                    name    : string ;
                    address : string ;
                    status  : (staff, student, other)
                 END ;
```

```
LoanRecord  = RECORD
                    catno   : NumberType ;
                    cardno  : NumberType ;
                    datedue : datetype
              END ;
BookRel   = RELATION <catno> OF BookRecord ;
BorrowerRel = RELATION <cardno> OF BorrowerRecord ;
LoanRel   = RELATION <catno> OF LoanRecord ;

VAR
      Library : DATABASE
                    Books     : BookRel ;
                    Borrowers : BorrowerRel ;
                    Loans     : LoanRel
              END ;
```

The RELATION construct defines a relation type in terms of the specified record type. The inclusion, in the declaration of a relation type, of a list of key attributes, (e.g. <cardno>), is really an intra-relation integrity rule which imposes the constraint that no two tuples in an instance of this type may have the same value(s) in all the key attributes. Note that when defining attribute types one should be able to take advantage of whatever types are offered by the language, which may include subranges, enumerated types, or ideally abstract data types. Pascal/R however, in common with some other database programming languages, restricts attribute types to be simple types.

The DATABASE construct defines a new variable in the program whose value is a database consisting of three relations, Books, Borrowers and Loans.

Each of the languages provide operations for the insertion of new tuples into, and the deletion of tuples from a relation. Some also provide an operation to update the non-key fields of a tuple in a relation. All of the languages provide operations for retrieving information from relations, but some base these operations on tuple-oriented relational calculus, while others provide relational algebraic operations.

Let us now consider how database programming languages handle some of the more important issues involved in the development of database management systems; in particular, data manipulation, integrity preservation, data abstraction, and view definition. We begin our discussion by considering the differences between the algebra- and calculus-based approaches to database programming.

5.6.1 Data manipulation in database programming languages

A database programming language may be classified as either calculus- or algebra-based depending on whether it employs calculus- or algebra-based operations to manipulate its relations. The languages RAPP and PLAIN show a strong preference for the algebraic operations, in contrast to Pascal/R, Modula/R and RIGEL, which have chosen calculus-like operations. ASTRAL contains both calculus and algebraic operations.

Pascal/R and Modula/R provide existential and universal quantifiers. As a consequence, Boolean expressions of the power of first-order predicate calculus can be defined, and relational expressions can be formed to select tuples fulfilling some predicate. For example, the predicate

'Have all borrowers at least one book on loan?'

may be represented by the expression:

```
ALL b IN Borrowers : SOME l IN Loans : (b.cardno = l.cardno)
```

It is possible to iterate over relation elements (tuples) which satisfy some predicate, by means of the FOREACH statement. For example, to list the names of all borrowers who have not returned a book by the date due, we may write:

```
FOREACH b IN Borrowers : SOME l IN Loans :
    ((b.cardno = l.cardno) AND (l.datedue < CurrentDate)) DO
    WriteLn (b.name)
END ;
```

The reader should note the strong similarity between these examples and tuple-oriented relational calculus, as described in Chapter 4.

The assignment statement is applicable to relation variables and relational expressions. In addition to the normal assignment operator (:=), Pascal/R and Modula/R provide operations for insertion (:+), deletion (:-) and replacement (:&). For example, the following code selects all student borrowers and assigns them to a relation Students:

```
VAR
    Students : BorrowerRel ;
BEGIN
    Students := [EACH b IN Borrowers : b.status = student] ;
END ;
```

To delete all the tuples in the Loans relation corresponding to books borrowed by Smith, we may write:

```
Loans :- [EACH l IN Loans : l.name = 'Smith'] ;
```

To insert a new record newbook into the Books relation requires the following code:

```
VAR
    newbook : BookRecord ;
BEGIN
    Books :+ [newbook] ;
END ;
```

Relation variables are fully integrated into the language. Not only can they be part of a permanent database, but they may be declared as local variables in modules and procedures. In addition they may be used as both value and variable parameters in procedures.

The notation for expressing queries in RIGEL is similar to that used in Pascal/R and Modula/R. The language ASTRAL operates on table variables consisting of a table name followed by an associative index which is optional. The index is a first order predicate, and it may be used to express the select and join operations. The projection operation may be expressed by a table constructor. In addition, ASTRAL provides the set operations of relational algebra.

The designers of PLAIN believed that uniformity of syntax in a language is important, so that the database operations should blend easily with the other language features. Therefore, they argued, it seemed more appropriate to extend a procedural language (like Pascal) with a set of procedural database operations, such as the relational algebraic operations. The language RAPP adopted the same broad design goals as those of PLAIN, and thus both languages provide explicitly the algebraic operators of product, join, select, and project, as well as the set operators union, intersection and minus. Thus, to find the names of all borrowers who have not returned a book by the date due, we might write (using RAPP syntax):

```
VAR
    result : RELATION [] OF RECORD name : string END ;
BEGIN
    result := (Borrowers join (Loans where datedue < currentdate))
                [name] ;
END ;
```

As we noted in Chapter 4, the result of a relational algebraic operation is always another relation. Thus in the above example we declare a temporary relation to hold the result of the query. The relational expression involves a selection on the Loans relation, followed by a join with the Borrowers relation, and finally a projection on the name attribute. The syntax is very similar to that used in Chapter 4.

In most relational systems the major effort in gaining efficiency is built into the database management system in the form of query decomposition and optimisation algorithms, and provision for the selection, creation and maintenance of index files. For example, in many commercial systems over 60 per cent of the compilation time of a typical SQL statement is devoted to optimisation. With this approach, the database management system fails to take advantage of the programmer's knowledge of the database. By providing the programmer with language mechanisms which allow him more control over the efficiency of his programs, the database management system can be greatly simplified, and its size reduced considerably. Thus, both RAPP and PLAIN place query optimisation largely in the hands of the programmer, by providing him with a set of procedural relational operations. The programmer is also given the ability to specify and create indexes on his relations, in addition to those automatically maintained on a primary key. The anticipated programmer of both RAPP and PLAIN is assumed to be familiar with database concepts, and those of high-level programming languages. Therefore, he should be well capable of optimising the database operations, and making efficient use of indexes on the defined relations.

However, in database programming languages such as Pascal/R and Modula/R, query decomposition and optimisation are performed by the database management system. As described above, such languages provide the programmer with a set of calculus-based operations with which he can describe the data required in terms of a collection of predicates. He need not be aware of the actual sequence of operations employed in obtaining the data from the database. In Pascal/R and Modula/R a run-time system has been produced for the execution of the relational expressions. This basically consists of an algorithm derived from that of Palermo (1972), with additional optimisation, and supported by more advanced access methods. The interface to the run-time system, which evaluates the relational expressions, represents predicates in disjunctive normal form prefixed by all quantifiers occurring in the predicate. The compilers of the two languages transform any non-normalised predicate into an equivalent one in disjunctive normal form, by means of logic theorems.

5.6.2   Integrity rules in database programming languages

As we have already seen, some of the integrity rules discussed in section 5.2.1, such as key uniqueness, may be enforced by means of the data structure relation. Also, the concept of strong type checking is central to each of the database programming languages under discussion in this chapter. Therefore, in each of them, every attribute in a relation must be defined with a specific type. The languages then ensure that the constraints associated with this type are enforced.

However, as described in Section 5.3.3, even the strong type checking facilities of these languages are not capable of enforcing every attribute constraint. In addition, there are many intra- and inter-relational constraints not expressible by the data structure relation. There are two ways in which we might overcome these deficiencies in database programming languages:

1. We can extend the declarative type definition of the relation to include the necessary constraints.
2. We can use a data abstraction facility, such as the module of Modula-2, to encapsulate the relation type definition and the set of operations allowed on variables of the type. Additional attribute constraints and the constraints required for variables of the relation type (e.g. referential integrity constraints) can then be programmed into these operations.

All of the database programming languages under discussion, with the exception of ASTRAL and Pascal/R have chosen the latter approach. In ASTRAL an access control statement is specified for each table (i.e. relation), and is executed prior to each access of the table. All constraints relevant to the table are defined in its access control statement. Pascal/R does not broach the problem, and like Pascal it has no module facility.

5.6.3   Data abstraction in database programming languages

The form of the abstract type in the different languages varies considerably. Modules in Modula/R are identical to those of Modula-2. In PLAIN the Module type permits the encapsulation of a single type, and the valid operations allowed on instances of that type. RIGEL and RAPP allow several types, and the operations permitted on instances of those types, to be declared together in the one module (in RAPP a module is referred to as an *envelope*).

The module of PLAIN has an export clause, giving the names of all operations visible outside the module, and an import clause, which specifies for each variable identifier imported whether it is a read-only variable (read-only), a read/write variable (modified), or a program unit that will be called (invoked). A program unit may be a procedure, a function, an exception handling routine, or another module. The module type definition may optionally contain a *rep* part, in which the representation of the type is declared. This is not visible to the user. If a module contains a rep part, then the module defines a new data type, and variables of this type may be declared. When such a variable is declared, the body part of the module is executed, if one exists in the module type definition. The body of the module performs any necessary initialisation. All operations on values of a variable declared to be of the module type must be performed by the program units exported from, and defined in the module, and the variable must be passed as a formal parameter to these program units. The operations defined on the type are declared in the opt part of the module: access rights to these operations are explicitly exported from the type definition. If a module has no rep part, then it is merely an encapsulation of its functions and procedures, and variables may not be declared to be of that type.

A module in RIGEL has three sections: *public, private* and *initialisation*. The public section defines the objects that can be accessed by the user of the module. The private section implements the objects defined in the public section. The initialisation section contains any necessary initialisation operations, and is executed when the module is defined. In RIGEL, modules are used to provide a convenient notation for specifying program interfaces to databases. Only those relations and views which a programmer may access are declared in the public section. High-level operations can be associated with the data by declaring them in the module, thus providing a complete specification of the database interface. After importing the module to a program the exported (i.e. public) relations, views and procedures can then be accessed.

The module facility of RAPP is identical to the *envelope* construct of the modular, multiprocessing language Pascal Plus (Welsh and Bustard, 1979). The envelope does not have a public or definition section, rather it prefixes all objects which are visible outside the envelope with a star (*). The starred objects of the envelope are accessible to any block enclosing an instance of the envelope. In Modula/R variables may be imported into a module, from another module, with read/write access. This is in contrast to the envelope of RAPP, wherein no such import facility exists. Instead an envelope may use the identifiers defined in blocks which enclose the envelope definition, by the normal Pascal rules of scope, but may not assign values to these global variables. If a type is declared in a definition module of Modula/R, or in a public section of a module in RIGEL, the full details of the declaration are visible in importing modules (or programs). Thus, if a record type is declared, all the record fields are visible in importing modules (or programs). The envelope feature of RAPP, on the other hand, allows the programmer to select which fields of the record are to be visible outside of the envelope. This is particularly useful for defining views which are a projection on a single base relation.

5.6.4   Views in database programming languages

A view, in its most general form, is an abstract relation which may be derived from one or more underlying base relations. The definition of a view comprises the declaration of the abstract relation which the view simulates, called the *abstract relation declaration*; and the specification of how the tuples of the view are to be constructed from the tuples of the underlying base relations, called the *mapping specification*. The user of the view should only see the abstract relation declaration. This can be achieved by placing the abstract relation declaration inside the visible (or exported) part of a module, and the mapping specification inside the hidden part. Thus a view is directly analogous to an abstract data type.

For performance and consistency reasons, views are maintained only at the *logical* level. That is, they do not exist at the physical storage level. Thus queries on views must be translated into queries on the base relations, rather than executing them directly on a materialisation of the view. While this translation is always possible for retrieval operations, it is not always possible for updates. That is, views exist for which an update of the view cannot be safely and unambiguously translated to a sequence of update operations on the base relations. Let us consider four ways in which a view update facility could be provided in a database programming language (Rowe and Shoens, 1979):

1. Views may not be updated. Although this approach seriously restricts the utilisation of views, it is the approach taken in ASTRAL.
2. Views may be updated but the programmer must specify precisely how the update is to be carried out. That is, he must specify which base relations are to be updated and provide the view updates as high level operations within the view module. This is the approach taken in RIGEL and RAPP.
3. Views may be updated only by updates that can be unambiguously translated to base relation updates. The problem with this approach is that the programmer would not know until compile time, or in some cases execution time, whether a particular view update was legal or not. Also, the update translation requires the user to have access to the 'hidden' mapping specification.
4. All updates are allowed, and language constructs are provided to allow the programmer to specify the translation of ambiguous and undefined

updates. This alternative could result in significant language complexity.

In RIGEL and RAPP views are specified as an abstract type which separates the view representation and its implementation. In both languages updates on views are specified as high-level abstract operations. However, the two languages differ in that RIGEL supports views as a built-in type, while RAPP defines a view structure like any other relation type. The use of the term *view* in PLAIN is somewhat different from its use in other languages, such as RAPP and RIGEL. In PLAIN, a set of operations on a relation may be encapsulated in a module, so defining a new data type with a restricted set of structured, pre-defined operations on it. In this way the user does not *see* an artificial database organisation but merely a set of permissible operations on the data type. The user does not in fact see any database organisation, as the representation of the relation is hidden from his view.

R.T.C. LIBRARY
LETTERKENNY

5.7   PERSISTENCE

In persistent programming languages, persistence is an orthogonal property of data. That is, any data object, regardless of type, may exist beyond the lifetime of the program in which it is created. The language PS-Algol (Atkinson et al., 1983) is designed to support persistence, and thereby offers a contrasting approach to database applications programming. Unlike the languages mentioned in the previous section, PS-Algol does not involve the addition of new data structures to a language, but rather provides persistence as a property applicable to all existing data structures.

One of the primary motivations for persistent programming languages is to relieve the database applications programmer of the considerable effort normally required to transfer data between the database storage system and his program. In programming database applications with conventional programming languages, a large fraction of the code is devoted to performing translations between the form of data in the program (arrays, records, sets etc.) to the form required for external storage. The database programming languages which we discussed earlier in this chapter, go some way towards alleviating the programmer's burden to provide this mapping code, in that they integrate the data type relation, which has the property of persistence, into the programming language. PS-Algol adopts the principle of data type completeness, by which the rules governing the manipulation of all data objects should be consistent. Thus all data types in PS-Algol have the property of persistence.

Consider the entity-relationship diagram for a simple library database shown in Figure 5.1. This consists of two entity types, BOOK and MEMBER, and a single 1:N relationship LOAN (only current loans are recorded).

A data structure in PS-Algol for this database might be defined as shown in Figure 5.2.

Figure 5.1   A simple library database

```
structure date ( int day, month, year )
structure book ( int catno,            ! unique catalogue no.
              string title,            ! title of book
                   author )            ! author of book
structure member ( int cardno,         ! unique id no.
                string name,           ! member's name
                  address )            ! member's address
structure loan ( pntr loaned,          ! to a book record
               borrower,               ! to a member record
               datedue )               ! to a date record
```

Figure 5.2   A PS-Algol data structure for the library database

The **structure** construct defines a record class. The **pntr** construct defines a type which ranges over tokens for all the existing instances of those classes, together with the special token **nil**. Note that pointers are not constrained to a particular type (as in Pascal and Modula-2), and thus it is necessary for the programmer to use comments to clarify their meaning.

PS-Algol is implemented as a number of functional extensions to S-Algol (Morrison, 1982). This language offers the following data typing facilities:

1. The scalar data types are integer, real, Boolean, string, picture and file.
2. For any data type T, *T is the data type of a vector with elements of type T.
3. The pointer data type comprises a structure with any number of fields, and any data type in each field.

Very complex data structures may be defined by the recursive application of rules 2 and 3.

The language itself does not change to accommodate persistence. The implementation takes care of storing and retrieving persistent data, and of checking type equivalence when data is re-used in different programs. PS-Algol provides a variety of procedures for managing persistence and also a set of procedures for manipulating indexes.

5.8   FUNCTIONAL DATABASE LANGUAGES

It has been demonstrated by many authors (e.g. Sibley and Kerschberg, 1977; Buneman and Frankel, 1979; Shipman, 1981) that the relationships among data, as described in Chapter 2, can simply be represented by means of the mathematical notion of a function. In this section we shall follow closely the notation of Shipman, and the functional programming language DAPLEX. Implementations of this language are provided by Fox et al. (1984) and Atkinson and Kulkarni (1984). A subset of DAPLEX embedded in Ada, called ADAPLEX has also been implemented (Smith et al., 1981).

The relationship between an entity set and an attribute, for example, is a function that maps the entities in that set into the domain of the attribute. Thus, for example, rather than defining an entity STUDENT with an attribute NAME which is a STRING, NAME may be regarded as a function which maps STUDENTs into STRINGs. In this way, a relation scheme specified in the form:

STUDENT (ID_NO, NAME, ADDRESS)

may be regarded as a set of functions:

STUDENT ( ) —> ENTITY
ID_NO (STUDENT) —> INTEGER
NAME (STUDENT) —> STRING
ADDRESS (STUDENT) —> STRING

Thus in this *Functional Data Model* we define an entity by means of the functions (or operations) that may be applied to it. The representation of the entity is left to the implementor and defined at a lower level of abstraction. The similarity to abstract data types is obvious.

The function STUDENT defined above, with zero arguments, evaluates to a set of entities. ENTITY is a system provided type and all entities are subtypes of that type. The other functions defined above return scalar values and define attributes or properties of the entity type STUDENT. The entity types INTEGER, STRING and BOOLEAN are built-in entity types.

Functions defined over entities may also return entities (single-valued functions), or sets of entities (multi-valued functions). Multi-argument functions are also permitted and these provide a convenient means for representing relationships involving several entities. Thus the introduction of artificial entities to model many-to-many relationships or non-binary relationships is unnecessary.

A DAPLEX schema for a simplified version of the college database, described in Chapter 2, is given in Figure 5.3. This is similar to the example given in Shipman's paper and we have used upper/lower case to conform with the conventions of that paper. A complete description of the syntax of DAPLEX is given in Appendix 3.

DECLARE Student ( )	—>>	ENTITY
DECLARE ID_No (Student)	—>	INTEGER
DECLARE Name (Student)	—>	STRING
DECLARE Address (Student)	—>	STRING
DECLARE Level (Student)	—>	INTEGER
DECLARE Course (Student)	—>>	Course
DECLARE Course ( )	—>>	ENTITY
DECLARE Course_No (Course)	—>	INTEGER

DECLARE Title (Course)	→	STRING
DECLARE Department (Course)	→	Department
DECLARE Lecturer (Course)	→	Lecturer
DECLARE Department ( )	→>>	ENTITY
DECLARE Name (Department)	→	STRING
DECLARE Head (Department)	→	Lecturer
DECLARE Lecturer ( )	→>>	ENTITY
DECLARE Name (Lecturer)	→	STRING
DECLARE Room (Lecturer)	→	INTEGER
DEFINE Lecturer (Student)	→>>	Lecturer(Course (Student))

Figure 5.3 A DAPLEX description of the college database

Following Shipman, we may schematically represent this functional description of the college database as shown in Figure 5.4.

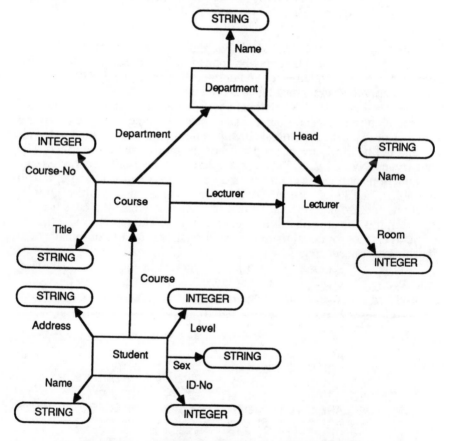

Figure 5.4 A functional model for the college database

A DECLARE statement introduces a new function which, if it has no arguments, is a new entity type. A single-headed arrow (—>) indicates a single-valued function, while a double-headed arrow (—>>) implies a multi-valued function. A DEFINE statement introduces a 'derived function' which is defined in terms of other declared or defined functions.

The statement:

DECLARE Department (Course) —> Department

indicates that Department is a function which, when applied to a Course entity, returns an entity of type Department. That is, a department entity is returned, not a department name or other identifier. The statement:

DECLARE Course (Student) —>> Course

is an example of a multi-valued function. That is, the Course function when applied to a Student entity returns a *set* of entities of type Course. An example of a multi-argument function might be:

DECLARE Marks (Student, Course) —> INTEGER

which returns the marks obtained by a Student entity on a Course entity.

Subtypes

An important concept in the functional data model is that of a *subtype*. For example, instead of declaring students and lecturers to be of type ENTITY as in the schema of Figure 5.3, we could introduce an entity type Person and declare Student and Lecturer to be subtypes of that type as follows:

DECLARE Person ( ) —>> ENTITY
DECLARE Name (Person) —> STRING
DECLARE Student ( ) —>> Person
DECLARE Lecturer ( ) —>> Person

These declarations imply that the set of Student entities, and the set of Lecturer entities, are subsets of the set of Person entities. The two sets (Students and Lecturers) may overlap (e.g. if a lecturer can also be a student), or they may be disjoint. Any Student entity and any Lecturer entity has the Name function defined over it, and the individual Name functions defined for these entities in the schema of Figure 5.3 are no longer necessary. Subtypes inherit all the properties of their supertypes.

Thus the functional data model arranges types into a *type hierarchy*. For example, we could extend the hierarchy defined above by introducing an entity type Professor which is a subtype of the type Lecturer (i.e. all professors are lecturers and share the properties of lecturers, but may have additional properties of their own).

As shown in Chapter 2, the same kind of hierarchy could be represented in the relational model with a schema of the following form:

PERSON (ID#, NAME, ADDRESS, SEX)

STUDENT (ID#, LEVEL)

LECTURER (ID#, ROOM#, APPOINTMENT_DATE)

PROFESSOR (ID#, CHAIR_TITLE)

In this schema the PERSON relation holds an identifying number (ID#) for all the persons in the database, together with their names, addresses and sex. The LECTURER relation holds a subset of these ID#s, for all those persons who are lecturers, together with attributes which apply specifically to lecturers, namely room number and date of appointment. The PROFESSOR relation holds a subset of the lecturer ID#s together with the attribute CHAIR_TITLE, an attribute which pertains only to professors. Thus the complete set of attributes held for a professor includes ID# and CHAIR_TITLE (in the PROFESSOR relation), ROOM# and APPOINTMENT_DATE (in the LECTURER relation), and NAME, ADDRESS and SEX (in the PERSON relation). This arises by virtue of the fact that a professor is a lecturer who is a person.

It should be obvious to the reader that, in a database such as that defined by the above schema, the maintenence of referential integrity (as discussed in Section 5.2.3), is of crucial importance. That is, the database management system must not allow a situation to arise in which a 'subtype relation' contains a tuple which has no corresponding tuple in the appropriate 'supertype relation'. Similarly, for example, if we delete a PROFESSOR tuple, the system must ensure that the corresponding LECTURER and PERSON tuples are also deleted. In the functional data model such referential integrity constraints are *implicit* in the model itself. This is an important advantage of the functional approach over the relational data model.

Data manipulation in DAPLEX

Consider the following simple query:

'Print the names of all students taking a course in the Computer Science department.'

In DAPLEX we could write this query in the following form:

```
FOR EACH Student
    SUCH THAT FOR SOME Course (Student)
        Name (Department (Course)) = 'Computer Science'
    PRINT Name (Student)
```

The FOR EACH statement iterates over the set of entities of type Student, executing the PRINT statement for each member of that set for which the qualification specified in the SUCH THAT clause is satisfied. The SUCH THAT clause here contains a further quantification indicated by the phrase 'FOR SOME Course(Student)'. This implies that if the following predicate is true for at least one of the Course entities returned by applying the Course function to the current Student entity under consideration, then the Name of that Student entity will be printed.

Note the use of nested function application and the absence of explicit looping variables. This gives the language a format which is closer to 'natural' language than, for example, the relational data languages discussed in this and earlier chapters.

Data entry and update in DAPLEX are illustrated by the following two examples:

1. 'Add a new student named Joe Smith and enrol him in the courses Database Technology and Concurrent Systems':

```
FOR A NEW Student
  BEGIN
    LET Name (Student) = 'Joe Smith'
    LET Address (Student) = '1 Anywhere Street'
    LET Sex (Student) = 'Male'
    LET Level (Student) = 1
    LET Course (Student) =
        ( THE Course SUCH THAT Name (Course) =
                                'Database Technology',
          THE Course SUCH THAT Name (Course) =
                                'Concurrent Systems' )
  END
```

2. 'Move the student Tom Brown from the course in Data Processing to the course in Software Engineering':

```
FOR THE Student SUCH THAT Name (Student) = 'Tom Brown'
  BEGIN
    EXCLUDE Course (Student) =
      THE COURSE SUCH THAT Name (COURSE) =
                                'Data Processing'
    INCLUDE Course (Student) =
      THE Course SUCH THAT Name (Course) =
                                'Software Engineering'
  END
```

EXERCISES

5.1 An estate agent maintains a database on houses that are for sale in his area. The database contains a relation for the entity type HOUSE which has the following attributes:

REF#	A unique 5-digit positive integer;
ADDRESS	The address of the house;
AREA	The area of the property in square metres;
STYLE1	Detached, semi-detached or terraced;
STYLE2	Two-storey, bungalow, chalet, etc.
PRICE	The asking price of the house;
BEDROOMS	The number of bedrooms;
GARAGE	Whether or not the house has a garage;
HEATING	The kind of heating (e.g. oil, coal, gas,

electricity or none)

ATTRACTIONS   A variable number of attractions chosen from a fixed set (e.g. nice garden, close to shops, close to schools, rural, urban, wooded etc.)

Using the data typing facilities of Modula-2 write a suitable set of domain definitions for each of these attributes. Each definition should be as precise as possible in order to facilitate the preservation of domain integrity.

5.2   Consider the following relational schema for a database concerning football teams, their players and the matches that they play:

TEAM (<u>TEAMNAME</u>, MANAGER)

PLAYER (<u>SQUAD#</u>, <u>TEAMNAME</u>, PLAYERNAME, POSITION)

MATCH (<u>TEAMNAME1</u>, <u>TEAMNAME2</u>, <u>DATE</u>, VENUE, SCORE1, SCORE2)

In the MATCH relation the attributes TEAMNAME1 and TEAM-NAME2 are foreign keys from the TEAM relation. The attributes SCORE1 and SCORE2 denote respectively the number of goals scored by TEAMNAME1 and TEAMNAME2.

(a)   Write a suitable set of domain definitions for this database using the typing facilities of Modula-2;
(b)   Write a complete set of referential integrity rules for this database in the form used in Section 5.2.3.
(c)   Outline any other integrity rules which are appropriate for this database but which are not covered by the rules given in your answers to parts (a) and (b).

5.3   Describe the ways in which modular programming can be used to facilitate the implementation of,

(a)   domain integrity rules;
(b)   referential integrity rules;
(c)   user views.

5.4   Give a DAPLEX schema for the football database defined in Exercise 5.2 above.

6

Physical Storage Organisation

6.1 INTRODUCTION

The fundamental problem in physical database design is to store a *file* consisting of *records*, each record having an identical format. A *record format* takes the form of a list of field names, with each field having an associated data type such as integer, real or character string. A record consists of values for each field. The typical operations that we wish to perform on a file are:

1. Add a new record to the file.
2. Delete a specified record from the file.
3. Retrieve records which have specified values in particular fields.

The ability to locate records in a file given the values of *any* fields is essential to the effective operation of a database system. The basic file organisations provided by most high-level languages, namely the sequential and random organisations, provide the minimal facility of access to records on the basis of their position in the file. Clearly however, higher-level file organisations are necessary to cope with the complex multifield information retrieval demands of database users.

In this chapter we shall review the basic file organisations before considering the more sophisticated, higher-level file structures found in modern database management systems.

6.2 A FILE ABSTRACTION IN MODULA-2

The definition of Modula-2 does not include a file type, but most implementations provide a utility module similar to that described below. The module Files is intended primarily for writing to and reading from disc files. Both random and sequential access are supported. Operations are also

131

provided for connecting logical files to external files, and for deleting and renaming external files.

To create a file, a variable of type File must first be declared:

VAR f : File ;

An external file is created and connected to a logical file by a call to the procedure Create:

PROCEDURE Create (VAR f : File ; name : ARRAY OF CHAR) ;

Existing files may be opened and connected to logical file variables through the procedure Open:

PROCEDURE Open (VAR f : File ; name : ARRAY OF CHAR ; m : Mode) ;

The mode can be read-only (Rmode), write-only (Wmode) or read-write (RWmode). When a program is finished with a file it should be closed through a call to the Close procedure:

PROCEDURE Close (VAR f : File) ;

Disc files may also be deleted or renamed using the Delete and Rename procedures:

PROCEDURE Delete (f : File) ;

PROCEDURE Rename (f : File ; NewName : ARRAY OF CHAR) ;

The status variable, of type FileStatus, exported by Files reports on the success or failure of the last operation. If successful status will be set to Done. Otherwise, the values that status may take have the following meanings:

```
TYPE FileStatus   =   (Done,            (* Operation successful *)
                       FileNotFound,    (* File could not be found *)
                       EndOfFile,       (* End of file encountered *)
                       ReadOnlyFile,    (* Write operation forbidden *)
                       WriteOnlyFile,   (* Read operation forbidden *)
                       StatusError,     (* File closed  *)
                       DeviceError,     (* Error in I/O device *)
                       UseError);       (* Invalid operation *)
```

The value of status should be checked after each operation.

The procedures ReadChar, ReadRecord, and ReadNBytes allow data to be read from a file.

PROCEDURE ReadChar (f : File ; VAR ch : CHAR) ;

PROCEDURE ReadRecord (f : File ; VAR rec : ARRAY OF WORD) ;

PROCEDURE ReadNBytes (f : File ; buffer : ADDRESS ;
                                 nbytes : CARDINAL);

ReadChar reads a single character from a file f. ReadRecord reads a word-aligned record from f starting at the current position. ReadNBytes will read the next nbytes from f starting at the current position and puts them at address buffer. For each of these procedures, the new position in the file after successful execution will be the byte immediately following the last byte read. The variable status is set to EndOfFile if the end of the file is encountered during execution of any of these procedures.

The procedures WriteChar, WriteRecord, and WriteNBytes may be called to write data to a file.

    PROCEDURE WriteChar (f : File ; ch : CHAR) ;

    PROCEDURE WriteRecord (f : File ; VAR rec : ARRAY OF WORD) ;

    PROCEDURE WriteNBytes (f : File ; buffer : ADDRESS ;
                                    nbytes : CARDINAL) ;

WriteChar writes a single character ch to the file f. WriteRecord writes a word-aligned record to the file starting at the current position. WriteNBytes takes nbytes starting at address buffer and writes them to the file starting at the current position. For each of these operations, the new position in f after successful execution will be the byte immediately following the last byte written.

Random access to a file is made possible through the procedures SetPosition and GetPosition.

    PROCEDURE SetPosition (f : File ; position : LONGINT) ;

    PROCEDURE GetPosition (f : File ; VAR position : LONGINT) ;

SetPosition sets the current file position in f to the specified value of the parameter position. If this position is beyond the current end of file position, then the variable status returns the value EndOfFile. The procedure GetPosition returns the current position in the file f. The current size of a file may be determined with the procedure FileSize:

    PROCEDURE FileSize (f : File ; size : LONGINT) ;

The complete Files definition module is given in Figure 6.1.

6.2.1 Implementation of the files module

The implementation of the operations described in the Files definition module will obviously vary considerably from one system to another. However, it is important to note that disc files are opened as block devices. This means that data are read from or written to a disc file in blocks of bytes, where the block size varies typically from 2^9 to 2^{12} bytes. Thus for example, when a program calls the procedure ReadNBytes and requests it to read 50 bytes from a disc file, the procedure will read the appropriate block from the disc and put the contents into a buffer. The 50 bytes are then extracted from the buffer and sent to the calling program. If the program requests further bytes, the Files module will continue to extract them from the buffer until it has been exhausted. The next block will then be read to re-fill the buffer. This process clearly saves on time-consuming disc operations.

Thus the basic external storage operation is the transfer of a block from secondary storage to main memory. In most modern systems such a transfer takes much longer than searching the block for information once it is in main memory. Thus the speed of algorithms for accessing data may be measured in terms of the number of block transfers necessary.

```
DEFINITION MODULE Files ;

FROM SYSTEM IMPORT WORD, ADDRESS;

EXPORT QUALIFIED
        File, status, FileStatus, Mode, Create, Open, Close, Delete,
        Rename, SetPosition, GetPosition, FileSize, ReadChar,
        ReadRecord, ReadNBytes, WriteChar, WriteRecord,
        WriteNBytes;

TYPE    File ;
        (* File is an opaque type *)
        Mode = (Rmode, Wmode, RWmode) ;
        FileStatus = (Done, FileNotFound, EndOfFile, ReadOnlyFile,
                      WriteOnlyFile, StatusError, DeviceError,
                      UseError) ;

VAR     status : FileStatus ;


PROCEDURE Create (VAR f : File ; name : ARRAY OF CHAR ) ;

PROCEDURE Open (VAR f : File ; name : ARRAY OF CHAR ;  m : Mode ) ;

PROCEDURE Close (VAR f : File) ;

PROCEDURE Delete (f : File) ;

PROCEDURE Rename (f : File ; NewName : ARRAY OF CHAR) ;

PROCEDURE ReadChar (f : File ; VAR ch : CHAR) ;

PROCEDURE ReadRecord (f : File ; VAR rec : ARRAY OF WORD) ;

PROCEDURE ReadNBytes (f : File ; buf : ADDRESS ; nbytes : CARDINAL);

PROCEDURE WriteChar (f : File ; ch : CHAR) ;

PROCEDURE WriteRecord (f : File ; VAR rec : ARRAY OF WORD) ;

PROCEDURE WriteNBytes (f : File ; buf : ADDRESS ; nbytes : CARDINAL) ;

PROCEDURE SetPosition (f : File ; position : LONGINT) ;

PROCEDURE GetPosition (f : File ; VAR position : LONGINT) ;

PROCEDURE FileSize (f : File ; size : LONGINT) ;

END Files.
```

Figure 6.1   Definition module for a file abstraction

6.3   FILE STRUCTURES FOR SINGLE KEY PROCESSING

As we have seen, the Files module provides either random or sequential access to records on the basis of their position in the file. For database applications, a more useful mode of access is one based on key values. That is, given a unique record identifier (key value), we wish to locate the record in the file. An organisation which provides direct access to records given their key values is often called a *direct access file*. A definition module to provide such an organisation in Modula-2 is given in Figure 6.2. This module, in common with other modules in this chapter, assume that the user provides definitions for keytype and rectype, where the definition of rectype takes the form:

```
TYPE
    rectype  =  RECORD
                     keyvalue : keytype ;
                     . . . { definition of non-key fields } . . .
                END ;
```

We shall also assume that the relational operators '=', '<', '>', etc. are defined for variables of type keytype and rectype. If this is not the case then it is quite easy to write Boolean functions of the form:

```
PROCEDURE EQUALKEYS ( k1, k2 : keytype ) : BOOLEAN ;

PROCEDURE LESSTHAN ( k1, k2 : keytype ) : BOOLEAN ;
```

etc., which perform comparisons on variables of a structured type and return the appropriate Boolean result.

```
DEFINITION MODULE DirectFile ;

FROM SYSTEM IMPORT WORD, ADDRESS;

FROM Files IMPORT
    File, status, FileStatus, Mode, Create, Open, Close,
    SetPosition, GetPosition, FileSize, ReadRecord, WriteRecord;

EXPORT QUALIFIED
    CreateFile, OpenFile, CloseFile, FindRecord, InsertRecord,
    DeleteRecord, ReplaceRecord ;

PROCEDURE CreateFile (VAR f : File ; name : ARRAY OF CHAR ) ;

PROCEDURE OpenFile (VAR f : File ;  name : ARRAY OF CHAR ;
                                m : Mode ) ;

PROCEDURE CloseFile (VAR f : File) ;

PROCEDURE FindRecord (f : File ; k : keytype ;  VAR r : rectype ;
                                VAR found : BOOLEAN) ;

PROCEDURE InsertRecord (f : File ; k : keytype ;  r : rectype ;
                                VAR found : BOOLEAN) ;
```

PROCEDURE DeleteRecord (f : File ; k : keytype ;
                                          VAR found : BOOLEAN) ;

PROCEDURE ReplaceRecord (f : File ; k : keytype ; newr : rectype ;
                                          VAR found : BOOLEAN) ;

END DIRECTFILES.

Figure 6.2   A direct file abstraction

The procedure FindRecord retrieves the record with key value k from the file f and assigns its value to the variable parameter r. If a record with key value k does not exist in the file, then the variable parameter found will be set to FALSE. Otherwise found is set to TRUE. Procedure InsertRecord will add the record value r, with key value k, to the file f provided a record with this key value does not already exist in the file. If such a record does already exist, the operation will not be performed and the value of found will be set to TRUE. Procedure DeleteRecord removes the record with key vale k from the file f. If such a record does not exist in f the value of found will be set to FALSE. Procedure ReplaceRecord will replace the record with key value k in file f, provided it exists, with the new record newr.

The implementation of the operations FindRecord, InsertRecord, Delete-Record and ReplaceRecord obviously require some means for converting key values to actual record addresses. The simplest approach would be to store the records as a 'heap'. In a heap file the records are stored in no particular order. A new record is inserted in the first available space in the first unfilled block, though records are not usually allowed to overlap block boundaries. To search for a given key value, the file must be scanned record by record. On average this will require N/2 block accesses, where N is the number of blocks required to store the file. In a database environment the cost of such an operation is usually prohibitive if the file is more than a few blocks long.

An alternative approach is to store the records in ascending order of key value. To search for a record with a given key value we may use a binary split search which will require on average $O(\log_2 N)$ block accesses. This is much better than the average of N/2 accesses required for a linear search, but may still be unacceptable if the file is large and real-time responses are required. The major disadvantage of this organisation however, is that insertion and deletion of records involve a complicated and time-consuming reorganisation of the file, in order to maintain the key sequence. For database applications the cost of such reorganisation may be unacceptable.

The remainder of this section is devoted to alternative file organisations which allow arbitrary retrievals on the basis of key values, without scanning more than a small fraction of the file. In designing better organisations we must try to avoid using too much extra storage space, and we must avoid making insertion and deletion operations too complicated. The following sections describe some useful ideas that have been successfully employed in database systems.

6.3.1   Hashed   files

In a hashed file the records are stored in *buckets* which may consist of a number of physical blocks. A *hash function* H(k), takes as its argument a value for a key and produces as its result the number of the bucket in which the record with key value k is to be found (or inserted). The fundamental problem with hashed files is that the set of possible key values is generally much larger than the number of available buckets. Thus the hash function H is a many-to-one function.

It is desirable that H(k) computes rapidly, and takes on all possible values of bucket number with equal probability, so that we do not have too many keys hashing to the same bucket number. There are numerous alternative strategies for determining H(k) but the following technique gives very good results in many situations:

1.   Choose N, the number of buckets required to hold the file, to be a prime number (or at the very least a number with no small factors).

2.   Treat the key as a sequence of bits and divide the sequence into equal length portions. Add the portions together as integers, giving a single integer, say S_k, as result. This technique of splitting the key into parts which are then combined to give a single result is often called *folding*. Note that in programming this technique one must be careful to avoid integer overflow.

3.   Choose the hash function H(k) to be,

$$H(k) = (S_k \ \text{MOD} \ N) + 1$$

To insert a new record, we apply the hash function to its key value and store the record in the resulting bucket number. Each bucket holds a count of the number of records currently held in that bucket, and if this indicates that the bucket is already full then the record must be stored elsewhere. One obvious strategy is to store the record in a specially reserved *overflow* bucket which is then chained to the bucket of the main file. An advantage of chaining is that an overflowed record will be found quickly, but this technique may waste storage space since many overflow buckets may be partially filled. Numerous alternative strategies for resolving overflow have been proposed in the literature (Knuth, 1973).

To find a record with key value k, we again compute H(k) which gives us a bucket number. We transfer the blocks of this bucket one by one to main memory and search them sequentially for the desired record. If the bucket is full and the record is not found then we must search the overflow area.

A data structure for a hashed file might take the following form:

```
CONST
    recordsperbucket = { User supplied }

TYPE
    bucketaddress = { User supplied }
```

```
buckettype = RECORD
                noofrecords : 0..recordsperbucket ;
                recordlist : ARRAY [1..recordsperbucket] OF rectype ;
                overflowptr : bucketaddress ;
            END ;
```

Then assuming that we have a procedure:

```
GetBucket (f : File ; b : bucketaddress : VAR bucket : buckettype) ;
```

which copies from file f the contents of the bucket at address b into the variable bucket, the procedure FindRecord might be implemented as shown in Figure 6.3.

```
PROCEDURE FindRecord (f : File ; k : keytype ; VAR r : rectype ;
                                VAR found : BOOLEAN) ;
VAR
    h : bucketaddress ;

BEGIN
    h := HASH(k) ;
    GetBucket(f,h,bucket) ;
    continue := TRUE ;
    found := FALSE ;
    WHILE continue AND NOT found DO
        i := 1 ;
        WHILE (i < bucket.noofrecords) AND NOT found DO
            IF k = bucket.recordlist[i].keyvalue
            THEN
                found := true ;
                r := bucket.recordlist[i] ;
            ELSE
                i := i + 1 ;
            END ;
        END ;
        h := bucket.overflowptr ;
        continue := h > 0 ;
        IF continue
        THEN
            GetBucket(f,h,bucket)
        END
    END
END FindRecord;
```

Figure 6.3 Finding a record in a hashed file.

A detailed time analysis of hashing is complex, depending as it does on the hash function and the distribution of key values. Usually however, only a few block accesses are necessary to find the record with a given key.

Disadvantages of hashing may be summarised as follows:

1. It may be wasteful of storage space. Clearly in order to avoid excessive

overflow, we must set aside rather more buckets than are actually necessary to hold the file. As more records are inserted some buckets may remain sparsely occupied, while others become full and require overflow management.

2. Processing the file in key order is difficult. We may of course, apply a sorting procedure to the file if necessary, but if this is a frequent requirement the cost may be prohibitive.

6.3.2   Indexed files

An alternative to hashing which facilitates both sequential and random access to the file is the *indexed sequential organisation*. In this organisation the records in the file are sorted by their key values and arranged into blocks on secondary storage such that sufficient free space for several additional records is left in each block. A second file, called a *sparse index*, consists of entries of the form (key value, block address), again sorted by key values, where the entry (k, b) appears in the index if the highest key value in block b of the records file is k.

To find a record with key k_1, we search the index for the first entry (k_2, b) with $k_1 \leq k_2$. The value b then gives us the number of the block containing that record (if it exists), and so we copy this block from the records file to main memory and perform a linear or binary search of this block for the desired record. The index, being much smaller than the records file can often be copied to main memory and searched rapidly.

To insert a record with key value k, we look up the index for the appropriate block number as described above and, if space is available in that block we insert the record there, maintaining the sorted order. If the block is full then we must adopt some strategy for dealing with overflow. There are a variety of such strategies discussed extensively in the literature (see for example the book by Elder, 1984), and we shall not pursue the matter any further in this text.

From a database point of view, the indexed sequential organisation has a number of disadvantages. Firstly, the problem of overflowing records complicates the insertion process and may slow down retrieval; Secondly, the degree of access to the records file is still high, even for the important class of query known as *existence tests*. That is, in order to determine whether a record with a given key value exists, it is necessary to access the records file.

An organisation which overcomes both of these disadvantages, at the expense of additional storage space, is the *indexed random organisation*. With indexed random files (sometimes called 'files with a dense index'), the records are unsorted and the *dense primary index* contains an entry (k, b) for *every* key value k in the file. It is usual to maintain the index in sorted key order so that look-up may be done efficiently using, for example, the binary split method. To illustrate this method, suppose that we have copied the index into the array Index, defined by the following declarations:

```
TYPE
    IndexRecord =    RECORD
                         keyvalue : keytype;
                         address  : blockaddress;
                     END;
VAR
    Index : ARRAY[1..N] OF IndexRecord;
```

To search for key value k, we compare k with the key value of the middle index element. If k < Index[N/2].keyvalue then we repeat the process on the lower half of the index. If k >= Index[N/2].keyvalue then we repeat the process on the upper half of the index. Eventually only one element will remain to be considered. The Modula-2 procedure in Figure 6.4 implements a binary split search.

```
PROCEDURE FindKey (key : keytype ; VAR position : blockaddress ;
                                    VAR found : BOOLEAN ) ;
VAR
    upper, lower, middle : CARDINAL ;
BEGIN
    found := FALSE ;
    lower := 1 ;
    upper := N ;
    WHILE NOT found AND (lower <= upper) DO
        middle := (upper + lower) DIV 2 ;
        IF key = Index[middle].keyvalue
        THEN  found := TRUE
        ELSIF key < Index[middle].keyvalue THEN upper := middle - 1
        ELSE  lower := middle + 1
        END
    END ;
    IF found THEN
        position := Index[middle].address ;
    END ;
END FindKey ;
```

Figure 6.4   A binary split search procedure

A data file and its associated dense primary index are a closely related pair of entities which should be created, opened and closed together. The definition module for an indexed file abstraction should reflect this close association and so we modify our original DIRECTFILES module so that the index file is specified in each operation. The resulting module is shown in Figure 6.5.

An advantage of the indexed random organisation is that by maintaining the records file in unsorted order, we do not have the problems of partially filled blocks or of overflow. In addition, existence tests can now be carried out by searching only the index file.

The dense index however, is much larger than for the indexed sequential organisation since it contains an entry for every record. Thus, searching the dense index can itself become quite time-consuming. A possible solution to this problem is to use *multilevel indexing.*

```
DEFINITION MODULE INDEXEDFILES ;

FROM SYSTEM IMPORT WORD, ADDRESS;

FROM FILES IMPORT
      File, status, FileStatus, Mode, Create, Open, Close,
      SetPosition, GetPosition, FileSize, ReadRecord, WriteRecord;

EXPORT QUALIFIED
      CreateFile, OpenFile, CloseFile, FindRecord, InsertRecord,
      DeleteRecord, ReplaceRecord ;

PROCEDURE CreateFile (VAR f, index : File ;
                            fname, indexname : ARRAY OF CHAR ) ;

PROCEDURE OpenFile (VAR f, index : File ;
                          fname, indexname : ARRAY OF CHAR ;  m : Mode ) ;

PROCEDURE CloseFile (VAR f, index : File) ;

PROCEDURE FindRecord (f, index : File ; k : keytype ;  VAR r : rectype ;
                            VAR found : BOOLEAN) ;

PROCEDURE InsertRecord (f, index : File ; k : keytype ;  r : rectype ;
                            VAR found : BOOLEAN) ;

PROCEDURE DeleteRecord (f, index : File ; k : keytype ;
                            VAR found : BOOLEAN) ;

PROCEDURE ReplaceRecord (f, index : File ; k : keytype ; newr : rectype ;
                            VAR found : BOOLEAN) ;

END INDEXEDFILES.
```

Figure 6.5   An indexed file abstraction

6.3.3   Multilevel indexing: B-trees

Since an index is a file, we may treat it like an ordinary file of records, maintained in sorted order, and build a sparse index to it. This idea may be carried to as many levels as we wish, leading to a tree-structured multilevel index. Each level of the index acts as a sparse index to the level below, with the first level (the *root node*) fitting onto a single block. Such an organisation can be considerably more efficient than a file with a single level dense index.

Multilevel indexing based on *B-tree* structures is now probably the most popular storage organisation of all in modern database systems. B-trees were first described by Bayer and McCreight (1972), and since that time numerous variations on the original idea have been proposed. The B-tree of Bayer and McCreight forms a dense index to the data file and the nodes of the tree contain pointers to the data records as well as to nodes on the next level of the tree. In the variation proposed by Knuth (1973) however, the sorted, single-level dense index is retained and the B-tree forms a multilevel sparse index to this dense index. This structure is often called a B$^+$-tree, and its advantage is that the retention of the sorted dense index provides fast *sequential* access to the indexed data. In the following discussion we shall concern ourselves with the original structure as proposed by Bayer and McCreight.

A fundamental property of a B-tree is that it is always *balanced*. That is, every path from the root node to a leaf node is of the same length, and insertion and deletion algorithms maintain this balance. In addition, the strategies for insertion and deletion ensure that no node, except possibly the root, is ever less than half full. Thus storage utilisation is at least 50 per cent at any time and should be considerably better on average. A B-tree also maintains the order of the keys so that the file may be processed in both sequential and random modes.

Definition of a B-tree

Let m be a natural number. A B-tree, T, of order m is either empty or has the following properties:

1. Every node has at most $2m$ keys.
2. Every node, except for the root has at least m keys. The root node has at least one key.
3. Every path from the root to a leaf node has the same length h, the height of the tree (i.e. the tree is always balanced).
4. A non-leaf node which contains k keys has $k+1$ children. That is, to save space the first key value is omitted from each node.

(Note that the definition of the order of the tree tends to vary from author to author. We have followed the definition of Bayer and McCreight.) Thus a non-leaf node P with n keys ($m \leq n \leq 2m$) is an ordered set of the form,

$$(p_0 , k_1 , d_1 , p_1 , k_2 , d_2 , p_2 , \ldots , k_n , d_n , p_n)$$

where k_i ($i = 1..n$) are key values, d_i ($i = 1..n$) are pointers to the associated data records and p_i ($i = 0..n$) are pointers to the children of P as follows:

p_0 is a pointer to the subtree for keys less than k_1;
p_i ($i = 1..n-1$) are pointers to the subtrees for keys greater than or equal to k_i and less than k_{i+1} ;
p_n is a pointer to the subtree for keys greater than or equal to k_n.

Thus a node can be considered as consisting of *items* of the form shown in Figure 6.6. Each node, of course, has one extra node reference. To facilitate insertion and deletion of key values in the tree we might also include in the description of a node, the number of items currently held in the node.

An example of a B-tree of order 1 is shown in Figure 6.7. (Note: For clarity the pointers to the data records d_i are not shown.)

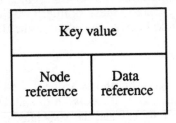

Figure 6.6 An item in a B-tree

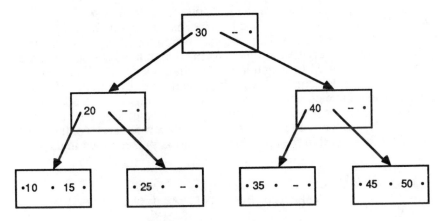

Figure 6.7 A B-tree of order 1

Thus in Modula-2 we might represent items and nodes using the following structures:

```
CONST
    order   = {Order of the B-tree}
    maxnode = {max. number of keys in a node = 2*order}
TYPE
    keytype = {User supplied}
    nodeptr = POINTER TO node ;
    item  =   RECORD
                keyvalue : keytype ;
                noderef : nodeptr ;
                dataref : blockaddress ;
              END ;
    node  =   RECORD
                noofitems : [0..maxnode] ;
                firstnoderef : nodeptr ;
                items : ARRAY [1..maxnode] OF item ;
              END ;
    Btree =   nodeptr ;
```

This representation assumes that the B-tree, which is normally held in secondary storage, has been copied into a dynamic data structure held in main memory. Thus the node pointers can be represented by the type POINTER TO node. On secondary storage these pointers would be replaced by the actual or relative block addresses of the nodes in the B-tree file.

Searching a B-tree

To search a B-tree for a record with key value v, we begin at the root node and find the first key value k_i (if it exists) in this node such that $k_i >= v$. If $k_i = v$ then we have found the key and the associated data reference is given by d_i. Otherwise we then follow the pointer p_{i-1} to the next index level and repeat the process until we come to a leaf node. If there is no key value k_i such that $k_i > v$, then we follow the last pointer in the node p_n. If we reach a leaf node and v is not in that node then it does not exist in the tree.

If the order of the tree is large we may search for a key in a node using a binary search. Otherwise a simple sequential search will suffice. In either case the time required to search a node in main memory will almost certainly be negligible compared with the time it takes to copy a node from secondary to main memory.

A procedure for searching a B-tree, r, for key value k is given in Figure 6.8. If the key value is found the associated data reference (i.e. the block address of the record in the main file with this key) is returned in the variable d.

```
PROCEDURE Search ( r : Btree ; k : keytype ;
                VAR found : BOOLEAN ; VAR d : blockaddress ) ;
VAR
    p : nodeptr ;
    lower, upper, middle : CARDINAL ;
BEGIN
    p := r ;
    IF p = NIL
    THEN found := FALSE ;
    ELSE
        WITH p^ DO
        lower := 1 ; upper := noofitems + 1 ;
        WHILE lower < upper DO
            middle := (lower + upper) DIV 2 ;
            IF k >= items[middle].keyvalue
            THEN lower := middle + 1
            ELSE upper := middle
            END
        END ;
        upper := upper - 1 ;
        IF upper = 0
        THEN  (* k less than all key values in node *)
            p := firstnoderef ;
        ELSIF k = items[upper].keyvalue
            THEN found := TRUE ;
```

```
                    d := items[upper].dataref
           ELSE p := items[upper].noderef
           END
    END ;
    IF NOT found
    THEN Search(p,k,found,d)  END
END Search ;
```

Figure 6.8   A procedure for searching a B-tree

Time analysis of B-trees

Let N_{min} and N_{max} be the minimal and maximal number of nodes in a B-tree of order m and height h. Then we have that:

$$N_{min} \quad = \quad 1 + 2((m+1)^0 + (m+1)^1 + \ldots + (m+1)^{h-2})$$

$$= \quad 1 + 2((m+1)^{h-1} - 1)/m$$

and

$$N_{max} \quad = \quad \sum_{i=0}^{h-1}(2m+1)^i \quad = \quad ((2m+1)^h - 1)/2m$$

where we have used the well known formula for the sum of a geometric progression. These expressions for N_{min} and N_{max} follow very simply from the fact that the minimum (maximum) number of nodes arises by allowing each node to have the minimum (maximum) number of pointers. (Recall that the root node may have only one key and two pointers.)

Thus the minimum and maximum number of keys in a B-tree, K_{min} and K_{max} are given by,

$$K_{min} \quad = \quad 1 + mN_{min} \quad = \quad 1 + m + 2(m+1)^{h-1} - 1$$

$$K_{max} \quad = \quad 2mN_{max} \quad = \quad (2m+1)^h - 1$$

If we have an index of size K, we have that

$$2(m+1)^{h-1} - 1 \; < \; K \; < \; (2m+1)^h - 1$$

Re-arranging this we obtain an upper bound for h, the height of the tree and therefore the maximum number of node accesses required to find a key:

$$h \; < \; 1 + \log_{m+1}((K+1)/2)$$

for $K > 1$. The minimum number of node accesses is clearly 1, when the key being searched for is in the root node.

Example
Let $K = 100,000$ and $m = 10$, then from the inequality for h derived above, we have that,

$$h \; < \; 1 + \log_{11}(50,000.5) \; \approx \; 5.5$$

That is, the maximum number of block accesses required to find a key is only 5. A serial search of the index with 20 keys per block would require on average $(100,000/20)/2 = 2500$ accesses. A binary split search of a sorted, single-level index would require, on average, the order of $\log_2(100,000/20) \approx 12.3$ accesses.

Inserting keys into a B-tree

Inserting a key value into a B-tree involves searching the tree as described above to find the appropriate node and inserting the key value and its associated pointer into this node.

If the node is full however, we introduce a new node and redistribute the $2m+1$ keys across the two nodes. The m smallest keys stay in the old node and the m largest are moved to the new node. The middle $(m+1)$th key is moved up to an ancestral node on the previous level. If the ancestral node is full, then it too must be split. In this way splitting may propagate all the way back to the root. If the root node is split then a new root is created and the tree grows in height by one. This scheme preserves the order of keys in the B-tree and keeps the tree balanced.

A Modula-2 procedure which implements this insertion scheme is given in Figure 6.9. The basic algorithm is adapted from Wirth (1986). The procedure is annotated to explain its operation.

```
PROCEDURE insert ( VAR r : Btree ; k : keytype ; d : blockaddress ;
                              VAR found : BOOLEAN ) ;
VAR
    newitem : item ;
    higher : BOOLEAN ;
    s : nodeptr ;
    i, pos : CARDINAL ;


    PROCEDURE newroot (newitem : item);
    (* Creates a new root when the tree grows in height by 1 *)
    VAR
        p : nodeptr ;

    BEGIN
        ALLOCATE(p,SIZE(node)) ;
        WITH p^ DO
            noofitems := 1 ; firstnoderef := r ; items[1] := newitem
        END ;
        r := p
    END newroot;


    PROCEDURE insert2 ( s : nodeptr ; VAR higher : BOOLEAN ;
                                VAR newitem : item ) ;
    VAR
        lower, upper, pos : CARDINAL ;
        u : item ;
```

```
PROCEDURE Splitnode ( s : nodeptr ) ;
(* Splits a node, passing the middle key value up the tree *)
VAR
    i : CARDINAL ; newnode : nodeptr ;
BEGIN
    ALLOCATE(newnode,SIZE(node)) ;
    (* Move 'order' largest key values to new node, keeping
        'order' smallest key values in existing node s*)
    IF pos <= order
    THEN
        IF pos = order
        THEN newitem := u
        ELSE
            newitem := s^.items[order] ;
            FOR i := order TO pos+2 BY -1 DO
                s^.items[i] := s^.items[i-1]
            END
            s^.items[pos+1] := u
            FOR i := 1 TO order DO
                newnode^.items[i] := s^.items[i+order]
            END ;
        END ;
    ELSE
        pos := pos - order ;
        newitem := s^.items[order+1] ;
        FOR i := 1 TO pos-1 DO
            newnode^.items[i] := s^.items[i+order+1]
        END ;
        newnode^.items[pos] := u ;
        FOR i := pos+1 TO order DO
            newnode^.items[i] := s^.items[i+order]
        END ;
    END ;
    s^.noofitems := order ;
    newnode^.noofitems := order ;
    newnode^.firstnoderef := newitem.noderef ;
    newitem.noderef := newnode
END  Splitnode;

BEGIN
    IF s = NIL
    THEN
        higher := TRUE ;
        found := FALSE ;
        WITH newitem DO
            keyvalue := k ; noderef := NIL ; dataref := d ;
        END
    ELSE
        WITH s^ DO
            lower := 1 ; upper := noofitems + 1 ;
            WHILE lower < upper DO
                pos := (lower + upper) DIV 2 ;
                IF k >= items[pos].keyvalue
```

```
                        THEN lower := pos + 1
                        ELSE upper := pos
                        END
                END ;
                pos := upper - 1 ;
                IF (pos > 0) AND (items[pos].keyvalue = k)
                THEN
                        found := TRUE  (* key value already in tree *)
                ELSE
                        IF pos = 0
                        THEN (* k less than all key values in node *)
                                insert2(firstnoderef,higher,u)
                        ELSE
                                insert2(items[pos].noderef,higher,u)
                        END ;
                        IF higher
                        THEN
                                IF noofitems = maxnode
                                THEN (* overflow - node must be split *)
                                  Splitnode(s)
                                ELSE
                                   higher := FALSE ;
                                   FOR i := noofitems+1 TO pos+2 BY -1 DO
                                           items[i] := items[i-1]
                                   END ;
                                   items[pos+1] := u ;
                                   noofitems := noofitems + 1
                                END
                        END
                END
        END
    END
    END insert2;

BEGIN
    higher := FALSE ;
    insert2(r,higher,newitem) ;
    IF higher THEN newroot(newitem) END
END  insert;
```

Figure 6.9   A procedure for inserting a key k in a B-tree

To illustrate the node-splitting scheme, Figure 6.10 shows how our original B-tree grows as keys are inserted into a tree that is initially empty.

Insert 30
A new node (the root node) is created and 30 is inserted into the first key
position (Figure 6.10(a)).

Insert 10
This value is inserted into the root node but the keys are maintained in
ascending order (Figure 6.10(b)).

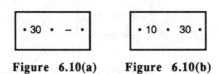

Figure 6.10(a)   Figure 6.10(b)

Insert 35
In this case there is insufficient space in the root node for the new key value
and so the node must be split. The middle key value, 30, moves to the level
above, necessitating the creation of a new root node (Figure 6.10(c)).

Insert 40
This is a straightforward insertion into the rightmost leaf node (Figure
6.10(d)).

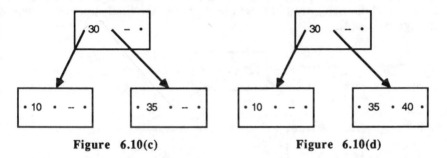

Figure 6.10(c)   Figure 6.10(d)

Insert 45
A search for the key value 45 brings us again to the node on the right hand
branch. However, this node is full and so the key values 35, 40 and 45
must be redistributed. The key value 35 stays in the existing node, 45 is
placed in a new node, and the middle value, 40, moves up to the root node
(Figure 6.10(e)).

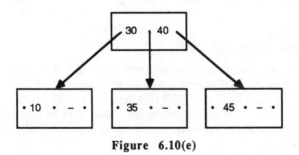

Figure 6.10(e)

Insert 20
This is a straightforward insertion into the leftmost leaf node (Figure
6.10(f).

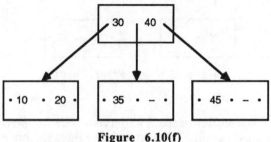

Figure 6.10(f)

Insert 25
This insertion requires the key values 10, 20 and 25 to be redistributed. The value 10 remains in the existing node and 25 moves to a newly created leaf node. The middle value, 20, moves to the level above. However, the node at this level (the root) is full and must also be split. Thus a new root is created and the tree grows in height by 1, giving the final structure shown in Figure 6.10(g).

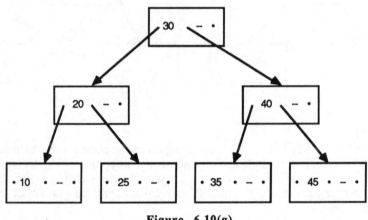

Figure 6.10(g)

Deleting keys from a B-tree

For database applications we must have the capability of deleting keys from an index, and our deletion algorithm must preserve the structure of the B-tree. If the key is on a leaf node then it is simply deleted and the only problem that may arise is that the resulting leaf node may be left with too few keys. This problem is called *underflow* and we shall describe how to deal with it presently.

If the item is not on a leaf but rather on some non-terminal node P, then it is replaced by the largest key on the subtree for which P is the root. This largest key is then deleted from its node, again resulting in the possibility of underflow.

When an underflow situation arises in a node P we fetch an *adjacent* node, say Q, and *redistribute* the keys on nodes P and Q, together with the separating key value from the parent node. (An adjacent node is a node with the same parent and pointed to by an adjacent pointer in this parent node.) However, if the number of keys in Q is already at its minimum then we cannot redistribute the keys and maintain the properties of a B-tree. Instead we *merge* nodes P and Q together with the separating key of their parent node. This process of node merging is the inverse process of node splitting which we described in the previous section, and of course it may propagate all the way back to the root.

A procedure which implements the deletion algorithm described above is given in Figure 6.11. Again, the basic algorithm is due to Wirth (1986). Examples follow the procedure illustrating deletion for cases where redistribution and merging are necessary.

```
PROCEDURE Delete (VAR r : Btree ; k : keytype ; VAR found : BOOLEAN) ;
    (* Deletes key value k (if found) from B-tree r *)
VAR
    q : nodeptr ; undersize : BOOLEAN ;

    PROCEDURE Delete2 ( r : nodeptr ;  VAR undersize : BOOLEAN ) ;
        (* Recursive procedure to search and delete *)
    VAR
        p : nodeptr ;
        lower, upper, pos, i : CARDINAL ;

        PROCEDURE underflow (p,r : nodeptr ; pos : CARDINAL ;
                                    VAR undersize : BOOLEAN ) ;
            (* A procedure to deal with underflow *)
        VAR
            q : nodeptr ;
            i, j, np, nq : CARDINAL ;
        BEGIN
            np := p^.noofitems ;
            IF pos < np
            THEN
                pos := pos + 1 ;
                q := p^.items[pos].noderef ;
                nq := q^.noofitems ;
                j := (nq - order + 1) DIV 2 ;
                r^.items[order] := p^.items[pos] ;
                r^.items[order].noderef := q^.firstnoderef ;
                IF j > 0
                THEN  (* move j items from q TO r *)
                    FOR i := 1 TO j-1 DO
                        r^.items[i+order] := q^.items[i]
                    END ;
                    p^.items[pos] := q^.items[j] ;
                    p^.items[pos].noderef := q ;
                    q^.firstnoderef := q^.items[j].noderef ;
                    nq := nq - j ;
                    FOR i := 1 TO nq DO
                        q^.items[i] := q^.items[i+j]
```

```
                    END ;
                    q^.noofitems := nq ;
                    r^.noofitems := order - 1 + j ;
                    undersize := FALSE
                ELSE  (* merge nodes r AND q *)
                    FOR i := 1 TO order DO
                        r^.items[i+order] := q^.items[i]
                    END ;
                    FOR i := pos TO np-1 DO
                        p^.items[i] := p^.items[i+1]
                    END ;
                    r^.noofitems := maxnode ;
                    p^.noofitems := np - 1 ;
                    undersize := np <= order ;
                    DEALLOCATE(q)
            END
        ELSE
            IF pos = 1
            THEN q := p^.firstnoderef
            ELSE q := p^.items[pos-1].noderef
            END ;
            nq := q^.noofitems + 1 ;
            j := (nq - order) DIV 2 ;
            IF j > 0
            THEN  (* move j items from q TO r *)
                    FOR i := order-1 TO 1 BY -1 DO
                        r^.items[i+j] := r^.items[i]
                    END ;
                    r^.items[j] := p^.items[pos] ;
                    r^.items[j].noderef := r^.firstnoderef ;
                    nq := nq - j ;
                    FOR i := j-1 TO 1 BY -1 DO
                        r^.items[i] := q^.items[i+nq]
                    END ;
                    r^.firstnoderef := q^.items[nq].noderef ;
                    p^.items[pos] := q^.items[nq] ;
                    p^.items[pos].noderef := r ;
                    q^.noofitems := nq - 1 ;
                    r^.noofitems := order -1 + j ;
                    undersize := FALSE
            ELSE  (* merge r AND q *)
                    q^.items[nq] := p^.items[pos] ;
                    q^.items[nq].noderef := r^.firstnoderef ;
                    FOR i := 1 TO order - 1 DO
                        q^.items[i+nq] := r^.items[i]
                    END ;
                    q^.noofitems := maxnode ;
                    p^.noofitems := np - 1 ;
                    undersize := np <= order ;
                    DEALLOCATE(r)
            END
        END
    END underflow;
```

```
            PROCEDURE Del( p : nodeptr ; VAR undersize : BOOLEAN) ;
            VAR
                q : nodeptr ;
            BEGIN
                WITH p^ DO
                    q := items[noofitems].noderef ;
                    IF q <> NIL
                    THEN
                        Del (q,undersize) ;
                        IF undersize
                        THEN underflow(p,q,noofitems,undersize)
                        END
                    ELSE
                        p^.items[noofitems].noderef :=
                                                    r^.items[pos+1].noderef ;
                        r^.items[pos+1] := p^.items[noofitems] ;
                        noofitems := noofitems - 1 ;
                        undersize := noofitems < order
                    END
                END
            END Del;

BEGIN
    IF r = NIL
    THEN undersize := FALSE
    ELSE
        WITH r^ DO
            lower := 1 ; upper := noofitems + 1 ;
            WHILE lower < upper DO
                pos := (lower + upper) DIV 2 ;
                IF k > items[pos].keyvalue
                THEN lower := pos + 1  ELSE upper := pos
                END
            END ;
            pos := upper - 1 ;
            IF pos = 0
            THEN p := firstnoderef
            ELSE p := items[pos].noderef
            END ;
            IF (pos <= noofitems-1) AND (k = items[pos+1].keyvalue)
            THEN
                found := TRUE ;
                IF p = NIL
                THEN
                    (* key value in leaf node *)
                    noofitems := noofitems - 1 ;
                    FOR i := pos+1 TO noofitems DO
                                items[i] := items[i+1]
                    END ;
                    undersize := noofitems < order
                ELSE
                    (* key value in non-leaf node *)
                    Del(p,undersize) ;
```

```
                                        IF undersize
                                        THEN underflow(r,p,pos,undersize)
                                        END
                                    END
                                ELSE
                                    Delete2(p,undersize) ;
                                    IF undersize
                                    THEN underflow(r,p,pos,undersize)
                                    END
                                END
                            END
                        END
                    END Delete2;

BEGIN
            found := FALSE ;
            Delete2(r,undersize) ;
            IF undersize
            THEN IF r^.noofitems = 0
                    THEN
                        q := r ;  r := r^.firstnoderef ;
                        DEALLOCATE(q)
                    END
            END
        END Delete;
```

Figure 6.11   A procedure for deleting keys from a B-tree.

To illustrate the deletion algorithm, consider again the B-tree in Figure 6.6 and suppose that we wish to delete the key value 35. The causes underflow, but an adjacent node is more than minimally full (i.e. the node containing key values 45 and 50), Thus we redistribute the key values 45 and 50, together with 40, the separating key value from the parent node. This results in the tree shown in Figure 6.12.

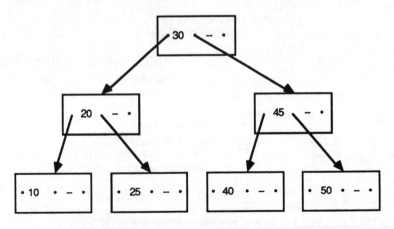

Figure 6.12   B-tree of Figure 6.6 with 35 deleted

Suppose that we now wish to delete key value 40. This also causes under-flow, since the resulting node is too small (in this case empty). This time however, we cannot solve the problem by redistribution since the only available adjacent node (i.e. the node with key value 50) contains the mini-mum number of keys. Thus we merge into the adjacent node, the keys from the node which has underflowed (none in this case), the keys from the adjacent node (50) and the separating key value from the parent node (45). This causes underflow at the level above since the parent node (that which contained 45) is now empty. Once again merging is the solution, causing the tree to shrink in height by 1. The resulting tree is shown in Figure 6.13.

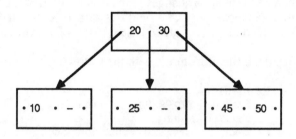

Figure 6.13   The B-tree of Figure 6.11 with 40 deleted

6.4   FILE STRUCTURES FOR NON-KEY PROCESSING

Let us now consider the problem of finding records in a file for which the values of non-key fields have been specified. In formal terms we are re-quired to find the records with the value v_1 in field F_1, v_2 in field F_2, . . ., v_n in field F_n. If S_i is the set of records with value v_i in field F_i ($i = 1..n$), then we require the set of records S where,

$$S = S_1 \cap S_2 \cap \ldots S_n.$$

Database management systems have adopted a variety of techniques to solve this problem. By far the most popular method, and the most generally applicable is that of file inversion, which extends the idea of indexing to cover non-key as well as key fields. We shall study inversion in some de-tail in the following section.

Other methods which have been adopted, and which we shall consider only briefly, include:

1. Multiple-linked lists (also called a *threaded* organisation) in which pointers are embedded within records to link together records with the same values in certain fields.
2. Partitioned hash functions - a relatively new technique in which the hash function takes as argument a combination of key and non-key fields.

6.4.1   File inversion

Consider a file whose records have a field F whose possible values are taken from a set of values D, the domain of F. A secondary index for field F is a file with record format,

(value from D, {record pointer})

That is, each entry in the secondary index consists of a value from the domain of F followed by a variable length list of pointers to the records of the file which have that value in field F. It is desirable that the pointers in the secondary index be logical identifiers rather than actual addresses, since the index may then be immune to changes in the organisation of the main file.

A file with a secondary index on field F is said to be inverted on field F. A file which is inverted on every field is said to be fully inverted.

Example. Consider a file of lecturers with the following record format:

```
lecturer  =  RECORD
              Staff_no   : [0..99999] ;   (* unique *)
              Name       : String ;
              Dept       : (Physics, Maths, CompSci) ;
              Age        : [21..65] ;
              Degree     : (BSc, MSc, PhD)
           END ;
```

Suppose we have an instance of this file as shown in Figure 6.14.

Record No.	Staff_no	Name	Dept	Age	Degree
1	12453	Bates,D	Maths	35	PhD
2	16752	Higgens,J	Maths	26	BSc
3	27453	Adams,D	CompSci	37	PhD
4	34276	Smyth,N	Physics	55	PhD
5	37564	Jones,C	CompSci	45	BSc
6	43257	Burns,M	Maths	32	MSc
7	45643	Collins,M	Physics	24	BSc
8	56321	Peters,N	CompSci	34	PhD
9	57432	Dale,T	Maths	52	PhD
. . .	. . .	. . .	. . .	. . .	. . .

Figure 6.14   An instance of the lecturers file

Inverting this file on every field except Name we get a dense primary index on Staff_no, shown in Figure 6.15, and three secondary indexes for the fields Dept, Age and Degree (Figure 6.16). Note that for Age we index over subranges, rather than on individual values.

Dense Primary Index

Key Value	Record Pointer
12453	1
16725	2
27423	3
34276	4
37564	5
43257	6
45643	7
56321	8
57432	9

Figure 6.15   A dense primary index for the lecturers file

Age	Record Pointer	Dept	Record Pointer	Degree	Record Pointer
21-30	2,7	Physics	4,7	BSc	2,5,7
31-40	1,3,6,8	CompSci	3,5,8	MSc	6
41-50	5	Maths	1,2,6,9	PhD	1,3,4,8,9
51-65	4,9				

Figure 6.16   Secondary index files for the lecturers file

The inverted fields may be absent from the main file since this information is held now in the index files. However unless storage space saving is of primary importance it is not usually advisable to omit inverted fields from the records since:

1.   It is advantageous to keep the main file independent of the indexes.
2.   Degradation of response time will occur if records have to be reconstructed from the information held in the indexes.

Secondary pinning

The records in the previous example are said to be pinned, since the secondary indexes contain actual record addresses. Thus the main file cannot be reorganised independently of the indexes.

Pinning can be avoided by using *key values* as pointers in the secondary index files as illustrated in Figure 6.17. Note, however, that this will degrade response time since the primary index must be searched to convert key values to actual addresses.

Dept	Record Pointers
Physics CompSci Maths	34276, 45643 27423, 37564, 56321 12453, 16725, 43257, 57432

Figure 6.17   A secondary index without pinning

Advantages of inversion

A great advantage of the inverted organisation is its ability to answer
queries of the form:

'Are there any records in the file that <qualification-part>?'

and

'How many records are there in the file that <qualification-part>'

by searching only the index files.

For example, consider the query:

'How many lecturers in Computer Science have a PhD?'

This query may be answered by searching the Dept and Degree secondary
index files for the pointer lists corresponding to the values 'CompSci' and
'PhD' respectively. This yields the pointer list (3,5,8) from the Dept index,
and the list (1,3,4,8,9) from the Degree index. Intersecting these lists indicates that the records at locations 3 and 8 satisfy the query.

Updating inverted files

Both secondary and primary indexes must accurately represent the contents
of the main file at all times. This means that the index files must be maintained every time a change is made to the main file, whether that change
involves the insertion of a new record, or deletion or modification of an
existing record.

For inverted files, insertion, deletion and modification operations are
rather costly since they may involve time-consuming changes to the index
files. For example, on inserting a new record every index file must be
updated either to include a new domain value, if this is not already present,
or to add the address of the new record to an existing pointer list.

When a record is deleted from the main file every reference to this
record must be deleted from the index files. We could simply flag the
record as deleted in the main file (logical deletion) but the deletion must be
reflected in the index files. Logical deletion is simpler than physically
deleting records, especially if deletion is a frequent operation. In such

circumstances the space occupied by deleted records could be recovered periodically by a 'housekeeping' routine which reorganised the main file and its indexes. Alternatively the record insertion routine could try to re-use the space occupied by logically deleted records.

When a record is modified the index files corresponding to modified fields must be updated. For example, suppose Collins graduates with a PhD and we wish to record this information in our inverted file organisation. Besides altering the appropriate field in Collins' record in the main file, we must remove the pointer to Collins' record from the BSc list in the Degree index, and insert it into the PhD list.

An inverted file abstraction in Modula-2

We may extend our indexed file abstraction to cover inverted files simply by allowing duplicate key values in our B-trees. Equal key values may be stored adjacent to each other in the tree, ordered by their data references. This will normally correspond to the order in which the keys are entered, since new data records are usually added to the end of data files.

The alterations necessary to the B-tree procedures are straightforward and are left as an exercise for the reader (see Exercise 6.3).

6.4.2   Multiple linked-lists

In the multiple linked-list organisation (sometimes called a *threaded* organisation) records are chained to other records in the file which have the same values in particular fields. For each field a list index contains a pointer to the head of the list corresponding to each value of that field present in the file. For example, considering the file which we inverted in the previous section, if we construct linked-lists (or threads) for the Dept and Degree fields we obtain the organisation illustrated in Figures 6.18 and 6.19.

Main File

Record No.	Staff_no	Name	Dept	Age	Degree	Degree Ptr	Dept Ptr
1	12453	Bates,D	Maths	35	PhD	3	2
2	16752	Higgens,J	Maths	26	BSc	5	6
3	27453	Adams,D	CompSci	37	PhD	4	5
4	34276	Smyth,N	Physics	55	PhD	8	7
5	37564	Jones,C	CompSci	45	BSc	7	8
6	43257	Burns,M	Maths	32	MSc	--	9
7	45643	Collins,M	Physics	24	BSc	--	--
8	56321	Peters,N	CompSci	34	PhD	9	--
9	57432	Dale,T	Maths	52	PhD	--	--

Figure 6.18   A multiple linked-list organisation

Degree	Head of List
BSc	2
MSc	6
PhD	1

Dept	Head of List
Physics	4
CompSci	3
Maths	1

Figure 6.19   List indexes for multiple linked-list organisation

Compared with the inverted organisation this method has the advantage that the structure of the index files is simpler since we do not have variable length pointer lists. However, for answering queries, access to the main file is generally considerably greater for this organisation than for inversion. For example, to find everyone in the Computer Science department with a PhD we have two possible strategies:

1. We could traverse the linked-list of Computer Science lecturers, and check each record that we encounter on the list to see if that person has a PhD.
2. We could traverse the PhD list and check each record to see if that person is also in the Computer Science department.

To choose the more economical of these strategies we would obviously need to know which was the shorter list. Thus it is desirable to include the length of the list with each entry in the list index files.

Updating operations may be complex and time-consuming in the multiple linked-list organisation. Each time a record is added to the file all the appropriate linked-lists must be extended, and if the record contains a field value not previously included in the file, a new entry in a list index will be required. Record deletion and modification may necessitate changes to many linked-lists. For example, consider again the changes required if Collins graduates with a PhD and we wish to record this fact in the database. Besides altering the degree field in Collins' record we must remove this record from the BSc linked-list and insert it into the PhD linked-list. This requires the modification of other records in the main file. For the equivalent inverted organisation, only the secondary index for degree had to be updated.

In general therefore retrieval and update operations using multiple linked-lists are slower and more complicated than for inversion. The method is generally only suitable for situations in which the allowable queries are fixed and well-defined, and where a high proportion of the records on a linked-list are likely to be required in answer to frequently specified queries. For example, the above organisation would be just as efficient as inversion for answering queries of the form: *'List the names of everyone in the Physics department '*, or *'List the names and ages of everyone with a PhD degree.'*

6.4.3   Partitioned hash functions

This technique extends the principles of hashing, as discussed earlier in this chapter, to cover a combination of both key and non-key fields (Ullman, 1982). Suppose that a bucket address is a sequence of B bits. The strategy is as follows:

1. Partition the B bits into groups: b_1 bits for field F_1, b_2 bits for field F_2, ..., b_k bits for field F_k.
2. Devise suitable hash functions, $H_i(v_i)$, $i = 1..k$, where H_i is a function for values v_i of field F_i whose result is a sequence of b_i bits.
3. Take the bucket address for the record $(v_1, v_2, \ldots, v_k)$ to be the concatenation,

$$H_1(v_1) \ H_2(v_2) \ldots H_k(v_k)$$

The contribution of a field to the hash function will depend on the size of its domain and the frequency with which it is specified in queries. That is, if the domain for a particular field is large then in order to discriminate among the many possible values of that field we require a large number of bits. More precisely, if a domain has 2^n values then ideally we require n bits for the associated field and a hash function which maps each value in the domain onto a different integer in the range $0..2^{n-1}$. However, given that the total number of bits is limited by the number of buckets, we have to rate each field according to its importance in users' queries and divide the number of available bits accordingly.

Example
Suppose we have a file of student records with the following structure:

```
Student =   RECORD
             idno   : CARDINAL ; (* a unique 5-digit number *)
             name  : STRING ;   (* up to 20 characters *)
             level  : [1..4 ];
             sex    : (M, F) ;
            END ;
```

We wish to store these records in 1024 (2^{10}) buckets. Suppose that we divide the 10 bits of a bucket address as follows: 4 bits for idno, 3 bits for name, 2 bits for level and 1 bit for sex. Consider the following hash functions, where $v_1 .. v_4$ represent values of the fields idno, name, level and sex respectively:

$$H_1(v_1) \ = \ v_1 \ \text{MOD} \ 16$$

$$H_2(v_2) \ = \ (\text{Number of characters in } v_2) \ \text{MOD} \ 8$$

$$H_3(v_3) \ = \ v_3 - 1$$

$$H_4(v_4) = ORD(v_4)$$

Then the bucket address for the record

(58651, Smith, 1, M)

is given by,

1 0 1 1 1 0 1 0 0 0 = 744

since we have that

58651 MOD 16 = 11	(1011 in binary)
5 MOD 8 = 5	(101 in binary)
1 – 1 = 0	(0 in binary)
ORD(M) = 0	(0 in binary)

Note that even if we do not know the values of all the fields which contribute to the hash function, we can still determine some information about the bucket address. In fact, if we know the value of a field F to which b bits have been assigned, we reduce the number of buckets to be searched by 2^b. For example, if we only know that the value of idno is 58651, then we need only search the 64 buckets corresponding to the 64 possible values of the remaining 6 bits in the bucket address. If we want a list of all male students, then we need only access evenly numbered buckets (i.e. those with a bit pattern whose final digit is 0)

Advantages of partitioned hash functions

The advantages of partitioned hash functions as compared with inverted files are that:

1. No space is required for index files.
2. Insertion, deletion and modification operations are much simpler since there are no index files to maintain.

However, for retrieval of records for which only a small amount of information has been specified, a much larger portion of the main file may still have to be searched compared with an inverted organisation. For this reason the method of partitioned hash functions is most suitable for moderately sized files which are highly volatile (i.e. those which are subject to frequent insertion, deletion and update operations).

EXERCISES

6.1 In Chapter 5, two aspects of integrity that we discussed were *key integrity* and *referential integrity*. The implementation of both of these require the database to perform *existence tests*, i.e. tests to determine whether a tuple with a given key value exists in a relation. Which of the techniques discussed in Section 6.3 would be most appropriate for the implementation of such existence tests. Give reasons for your answer.

6.2 Consider a file of records whose key values consist of two-character strings. A B-tree primary index of order 1 is to be maintained for this file. Suppose that the file is initially empty and records with the given key values are inserted in the following order:

   BD, GH, JY, AX, LM, CX, KL, ZY, HO, TS, PV

(a) Draw the B-tree as it appears after each of the above insertion operations.
(b) Show the new tree after each of the following deletion operations:

   1. Delete LM
   2. Delete AX
   3. Delete ZY

6.3 As described in Section 6.4.1, we may extend our indexed file abstraction to cover inverted files simply by allowing duplicate key values in our B-trees. Equal key values may be stored adjacent to each other in the tree, ordered by their data references. Rewrite the B-tree search, insertion and deletion procedures given in text to take account of duplicate key values.

6.4 Consider the following file containing information on cars:

Reg#	Make	Colour	Year	Engine-Capacity
BXI930X	Ford	White	1987	1100
ZIA987D	VW	Green	1983	1600
YIA453S	Nissan	Blue	1979	1200
TIZ653W	Ford	Green	1985	1100
RXT564Q	Ford	Red	1984	2000
HVW10X	Ford	Red	1987	1600
VCT543Z	VW	White	1983	2000
JKP612F	Mazda	Red	1984	1600
GFD73C	Nissan	Silver	1985	1100
TGF564S	VW	Gold	1981	1200

Show the main file and index structures necessary to organise this file as:

(i) A fully inverted file.
(ii) A multiple linked-list file in which lists are maintained for the fields Make, Colour, Year and Engine-Capacity.

Compare the relative efficiency of each of these organisations in answering a query which requires information on all red Fords registered before 1985.

6.5 A college wishes to maintain a file of student records with the following fields:

Student#	(a unique 5-digit integer)
Name	(up to 30 characters)
Level	(an integer in the range 1..4)
Sex	(M or F)

The records are to be stored in $2^{12} = 4096$ buckets. Devise a suitable partitioned hash function scheme which would facilitate access to the file on the basis of every field. Use your scheme to calculate the bucket addresses for records with the following field values:

(i)   (83104, 'John Robertson', 2, M)
(ii)   (82125, 'Mary Peters', 3, F)
(iii) (85324, 'Paul Smith', 1, M)

6.6 This chapter describes three techniques for accessing records in a file on the basis of non-key fields, namely file inversion, multiple linked-lists and partitioned hash functions. Compare the advantages and disadvantages of each of these methods for situations in which,

(i)   the database is highly volatile (frequent insertion, deletion and modification of records);
(ii)   rapid response times are required for *ad hoc* queries;
(iii) Storage space saving is of primary importance.

7

Implementation of Relational Operations

7.1 INTRODUCTION

The relational model of data provides a high degree of data independence by hiding from the user details regarding physical storage organisation of data and access paths. This places the entire burden of answering queries and performing updates efficiently on the database management system. Although considerable improvements in efficiency can be effected by means of high-level query optimisation, as discussed in Chapter 4, the DBMS must ultimately evaluate operations such as selection, projection and join at the physical level.

In this chapter we shall describe some of the techniques commonly employed for the evaluation of relational algebraic operations. In particular we concentrate on methods for executing the join operation, which is one of the most commonly used operations and also one of the most expensive to implement. We also consider methods for the optimisation, at the physical level, of complex queries involving more than one operator.

7.2 IMPLEMENTATION OF JOIN OPERATIONS

Consider the simple relations R_1 (A, B) and R_2 (B, C), with common attribute B. To evaluate the join of R_1 and R_2 and put the result in S, we could use the following simple *nested-loop* algorithm:

```
Create ( S, 'SName' ) ;
Open ( S, 'SName', Wmode ) ;
Open ( R1, 'R1Name', Rmode ) ;
Open ( R2, 'R2Name', Rmode ) ;
WHILE NOT EOF(R1) DO
```

```
ReadRecord ( R1, R1rec ) ;
WHILE NOT EOF(R2) DO
    ReadRecord ( R2, R2rec ) ;
    IF R1rec.B = R2rec.B
    THEN
        Srec.A := R1rec.A ;
        Srec.B := R1rec.B ;
        Srec.C := R2rec.C ;
        WriteRecord ( S, Srec ) ;
    END ;
END ;
SetPosition ( R2, 0 ) ;
END ;
```

In this algorithm, each time we read a record from R_1 we scan R_2 sequentially looking for tuples with the same value in the common attribute. For each such tuple found, we output the concatenated tuples to the result file. It is not difficult to appreciate that if R_1 and/or R_2 are even moderately large, this algorithm will be intolerably slow. For example, if R_1 and R_2 each contain of the order of 1000 blocks the total number of block accesses required will be of the order of 1,000,000.

We could of course improve matters by loading main memory with as many blocks of R_1 as possible, and restructure our loop to compare each tuple read from R_2 with each tuple of R_1 in main memory. When we have made all the necessary comparisons we load the next chunk of R_1 into main memory and repeat the process. This will reduce the number of block accesses to R_2 by a factor equal to the number of blocks of R_1 which will fit into main memory. This method is sometimes called the *nested block method* (Kim, 1980) and is particularly attractive if one of the relations is sufficiently small to be kept entirely in the main memory buffer. In this case the total number of block accesses required will be the sum of the number of blocks in each relation.

However, for the general case where the relations are much larger than the available amount of main memory, more significant improvements can be made by employing alternatives to the nested-loop method.

7.2.1   The sort-merge method

If we sort R_1 and R_2 on their common attribute(s) then the algorithm for the join takes the following form:

```
Create ( S, SName ) ;
Open ( S, 'SName', Wmode ) ;
Open ( R1, 'R1Name', Rmode ) ;
Open ( R2, 'R2Name', Rmode ) ;
WHILE NOT EOF(R1) AND NOT EOF(R2) DO
    ReadRecord ( R1, R1rec ) ;
    ReadRecord ( R2, R2rec )
    WHILE (R2rec.B < R1rec.B) AND NOT EOF(R2) DO
```

```
            ReadRecord ( R2, R2rec ) ;
        END ;
        GetPosition ( R2, P ) ;
        WHILE (R1rec.B = R2rec.B) AND NOT EOF(R2) DO
            Srec.A := R1rec.A ;
            Srec.B := R1rec.B ;
            Srec.C := R2rec.C ;
            WriteRecord ( S, Srec ) ;
            ReadRecord ( R2, R2rec )
        END ;
        SetPosition ( R2, P-1 ) ;
    END ;
```

Note that with this algorithm the relation R_2 need not be scanned for every tuple of R_1. That is, for a given R_1 tuple we skip over R_2 tuples until we reach the first position P in the file for which R1rec.B <= R2rec.B. At this point we check for equal common attributes and continue scanning R_2 until R1rec.B < R2rec.B; that is, there are no further tuples in R_2 with a value of B equal to that of the current R_1 tuple. We then get the next R_1 tuple, reset R_2 to position P, and repeat the same process until we reach the end of either R_1 or R_2.

Of course, sorting a large file of records may be a very time-consuming procedure. In general the number of records in the file to be sorted is much greater than the number that will fit into the available main memory. Thus the records cannot all be read into main memory and sorted there. Instead, we must adopt an efficient *external* sorting technique which usually involves distributing the records of the file to be sorted among a number of auxiliary files and then merging the records from these files to produce sorted *runs* of records. The length of these runs increases with each pass and the process stops when we have a single sorted run. This technique is called the *merge sort* method, and one commonly used variation of this method is described in the next section

Natural merge sort

Suppose we wish to sort a file of records, say F, in ascending order of a specified field A. Given a sequence of field values $a_1, \ldots, a_n$, an ascending ordered subsequence (called a *run*), $a_i, \ldots, a_j$ is such that

$$a_{i-1} > a_i$$
$$a_k \leq a_{k+1} \quad \text{for all } k \text{ in } [i..j-1]$$
$$a_j > a_{j+1}$$

The natural merge sort algorithm is made up of a number of passes, where each pass consists of a distribution phase and a merge phase. An N-way merge sort employs $2N$ auxiliary files and creates an ordered file by distributing runs to N of these files and then merging the runs to the remaining N files. The process is repeated until the file is sorted; that is, until one of the auxiliary files contains a single run consisting of all the records of the original file.

As a simple example consider a 2-way natural merge sort applied to the following file, F, of integers, using the auxiliary files T_1, T_2, T_3, and T_4:

F :   23   12   34   1   45   24   78   96   43   10   14

Pass 1: Distribute runs to T_1 and T_2. For clarity, runs are enclosed in brackets.

T_1 :   [23]   [1   45]   [43]

T_2 :   [12   34]   [24   78   96]   [10   14]

Merge runs from T_1 and T_2 to T_3 and T_4.

T_3 :   [12   23   34]   [10   14   43]

T_4 :   [1   24   45   78   96]

Pass 2: Merge runs from T_3 and T_4 to T_1 and T_2.

T_1 :   [1   12   23   24   34   45   78   96]

T_2 :   [10   14   43]

Pass 3: Merge runs from T_1 and T_2 to T_3 and T_4.

T_3 :   [1   10   12   14   23   24   34   43   45   78   96]

T_4 :   empty

The file is now sorted after only three passes. In the general case, merging r runs which are equally distributed on N files results in r/N runs. After p passes therefore there will be $r/(N)^p$ runs left. Thus the maximum number of passes required to sort n records using the natural N-way merge-sort is $p = [\log_N n]$.

We now develop a library procedure (adapted from Elder, 1984) which will perform a balanced 2-way merge sort of a file of records F. This procedure will have the heading:

```
PROCEDURE MergeSort ( VAR F, SortedFile : File ;
                              Ordered : OrderFunction ) ;
```

The procedure requires a user-supplied function procedure type of the following form:

```
TYPE
    OrderFunction = PROCEDURE ( recordtype, recordtype)
                              : BOOLEAN ;
```

The procedure call,

```
                    Ordered (r1, r2 )
```

returns the value TRUE if the records r1 and r2 are in the correct order for the sort, and FALSE otherwise.

The auxiliary files will be declared as an array of type File:

```
VAR
     auxfile : ARRAY [1..4] OF File ;
```

The structure of the procedure is as follows:

```
BEGIN
     Distribute initial runs from F to auxiliary files auxfile[1]..auxfile[2] ;
     REPEAT
          Merge runs from input files auxfile[1] and auxfile[2] to output
          files  auxfile[3] and auxfile[4] ;
          Switch input/output auxfiles ;
     UNTIL one run is obtained ;
     Copy sorted records from auxfile to sortedfile ;
END ;
```

Runs from F are distributed alternately to auxiliary files 1 and 2. A series of merges of runs are then performed from auxiliary files 1 and 2 to auxiliary files 3 and 4, and vice versa. On each pass each auxiliary file is alternately used as an input file and as an output file. The process terminates when only one run remains. This run is then copied from the appropriate auxiliary file to the file sortedfile.

The complete procedure is given in Figure 7.1.

```
PROCEDURE MergeSort ( VAR F, SortedFile : File ;
                                    Ordered : OrderFunction ) ;
TYPE
     FileRange = [1..4] ;
VAR
     auxfile : ARRAY FileRange OF File ;

     PROCEDURE Distribute ;
     VAR
          currentauxfile : FileRange ;
          record1, record2 : recordtype ;
          endofrun : BOOLEAN ;
     BEGIN
          currentauxfile := 1 ;
          WHILE NOT EOF (F) DO
              ReadRecord (F, record1) ;
              endofrun := FALSE ;
              WHILE NOT endofrun AND NOT EOF (F) DO
                  WriteRecord (auxfile[currentauxfile], record1) ;
                  ReadRecord (F, record2) ;
                  endofrun := NOT Ordered (record1, record2) ;
                  IF NOT endofrun THEN record1 := record2 END ;
              END ;
              IF currentauxfile = 1
              THEN currentauxfile := 2
              ELSE currentauxfile := 1
              END ;
          END ;
     END Distribute;
```

```
PROCEDURE Merge ;
VAR
    infile, outfile, temp : FileRange ;
    finished : BOOLEAN ;
    nextrecord : recordtype ;

    PROCEDURE Pass ( infile, outfile : FileRange ;
                                    finished : BOOLEAN ) ;
    VAR
        firstisactive, endofrun : BOOLEAN ;
        record1, record2 : recordtype ;

        PROCEDURE Copy ( i : FileRange ;  r : recordtype ) ;
        VAR
            temp : recordtype ;
        BEGIN
            IF firstisactive
            THEN WriteRecord ( auxfile[outfile], r ) ;
            ELSE WriteRecord ( auxfile[outfile+1], r ) ;
            END ;
            temp := r ;
            ReadRecord ( auxfile[i], record1 ) ;
            IF EOF (auxfile[i])
            THEN endofrun := TRUE ;
            ELSE endofrun := ordered ( record1, temp ) ;
            END ;
        END Copy;

        PROCEDURE CopyRun ( i : FileRange ; r : recordtype ) ;
        BEGIN
            REPEAT  Copy ( i, r )  UNTIL endofrun ;
        END CopyRun ;

    BEGIN
        firstisactive := TRUE ;
        ReadRecord ( auxfile[infile], record1 ) ;
        ReadRecord ( auxfile[infile+1], record2 ) ;
        finished := EOF (auxfile[infile]) OR EOF (auxfile[infile+1]) ;
        IF NOT finished
        THEN
            REPEAT
                REPEAT
                    IF ordered (record1, record2)
                    THEN
                        Copy (infile, record1) ;
                        IF endofrun
                        THEN CopyRun (infile+1, record2)
                        END
                    ELSE
                        Copy (infile+1, record2) ;
                        IF endofrun  THEN CopyRun (infile, record1)
                        END
                    END ;
```

```
                    UNTIL endofrun ;
                    firstisactive := NOT firstisactive ;
                UNTIL EOF (auxfile[infile]) OR EOF (auxfile[infile+1]) ;
                WHILE NOT EOF (auxfile[infile]) DO
                    CopyRun (infile, record1) ;
                    firstisactive := NOT firstisactive ;
                END ;
                WHILE NOT EOF (auxfile[infile+1]) DO
                    CopyRun (infile+1, record2) ;
                    firstisactive := NOT firstisactive ;
                END ;
            END ;
        END Pass ;

        PROCEDURE Resetauxfiles ;
        VAR
            i : FileRange ;
        BEGIN
            FOR i := 1 TO 4 DO Close (auxfile[i])  END ;
            Open (auxfile[infile], ' ', Rmode) ;
            Open (auxfile[infile+1], ' ', Rmode) ;
            Open (auxfile[outfile], ' ', Wmode) ;
            Open (auxfile[outfile+1], ' ', Wmode) ;
        END Resetauxfiles;

BEGIN
    infile := 1 ; outfile := 3 ;
    REPEAT
        Pass (infile, outfile, finished) ;
        IF NOT finished
        THEN temp := infile ;  infile := outfile ;  outfile := temp
        END ;
        Resetauxfiles ;
    UNTIL finished ;
    (* Sorted file is on auxfile[infile] - Copy this to SortedFile *)
    SetPosition (auxfile[infile], 0) ;
    ReadRecord (auxfile[infile], nextrecord) ;
    WHILE NOT EOF (auxfile[infile]) DO
        WriteRecord (SortedFile, nextrecord) ;
        ReadRecord (auxfile[infile], nextrecord) ;
    END ;
    END Merge ;

BEGIN
    Distribute ;
    Merge ;
END MergeSort ;
```

Figure 7.1   A merge-sort procedure

The procedure Distribute performs the initial distribution of runs from F to the auxiliary files 1 and 2. The procedure Merge performs the merges of runs from one pair of auxiliary files to the other. Note that each auxiliary file is alternately an input file and an output file in each merge pass, and so the file must be reset accordingly (by procedure Resetauxfiles). The variables infile and outfile are set alternately to 1 and 3 to indicate which files are currently input and output. Each pass begins by checking for the end-of-file condition in either of the input files. If end-of-file is not detected, then runs from each of the two input files are merged until the end of one of them is detected. The remaining runs on the other file must then be copied. Note that runs are sent to each of the two output files in turn. The Boolean variable firstisactive is true if the first output file is to receive the next run (i.e. either file 1 or 3), and false if the second output file is active.

The procedure CopyRun calls the procedure Copy to transfer a record from the input file specified by the parameter i until the end of a run on auxfile[i] is detected. This condition is represented by the Boolean variable endofrun, which is set in the procedure Copy. To determine the end of a run, the last record transferred from the active input file must be retained for comparison with the next record read.

7.2.2   Using indexes to evaluate joins

An obvious disadvantage of the sort-merge technique is that the time taken to perform the sorting may be unacceptable. An alternative technique is to take advantage of any indexes which may exist on the relations to be joined. For example, suppose that relation R_2 has a secondary index, I, on the common attribute B. Then the algorithm for performing the join involves scanning R_1 sequentially, and for each value of B found we look up the index to obtain a list of pointers to those tuples in R_2 with the same value of B. Each tuple thus pointed to is retrieved, concatenated with the current R_1 tuple (eliminating the duplicate B column), and output to the result file. In this way we access only those tuples in R_2 which participate in the join.

The algorithm for this method takes the following form:

```
Create ( S, 'SName' ) ;
Open ( S, 'SName', Wmode ) ;
Open ( R1, 'R1Name', Rmode ) ;
Open ( R2, 'R2Name', Rmode ) ;
Open ( I, 'IndexName', Rmode ) ;
WHILE NOT EOF (R1) DO
    ReadRecord ( R1, R1rec ) ;
    Lookup ( I, R1rec.B, PointerList ) ;
    WHILE PointerList <> NIL DO
        SetPosition ( R2, PointerList.address) ;
        ReadRecord ( R2, R2rec ) ;
        Srec.A := R1rec.A ; Srec.B := R1rec.B ; Srec.C := R2rec.C ;
        WriteRecord ( S, Srec ) ;
        PointerList := PointerList^.Next ;
    END ;
END ;
```

In this algorithm the procedure, Lookup (I, X, PointerList), looks up the index I for key value X, and returns a linked list of record addresses in the pointer variable PointerList. PointerList has the following form:

```
VAR
     PointerList = POINTER TO Item ;
     Item = RECORD
                 address : RecordAddress ;
                 Next : PointerList ;
            END ;
```

7.2.3   Hashing methods for evaluating joins

The simplest use of hashing as a strategy for performing joins is the following algorithm: build a hash table, in memory, of tuples from the smaller of the two relations (say R_1), hashed on the common attribute(s). Then scan the other relation, R_2, sequentially. For each tuple in R_2, calculate its hash value (based on the values of its common attributes), and use this value to probe the hash table of R_1 for tuples with matching common attributes. If a match is found, output the concatenated pair of tuples to the result relation. Otherwise, continue scanning R_2.

This hashing algorithm works best when the hash table for R_1 can fit into main memory. If this is not the case, then the algorithm can still be used in virtual memory but it behaves poorly since the probing of the hash table will necessitate many block accesses.

However, there are a variety of hashing algorithms which extend the simple approach described above, so as to take into account the possibility that a hash table will not fit into main memory. These are described in detail by Shapiro (1987) and references therein. The simplest strategy is to scan the smaller relation (R_1) repeatedly, each time partitioning off as much of R_1 as can fit into a hash table in main memory. After each scan of R_1, R_2 is scanned and a probe is made for a match. The steps involved in this algorithm (as described by Shapiro) are as follows (see Figure 7.2):

1. Let P = min(size of main memory, size of R_1). Choose a hash function h and a range of hash values such that P blocks of R_1 will hash into that range. Scan R_1 sequentially, and if a tuple hashes into the desired range insert it into the hash table in main memory. Otherwise write the tuple to a new file in secondary storage.
2. Scan the larger relation R_2 sequentially. If a tuple of R_2 hashes into the desired range, probe the hash table for matching R_1 tuples and output concatenated matching pairs of tuples to the result relation. Otherwise, write the tuple of R_2 to a new file.
3. Repeat steps (1) and (2), replacing relations R_1 and R_2 by the new files of tuples that were passed over. The process is at an end when no tuples of R_1 are passed over.

This method works well when a large amount of main memory is available, so that most of R_1 is processed on the first pass. Obviously, its performance will deteriorate as the size of main memory decreases and more passes are required.

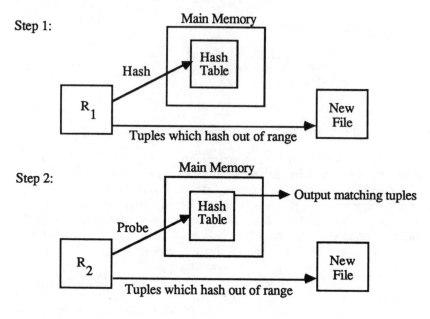

Step 3: Repeat steps 1 and 2 until no tuples of R hash out of range.

Figure 7.2 A simple hash-join method

7.2.4   Comparison of methods for implementing joins

If the two relations to be joined are already sorted on their common attributes then the merge-sort method seems to be the most efficient method for evaluating the join (Blasgen and Eswaran, 1977; Merrett, 1981). However, if one of the relations is small enough to fit into main memory then the nested block method is to be preferred. If one relation is much larger than the other and appropriate indexes are available, the nested loop method, making use of the indexes, is probably the best approach.

Techniques for the evaluation of *arbitrary* binary operations (e.g. set operations, theta-joins) tend to rely heavily on the dynamic creation of fast access paths, such as indexes and logical sorting. For example, while a relation is scanned for the evaluation of a unary operation on that relation (e.g. a simple selection or projection) an index may be dynamically constructed based on attributes required for a binary operation in the same query. A number of authors (e.g. Blasgen and Eswaran, 1976; Yao, 1979) have investigated a variety of general strategies for evaluating binary operations and compared them with respect to their efficiency. Their conclusion seems to be that no algorithm exists which is best for all situations. In general, the optimiser must either rely on heuristics or carry out expensive cost comparisons of the alternative strategies for each query.

7.3   IMPLEMENTATION OF SELECTION OPERATIONS

With regard to the implementation of selection operations we have little to add beyond the techniques described in Chapter 6, and we shall simply summarise the main ideas of that chapter.

The naive approach to the evaluation of selections would be to scan the relation sequentially and test every record to see if its attribute values satisfy each term of the selection predicate. Since this approach is very costly if the relations are large, various techniques have been devised to reduce the number of record accesses required. The principal idea is to utilise data structures that provide access paths based on both key and non-key attribute values.

File inversion employing multiple secondary indexes, (possibly combined with a partially threaded organisation), is probably the most flexible and efficient means for carrying out arbitrary selection operations on relations. Partitioned hash functions may have a role to play if the relations are not too large and storage space saving is of primary importance.

Selection operations are of course very commonly specified in queries and so it is essential that any index files employed are organised for efficient searching. Recall that in abstract terms an index is a binary relation which associates attribute values with references (or pointers) to records in the main relation. Thus the techniques which are employed for efficiently accessing relations may be applied recursively to indexes. The B-tree structure and its variants, as described in Chapter 6, are very widely used in relational database management systems and in database programming language implementations. In database management systems such access structures are normally invisible to the user. However some database programming languages (van de Riet et al., 1981; Hughes and Connolly, 1987) provide abstract representations of indexes, and other access paths, which can be very useful to applications programmers who demand intimate control over the efficiency of their programs.

7.4   IMPLEMENTATION OF PROJECTION OPERATIONS

At first sight projection might seem a rather straightforward operation in comparison with the join. However recall that the set property of relations requires that no two tuples may have the same values in all their attributes. Thus, when we perform a projection which does not keep the key of the relation intact we must remove any duplicate tuples that arise in the resultant relation. This can be a rather time-consuming operation if the relation to be projected is large.

For example, a typical 'nested loop' algorithm to perform the projection $R_1[A]$, might take the following form:

```
Create ( S, 'SName' ) ;
Open ( S, 'SName', RWmode ) ;
Open ( R1, 'R1Name', Rmode ) ;
WHILE NOT EOF (R1) DO
    ReadRecord (R1, R1rec) ;  found := FALSE ;
    SetPosition (S, 0) ;
    WHILE NOT EOF (S) AND NOT found DO
        ReadRecord (S, Srec) ;
        found := Srec = R1rec.A ;
    END ;
    IF NOT found THEN WriteRecord (S, R1rec.A) ; END ;
END ;
```

In this algorithm we scan the result relation S every time, looking for duplicate values, before inserting a new value of A. An alternative strategy would be as follows: We scan R_1 sequentially and each time we read a record R1rec, we scan the remainder of R_1 and 'mark' those tuples which contain the same value of A. The marked tuples are then passed over in the outer loop. An informal algorithm for this strategy is as follows:

```
WHILE NOT EOF (R1) DO
    ReadRecord (R1, R1rec) ;
    IF (R1rec is not marked) THEN
        WriteRecord (S, R1rec.A) ;
        GetPosition (R1, P) ;
        WHILE NOT EOF (R1) DO
            ReadRecord (R1, nextrec) ;
            IF R1rec.A = nextrec.A THEN mark nextrec END ;
        END ;
        SetPosition (R1, P) ;
        ReadRecord (R1, R1rec) ;
    END ;
END ;
```

Both of these algorithms are rather inefficient in that they involve repeated scans of all or part of either the result file or the original file. As in the case of the join however, significant improvements can be made by either sorting the original relation on the field(s) to be projected, or alternatively constructing a hash table on these fields.

For example, if we sort the relation R_1 on attribute A then we may evaluate the projection $R_1[A]$ by the following simple algorithm, which requires only a single pass through R_1.

```
Sort relation R on attribute A ;
ReadRecord (R1, R1rec) ;
WHILE NOT EOF(R1) DO
    WriteRecord (S, R1rec.A) ;
```

```
WHILE NOT EOF (R1) AND equal DO
    ReadRecord (R1, Nextrec) ;
    equal := Nextrec.A > R1rec.A ;
    IF NOT equal THEN R1rec := Nextrec ;
  END ;
END ;
```

7.5   OPTIMISATION OF COMPLEX QUERIES

In Chapter 4 we studied techniques for converting a relational algebraic expression into an equivalent, but more efficient form, using well-defined transformation rules. Many of these transformations are data independent and so can be performed at compile time. As noted in Chapter 4 however, full optimisation must ultimately take account of factors related to the physical storage organisation of the data, such as the size and distribution of relations and the existence of secondary indexes or other fast access paths.

The usual strategy when faced with a complex query involving a number of operations, is to transform the query into alternative sequences of elementary operations (such as selections, projections and joins) for which efficient implementations exist whose costs may be computed. The overall cost for each strategy is evaluated and the least expensive one is chosen for execution. Cost formulas are mainly concerned with the number of block accesses but some account of CPU time may also be taken. The costs will obviously be data dependent. For example the cost of a simple selection will be considerably reduced if indexes exist for the attributes specified in the selection predicate. The cost of a join operation will vary with the cardinality of the relations and with the implementation technique employed. Information such as the existence of indexes and the current cardinalities of relations normally resides in the data dictionary.

An important point to stress however, is that the elementary operations are not normally evaluated in isolation. For example in evaluating the expression,

$$((R1 \ join \ R2) \ join \ (R3 \ where \ A = 10)) \ [A, B]$$

it is not necessary to compute the inner join in its entirety before computing the second join and then the projection. Rather, each time a tuple is produced from the join of R1 and R2 it may be passed immediately to be joined with the selected tuples of R3, and the resulting tuple is projected immediately on its A and B attributes. Clearly this strategy may yield considerable savings in costs since the intermediate relations do not have to be stored and then re-scanned.

Palermo (1972) gives a general strategy for evaluating complex algebraic expressions which has been implemented successfully in some database management systems (Jarke and Schmidt, 1982). In this strategy no tuple is ever retrieved more than once and unnecessary values are discarded from retrieved tuples as soon as possible. Unnecessary values are those which are not referenced in the query and are not required for join operations (the values of all common attributes must be retained for natural join operations). The result relation is then constructed in such a way as to minimise the number of comparisons and the amount of intermediate storage required. As a given relation is scanned, all unary operations associated with that relation are evaluated completely and all binary operations involving the same relation are partially processed concurrently. For example, a join operation involving the relation is facilitated by the dynamic construction of a form of index which logically orders the tuples of the relation on the values of the common attributes.

Conclusion

Full optimisation of relational queries requires the use of both logical transformation techniques as described in Chapter 4, and efficient methods for the physical evaluation of operations as discussed in this chapter. However, although much progress has been made during the past decade, query optimisation is still a very active field of research. One promising area which is discussed in Chapter 9, is the application of specialised hardware (database machines) to the efficient processing of database transactions.

For a detailed description of query optimisation in relational database systems see the review article by Jarke and Koch (1984) and references therein.

EXERCISES

7.1   Rewrite the *nested loop* procedure to implement the *nested block* method as described in Section 7.2. Assume that a fixed number, N, records of relation R_1 can be held in a main memory buffer (i.e. an array).

7.2   Write a Modula-2 program which implements the simple hash-join algorithm described in Section 7.2.3. You may assume the existence of suitable hash functions Hash1 and Hash2, defined as follows:

    PROCEDURE Hash1 (r1 : R1Type) : HashRange ;

    PROCEDURE Hash2 (r2 : R2Type) : HashRange ;

Function procedure Hash1 (Hash2) hashes a record of relation R1 (R2) on the common attributes and yields a cardinal number in the range $0..P$, where P is a constant.

7.3   Suppose that a large amount of main memory is available for the implementation of relational queries (as is often the case with modern computers). Describe how this would facilitate the implementation of the join operation using the following techniques:

(i)   The nested-loop method.
(ii) The sort-merge method.
(iii) A method which utilises secondary indexes on the common attributes.
(iv) The simple hash-join algorithm described in Section 7.2.3.

(For a discussion of this question see Shapiro (1987).)

8

Database Administration

8.1 INTRODUCTION

In this chapter we shall be concerned with some of the operational issues related to database management. We focus on four main areas of interest, namely concurrency, recovery, security and distributed databases.

Three methods for concurrency control in database systems are described. These are, locking, optimistic scheduling and timestamping. Our treatment of concurrency also relates the problems of concurrent access in database management systems to the abstractions for concurrency control provided by programming languages such as Modula-2. These facilities are seen to be somewhat inadequate. However, some of the database programming languages discussed in Chapter 5 have high-level abstractions for concurrency control which are well-suited to database applications and these are described.

Recovery within the context of a database system refers to the process of restoring the system to a correct and consistent state after some failure has rendered its current state incorrect. The causes of such failures are numerous, especially in a large multi-user database system, and may range from errors or inconsistencies in individual transactions to catastrophic failures in the hardware or in the system software. The obvious way to provide a recovery service is to take regular back-up copies of the database. However, in addition to back-ups a DBMS must also provide a means for *redoing* transactions whose updates have been lost due to the reloading of a back-up copy, and for *undoing* transactions which have been the cause of inconsistent states. These operations are referred to respectively as *roll-forward* and *roll-back* and their implementation is described in this chapter.

The term security in a database context refers to the protection of the data against unauthorised disclosure, modification or destruction. There are of course, numerous aspects to the problem of providing security in a database system. A database administrator may have to concern himself with the legal and ethical aspects of security as well as the day-to-day operational controls on access to the system which are faced by any computer installation. In this chapter we shall be concerned primarily with those aspects of security which are within the realm of the software engineer. Thus we shall describe security techniques such as data encryption and restrictions on queries which are implemented in the database management software. A more general discussion covering many of the other aspects mentioned above can be found for example in the text of Fernadez et al. (1981).

In distributed databases the data are spread over a network of geo-graphically dispersed computers connected via communication links. Each site has its own local data and database management software and enjoys a high degree of local autonomy. The primary aim of the distributed database management software is to make the system appear to users as if it were a centralised system. This leads to significant complications for the DBMS in areas such as efficient query processing, concurrency control and recovery. In this chapter we describe some of the most important problems and the methods which have been proposed in the literature for their solution. However, many of these problems have yet to be completely solved at the current level of technology and in the commercial environment there are relatively few systems which can handle distribution to a satisfactory degree.

8.2 CONCURRENT ACCESS TO DATABASE SYSTEMS

In the context of a multi-user database system database procedures are often called *transactions*. A transaction (Gray, 1978) is a unit of work which corresponds directly to a single activity of the enterprise which is modelled by the database. A given database system may have many different classes of transactions ranging from simple interactive updates to very large and complex programs involving perhaps thousands of database operations. The property that all transactions must have in common is that they must all preserve the consistency and correctness of the data stored in the database. That is, the operations performed by an updating transaction should transform the database from one consistent state to another. Intermediate states, which exist after individual statements of an updating transaction have been performed, may be inconsistent. Therefore, to guarantee the consistency of the database, it must be required that updating transactions be processed entirely or not at all. A transaction which does not complete, due possibly to a program or system failure, must be backed up to its initial state and any changes which it has written to the database must be undone.

When several transactions are executed in parallel on a shared database their executions must be synchronised. That is, the effect on the database of a transaction must be that which would be obtained if no other transaction were executing concurrently. The effect of executing several transactions concurrently, therefore, must be the same as if they had been executed serially in some order. If the sequence of operations of a set of concurrently executing transactions is such that this condition is satisfied, the sequence is said to be *serialisable*. The problems associated with guaranteeing the serialisability of transactions will be discussed later in this section.

The need for concurrency control in a database system is illustrated by the following example (adapted from Amble et al., 1976).

Example

A relational database for an airline reservation system contains a relation DEPARTURES which contains information on the number of seats available on each flight on any given date. The relation scheme for DEPARTURES is as follows:

DEPARTURES (<u>FLIGHTNO, DATE,</u> CAPACITY, SEATS_LEFT)

A particular transaction on this database may involve booking several connecting flights on a particular date for a customer travelling with his family. Only if sufficient seats are available on all the required departures are the bookings confirmed. Otherwise an alternative group of flights has to be considered.

Thus the transaction must do the following:

1. Read the date, flight numbers and the number of seats required.
2. Check if each of the specified flights on the given date has sufficient seats available.
3. If sufficient seats are available, then reserve the seats. Otherwise report the failure.

An algorithm for the transaction might take the following form:

```
BEGIN
    read date_required, flights_required, no_seats_required ;
    failure := FALSE ;
    set F to first in flights_required ;
    WHILE NOT failure AND (not at end of flights_required list ) DO
        retrieve DEPARTURES tuple, d, where
            (d.FLIGHTNO = F) AND (d.DATE = date_required) ;
        IF d.SEATS_left < no_seats_required
        THEN failure := TRUE
        ELSE set F to next in flights_required
        END
    END ;
    IF failure
    THEN
        WriteString (' Flight ', F,' has insufficient seats')
    ELSE
        FOR (each F in flights_required ) DO
            update DEPARTURES tuple, d, where
                (d.FLIGHTNO = F) AND (d.DATE = date_required)
                with d.SEATS_LEFT := d.SEATS_LEFT - no_seats_required
        END ;
        WriteString (' Flights confirmed ')
    END
END ;
```

One difficulty with this transaction is that it is possible to complete the initial check for seats available successfully (i.e. with failure = FALSE) and yet overbook a flight. This could happen if another user updated one of the relevant DEPARTURES tuples after the above transaction had performed the initial check, but before it had carried out its updates.

A second problem with this transaction would arise if a program or system failure occurred while it was performing its updates. Thus some of the DEPARTURE tuples would have been updated but not others. Simply rerunning the transaction is not the answer since this would result in the customer and his family being booked twice on some flights. To maintain the consistency of the database therefore, the effect of the failed transaction on the database must be undone and the transaction rerun in its entirety. The techniques for undoing, or redoing, transactions will be considered in more detail later in this chapter.

The airline reservation example above illustrates just one of a number of problems that can arise if we allow transactions write-access to a database concurrently without some form of control. (Note that if a database is read-only, then no concurrency control is required.) The problems that can arise may be described more generally as follows:

The Lost Update
Consider the following sequence of events, where transactions T_1 and T_2 are executing concurrently:

1. Transaction T_1 reads record R from the database.
2. Transaction T_2 reads record R from the database.
3. Transaction T_1 updates record R and writes it back to the database.
4. Transaction T_2 updates record R and writes it back to the database.

The result of these events is that the update performed by transaction T_1 has been lost.

The Out-of-Date Retrieval
Consider the following sequence of events:

1. Transaction T_1 reads record R from the database with a view to updating its value.
2. Transaction T_2 reads record R for retrieval purposes.
3. Transaction T_1 modifies record R and writes it back to the database.

The result of these events is that transaction T_2 has retrieved an out-of-date value for record R.

An obvious solution to both of these problems would be to permit a transaction to *lock* a record during update, giving it exclusive access to that record while the update operation is in progress. However locking mechanisms can themselves give rise to serious problems in database systems and must therefore be carefully monitored and controlled. The following sections describe the typical locking mechanisms found in database management systems as well as some alternative strategies which have been proposed in the literature. The applicability of the concurrent features of high-level programming languages to database systems is also discussed.

8.2.1 Read- and write-locks

In order to prevent any transaction from reading or updating data that is being updated by another transaction we require a *locking* mechanism, which guarantees a transaction exclusive access to an item of data while a lock is in force. We can distinguish between two kinds of locks:

1. A *read-lock* which gives read-only access to a data item and prevents any other transaction from updating the item. This kind of lock is often called *read-sharable* since any number of transactions may hold a read-lock on an item.
2. A *write-lock* which gives read/write access to a data item and, while in force prevents any other transaction from reading or writing to the data item. This kind of lock is often called *write-exclusive* since it gives a transaction exclusive access to a data item.

Thus the problem of interfering transactions outlined in the example above, which could lead to overbooking a flight, is prevented if our transaction write-locks the relation DEPARTURES before execution. That is, the transaction takes the following form:

```
Write_Lock (DEPARTURES) ;
BEGIN
    ... as before ...
END ;
Unlock (DEPARTURES) ;
```

However, imposing a write-lock on the entire relation could have a serious effect on the degree of concurrency allowed in the system. Any other transaction which requires either read or write access to the DEPARTURES relation must wait until the write-lock is released. In fact it is easy to see that our transaction does not need to lock the entire relation, but rather only those tuples which correspond to the flights and date required by the customer.

The size of items that may be locked in a database system is referred to as the *degree of granularity*. If the items are large (e.g. relation level locking) the system overheads for concurrency control are small, but the degree of concurrency is low. With finer granularity (e.g. tuple-level locking), a high degree of concurrency is possible but at the cost of high system overheads. Items for concurrency control may be any composite collection of one or more of the abstract elements of the database. The only requirements are that they must not overlap (with regard to primitive data elements), and the collection of items must form a partition of the entire database. The natural choice for an item in most modern database management systems seems to be the record (or tuple). This is due to the fact that the DBMS already incurs overheads for the storage and processing of records. In addition, the record is a convenient conceptual unit of data, representing a single fact about the enterprise.

A data item, of course, need not necessarily be locked for the entire duration of the transaction, and the level of concurrency could be increased by locking a data item only for the duration of the actual data access. However, narrowing the sequence of statements for which a data item is locked increases the possibility of *deadlock* occurring, and involves the system in rather complex recovery procedures if locks are released before a transaction terminates.

8.2.2   Deadlock

A problem that can arise in a system which permits transactions to lock data items is a phenomenon known as *deadlock* or *deadly embrace*. This is best described by a simple example.

Example.
Consider two transactions T_1 and T_2 executing concurrently, and the following sequence of events takes place:

1. T_1 write-locks item A.
2. T_2 write-locks item B.
3. T_1 requests a lock on item B but must wait since T_2 has locked B.
4. T_2 requests a lock on item A but must wait since T_2 has locked A.

At this point neither T_1 nor T_2 can proceed - they are deadlocked.

There are a number of strategies which can be adopted to prevent deadlock occurring. For example, one could insist that each transaction requests *all* its locks before it begins execution and allow it to proceed only if every lock can be granted (the *preclaim* strategy). Otherwise it is forced to wait. This strategy would clearly have a detrimental effect on the level of concurrency in the system since transactions may have to wait a long time before they can start. Also, in a database environment the resource needs of a transaction (and therefore its locking requirements) may be dependent on factors known only at run-time. That is, the set of items to be locked by a transaction are generally determined dynamically by the logic of the transaction, its input data, and the current state of the database.

Thus it is clear that deadlock-free locking protocols, which may be effective in other concurrent environments such as operating systems, are generally inapplicable to database systems. A more effective strategy in a database environment therefore, may be to allow deadlocks to occur and to *detect* and *resolve* them when they do. To detect deadlock the system maintains a graph whose nodes consist of currently executing transactions and whose arcs are determined as follows: If transaction T_i requests a lock on an item that is locked by T_j, an arc is drawn from node T_i to node T_j. The arc is removed when T_j releases the lock. A deadlock situation is indicated by a cycle in this graph. This detection technique may be expensive if there is a high degree of granularity in the system.

Resolving deadlock involves choosing one of the deadlocked transactions and invoking a 'roll-back' procedure. The transaction is then restarted at some suitable later point in time. The roll-back procedure will involve the system in undoing any updates which the transaction has written to the database. Also, all the locks held by a transaction which is rolled back must be released, thereby allowing other deadlocked transactions to proceed.

A disadvantage of this strategy is that it involves costly run-time procedures for acquiring and releasing locks, testing for the disjointness of data items, and implementing roll-back operations. However, roll-back is a procedure which may also be required for crash-recovery in database management systems and the subject will be discussed in more detail later in this chapter.

8.2.3   Serialisability and the two-phase protocol

As stated earlier, the effect of executing several transactions concurrently must be the same as if they had been executed serially in some order. That is, if two transactions T_1 and T_2 are executed in parallel their effect on the database must be equivalent to $T_1;T_2$ (i.e. T_1 followed sequentially by T_2), or $T_2;T_1$. The following simple example shows that, if no restrictions are placed on the way in which transactions are scheduled, serialisability is easily violated.

Consider the following two transactions which update an item A.

T_1 :   BEGIN
            read(A) ; A := A + 1 ; write(A) .
         END ;

T_2 :   BEGIN
            read(A) ; A := A - 1 ; write(A)
         END ;

Clearly the effect of running these transactions serially in any order will be to leave the value of A unchanged. However, suppose the transactions are executed concurrently and the steps of each transaction are carried out in the following order:

T_1 :   read(A)
T_1 :   A := A + 1
T_2 :   read(A)
T_1 :   write(A)
T_2 :   A := A - 1
T_2 :   write(A)

The effect of this schedule of steps is to leave the value of A in the database decremented by 1. Obviously we could solve this problem for this simple example by allowing T_1 to write-lock item A while it carries out its update.

Transaction T_2 would then be required to wait until T_1 had written its updated value of A back to the database. However a locking mechanism is not in itself sufficient to guarantee serialisability.

A fundamental theorem of transaction scheduling (Eswaren et al. 1976) states that concurrent transactions can be guaranteed serialisable if, in any transaction, all locks precede all unlocks. Transactions obeying this protocol are said to be *two-phase*, (or equivalently to obey the *two-phase locking protocol*) in the sense that locks and unlocks take place in two separate phases during the execution of the transaction. If all transactions are two-phase, then all concurrent executions of those transactions are serialisable.

We may test for the serialisability of a given schedule of transactions with the following algorithm (Eswaran et al., 1976; Ullman, 1982).

Algorithm.
Construct a directed graph (called a precedence graph), with transactions as nodes, whose arcs are determined by the following rules (note that an arc from T_i to T_j implies that in any equivalent serial schedule T_i must precede T_j.):

1. If transaction T_i read-locks item A and transaction T_j is the next transaction (if any) to write-lock A, then draw an arc from T_i to T_j.

2. If transaction T_i write-locks an item A and T_j is the next transaction (if any) to write-lock A, then draw an arc from T_i to T_j.

3. If transaction T_k read-locks A between the write-locks of T_i and T_j then draw an arc from T_i to T_k. If transaction T_j does not exist (i.e. there are no further write-locks on A) then T_k is any transaction to read-lock A after T_i releases its write-lock.

If the precedence graph, constructed using the above rules, has a cycle then the schedule is not serialisable. If the graph has no cycles then the schedule is serialisable and any *topological sort* of the precedence graph yields an equivalent serial schedule.

An algorithm which performs a topological sort is as follows:

```
BEGIN
    Find the set S of nodes with no predecessors (i.e. no incoming
        arcs) ;
    WHILE (S is not empty) DO
        Remove a node T from S ;
        Remove T and its outgoing arcs from the graph ;
        Add any new members to S ;
    END ;
END ;
```

Example
Consider a schedule S of three concurrently executing transactions T_1, T_2 and T_3, consisting of the following steps:

1. T_1 :   write-lock (A) ;
2. T_2 :   write-lock (B) ;
3. T_1 :   unlock (A) ;
4. T_2 :   unlock (B) ;
5. T_1 :   write-lock (B) ;
6. T_3 :   read-lock (A) ;
7. T_1 :   unlock (B) ;
8. T_3 :   unlock (A) ;
9. T_2 :   write-lock (A) ;
10. T_3 :   read-lock (B) ;
11. T_2 :   unlock (A) ;
12. T_3 :   unlock (B) ;

This schedule has the precedence graph illustrated in Figure 8.1.

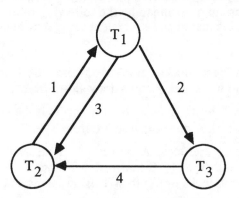

Figure 8.1   A precedence graph

In this graph the arcs 1 to 4 are due to the following rules:

Arc 1:   Rule 1 and steps 2 and 5 of the schedule;
Arc 2:   Rule 3 and steps 1 and 6;
Arc 3:   Rule 2 and steps 1 and 9;
Arc 4:   Rule 1 and steps 6 and 9.

Since the precedence graph has cycles, the schedule is not serialisable.

Proof of the two-phase locking protocol

We are now in a position to prove that the two-phase locking protocol guarantees serialisability. Recall that the theorem states that any schedule S of concurrent transactions can be guaranteed serialisable if, in any transaction, all locks precede all unlocks.

Suppose that S is not serialisable. Then the precedence graph for S will contain a cycle of the form:

$$T_i \longrightarrow T_j \longrightarrow T_k \longrightarrow \ldots \longrightarrow T_i$$

Thus from the rules for constructing arcs, a lock in T_j must follow an unlock in T_i, a lock in T_k must follow an unlock in T_j, and so on. Finally therefore we see that a lock in T_i must follow an unlock in T_i, which violates our assertion that the transactions are two-phase.

8.2.4   Optimistic scheduling

In many multi-user database environments, the system overheads incurred through lock management may be considerable, and not worth their expense if the competition for exclusive access to data items is low. In such circumstances, it may be better to take an optimistic approach to scheduling (Kung and Robinson, 1981), which does not involve any locking at all, and thereby removes the possibility of deadlock occurring.

In this optimistic approach transactions are allowed free access to data items but any updates are assigned to local copies or 'shadows' of the data items. Also, details of all read and write accesses by a transaction are recorded by the system. These are referred to respectively as the read and write sets of the transaction. Before any updates, carried out by a transaction on its local data items, are committed to the database, the transaction is put through a validation test. This test checks whether there has been any unserialisable interaction with other concurrently executing transactions which may have already committed their changes to the database. If so, the transaction is rolled back and restarted. Otherwise its changes are committed to the database. The roll back procedure is simplified by the fact that changes were made to local copies of data items and not to the actual database.

As transactions reach the validation phase they are sequentially assigned serialisation numbers. The validation test for a transaction T must then verify that at least one of the following criteria holds for every transaction T_i which precedes T in the serialisation order:

1. T_i committed before T started.
2. The write set of T_i does not overlap with the read set of T and T_i completes its commitment before T starts to commit.
3. The write set of T_i does not overlap with the read set or the write set of T.

Any one of these criteria ensures that serialisability is guaranteed.

Overheads for optimistic scheduling

The processing time overhead for optimistic scheduling is incurred in maintaining the read and write sets and shadow copies for each transaction, carrying out the validation phase, and finally committing those transactions which pass the validation test. The magnitude of these activities clearly depends on the degree of concurrency in the system and on the characteristics of the transactions. Aborting a transaction and restarting it in an optimistic environment are relatively simple in view of the use of shadow copies.

In terms of storage space, the overhead is incurred in storing the read and write sets for each transaction together with the shadow copies of updated items. These shadow copies may be discarded after the transaction has committed. However, for the validation phase the read and write sets must be retained of all transactions which completed after any currently running transaction began. In a highly concurrent database environment this could be a very large amount of information to store.

8.2.5   Timestamping

A third technique for dealing with concurrent transactions in a database system is timestamping (Bernstein and Goodman, 1980). The technique was originally proposed for dealing with concurrency control in distributed databases, but it appears to be applicable to centralised systems also. With this method, each transaction is assigned a unique *timestamp* which is some identification of the place the transaction occupies in a serialisation of the concurrently executing transactions. In the case of a single-processor system, the timestamp could simply be the time at which each transaction started. Clearly the clock used must be sufficiently fine-grained to ensure that timestamps will be unique.

The concurrency control system guarantees serialisability by ensuring that all read and write operations are performed in timestamp order. Thus the equivalent serial schedule is the chronological order of the commencement of each transaction. A read or write request by a transaction with a timestamp t_1 will not be granted if the data item concerned has been written by a transaction with a timestamp t_2, where $t_2 > t_1$. Similarly a write request will be rejected if the data item has been read by a transaction with a higher timestamp. (These rules correspond to those defined in Section 8.2.3 for guaranteeing serialisability in a locking environment.) When a transaction experiences a rejected request to read or write an item, it is rolled back and restarted with a new, higher timestamp. Thus any potential deadlock situations are avoided. However, rolling back a transaction every time a conflict occurs is likely to be more expensive than allowing it to wait until it can proceed (as is the case with locking).

Implementation of the method requires the system to maintain read and write timestamps with each item. These hold the timestamps of the transactions which last performed the corresponding operation on the item. The processing overheads are very low since it is only necessary to check and update the timestamps each time an item is accessed.

8.2.6   Concurrency in Modula-2

For concurrent programming, Modula-2 offers only some rather basic facilities which are somewhat inadequate for database applications. These facilities permit the representation of quasi-concurrent processes (or *coroutines*), which, although viewed as executing in parallel, actually share a single physical processor

A new process is created in a Modula-2 program by a call to the procedure NEWPROCESS:

```
PROCEDURE NEWPROCESS ( p : PROC ;
                WorkArea : ADDRESS ; WorkSize : CARDINAL ;
                VAR ProcessName : PROCESS ) ;
```

where p denotes the procedure that constitutes the process. This procedure must be parameterless and must be declared at the outermost level of the module; WorkArea specifies the base address of the area in memory which will serve as the workspace for the process. This workspace is usually created by declaring an ARRAY OF WORD; WorkSize is the size of the workspace in bytes; ProcessName is the result parameter where its type, PROCESS, is imported from the system module.

A transfer of control between two processes is effected by a call to the procedure TRANSFER:

```
TRANSFER ( VAR p1, p2 : PROCESS ) ;
```

Such a call suspends the current process, assigning it to the variable parameter p1, and activates the process p2. A program terminates when control reaches the end of a procedure which forms the body of a process.

As we saw in our discussion above, in database applications a process (transaction) may require that a certain condition exist in order for it to begin or continue execution. For example, the process may require access to a data item which is currently locked by another process. In many implementations of Modula-2 a Processes module supplies the procedures necessary for synchronising process execution using *signals*. The presence of a condition can be represented by variables of the type SIGNAL, and a signal can be sent through a call to the procedure SEND. By employing the procedure WAIT, a process can suspend its execution until it is informed, by a signal, that a particular condition has arisen. A common form for the Processes module, corresponding to the standard suggested by Wirth, is as follows:

```
DEFINITION MODULE Processes;

TYPE SIGNAL ;

PROCEDURE StartProcess ( P : PROC ;  WorkSize : CARDINAL ) ;
(* Defines and transfers control to a process*)

PROCEDURE SEND ( VAR Sent : SIGNAL ) ;

PROCEDURE WAIT ( VAR WaitingFor : SIGNAL ) ;

PROCEDURE AWAITED ( Check : SIGNAL ) : BOOLEAN ;
(* Indicates if any processes are currently waiting for a specified signal *)
```

```
PROCEDURE INIT ( VAR ASignal : SIGNAL ) ;
(* Initialises a signal *)

END Processes ;
```

For database applications, processes require access to shared data and the integrity of this data must be protected. In Modula-2 the solution to this problem is to create a separate module which contains the declarations of all the shared data objects together with procedures for performing all required operations on these shared data. Such a module is called a *monitor* (Hoare, 1974).

The definition module for a monitor which treats a database as a single data resource and implements read-sharable and write-exclusive locks might take the following form in Modula-2:

```
DEFINITION MODULE DatabaseAccessMonitor ;

TYPE
    AccessMode = (ReadAccess, WriteAccess, None) ;

PROCEDURE Acquire (AccessRequired : AccessMode) ;
(* Acquires database with the specified access mode. Provides read-
    sharable and write-exclusive locks*)

PROCEDURE Release ;
(* Releases a lock on the database.*)

{ Database Access Procedures }

END DatabaseAccessMonitor ;
```

A process may request read or write access to the database by calling the procedure Acquire with the appropriate value of the parameter AccessMode. A lock, whether sharable or exclusive is released by a call to the procedure Release. A process may have read access to the database if there are no processes using the database, or if other processes currently have read access *and* there are no processes waiting to write. This latter condition is necessary to ensure that a process waiting to write does not wait forever. Thus, the monitor must keep track of the current access mode, if any, together with details of all processes currently using the database or waiting to use it.

The implementation module in Figure 8.2 schedules the processes as follows: When a reading process releases its access to the database then if there are other current readers, no further action is required. Otherwise the first process waiting for write access is activated. When a writing process releases its access to the database, then all processes waiting for read access are activated. If there are no waiting readers, then the first waiting writer (if any) is activated. This scheduling algorithm should be adequate in practice, but alternative strategies are easily programmed.

```
IMPLEMENTATION MODULE DatabaseAccessMonitor ;

FROM Processes IMPORT SIGNAL, SEND, WAIT, AWAITED, INIT ;

TYPE
   AccessMode = ( ReadAccess, WriteAccess, None) ;

VAR
    {Declarations of database objects}
    ReadAllowed  : SIGNAL; (*Sent when read access is possible *)
    WriteAllowed : SIGNAL; (*Sent when write access is possible *)
    CurrentAccessMode : AccessMode ;
    NoOfReaders : 0..MaxInt ;

PROCEDURE Acquire ( AccessRequired : AccessMode ) ;
BEGIN
   CASE CurrentAccessMode OF
   None :    BEGIN
                 CurrentAccessMode := AccessRequired ;
                 IF AccessRequired = ReadAccess
                 THEN NoOfReaders := 1;
                 END ;
             END ;
   ReadAccess :   IF AccessRequired = Write
                  THEN WAIT(WriteAllowed)
                  ELSIF NOT AWAITED(WritePossible)
                      THEN NoOfReaders := NoOfReaders + 1 ;
                  ELSE WAIT(ReadPossible)
                  END ;
   WriteAccess :  IF accessRequired = Read
                  THEN WAIT(ReadAllowed)
                  ELSE WAIT(WriteAllowed);
                  END ;
   END ;
END Acquire;

PROCEDURE Release ;
VAR
    NoCurrentReaders : Boolean ;
BEGIN
    IF CurrentAccessMode = Read
    THEN
      NoOfReaders := NoOfReaders - 1 ;
      NoCurrentReaders := NoOfReaders = 0 ;
      IF NoCurrentReaders
      THEN  IF AWAITED(WriteAllowed)
              THEN SEND(WriteAllowed)   END ;
      END ;
    ELSE
      IF AWAITED(ReadAllowed)
      THEN
        WHILE AWAITED(ReadAllowed) DO
```

```
              SEND(ReadAllowed) ;
              NoOfReaders := NoOfReaders + 1 ;
          END ;
          CurrentAccessMode := ReadAccess ;
      ELSIF AWAITED(WriteAllowed)
          THEN
              SEND(WriteAllowed) ;
              CurrentAccessMode := WriteAccess ;
      END ;
      END ;
  END Release ;

  { Implementation of database access procedures }

BEGIN
  CurrentAccessMode := None ;
  NoOfReaders := 0 ;
  INIT (ReadAllowed) ;
  INIT (WriteAllowed) ;
END DatabaseAccessMonitor ;
```

Figure 8.2 A monitor for database access

Obviously the greatest drawback to the above monitor is that the entire database is treated as a single resource. For a finer degree of granularity, for example at the relation level, we would require a separate monitor such as that illustrated above for each relation. Record-level locking would clearly be impractical to implement using this method. Another drawback is that the programmer would have to implement his own integrity preservation system, treating processes as units for recovery, and ensuring that they follow a locking protocol which guarantees serialisability.

8.2.7 Concurrency in database programming languages

Recall that in database programming languages, as described in Chapter 5, a database is treated as a data abstraction with appropriate operations. A transaction construct may be added to provide both a high-level procedural abstraction for activities which may take place in parallel on the database, and also to provide a mechanism for recovery in the event of failure. In this way transactions are defined at the same level of abstraction as are the items upon which they operate.

To overcome the difficulties with standard concurrent programming languages, as outlined in the previous section, Modula/R (Reimer, 1984) extends Modula-2 with an explicit transaction construct which acts as a unit for recovery and concurrency. Fine grained concurrency can be achieved by selecting the tuples of a relation to be locked by means of a selection predicate.

To define a selection, the reserved word SELECTOR is used to introduce a selector name (s), which may be parameterised, and which is bound to a relation type (RelType), and is defined by a predicate (p).

```
SELECTOR s ( <formal parameter list>)
FOR rel: RelType ;
BEGIN
      EACH r IN rel : p
END ;
```

R.T.C. LIBRARY
LETTERKENNY

For example, a suitable selection for the airline reservation example described in Section 8.2.1 might be defined by,

```
SELECTOR ofdepartures (FlightSet : SET OF FlightType;
                                        Date : DateType)
FOR dep : DeparturesRelType
BEGIN
      EACH d IN dep : (d.FlightNo IN FlightSet) AND (d.Date = Date)
END ;
```

The transaction might then take the following form:

```
TRANSACTION Book ( FlightsRequired : SET OF FlightType ;
                DateRequired : DateType ; NoSeats : CARDINAL ) ;
IMPORT
      DepRequired = Departures [of(FlightsRequired, DateRequired)]
                                        WRITE;


BEGIN
      . . .

END Book ;
```

The effect of the IMPORT statement in this transaction is to write-lock those tuples in the Departures relation which satisfy the predicate specified in the SELECTOR statement, with the formal parameters FlightSet and Date replaced by the actual parameters FlightsRequired and DateRequired. Selected relations may be imported into a transaction with one of the specific access rights, READ, READWRITE and WRITE. These access rights are interpreted as read-sharable and write-exclusive. Exclusive in this context means that while a transaction holds exclusive access to a selected relation, access rights granted to other transactions must relate to *disjoint* relations. Two selected relations are defined to be disjoint if and only if there is no expression such that its assignment to one of the selected relations changes the value of the other.

The languages ASTRAL (Amble et al., 1979) and RAPP (Hughes and Connolly, 1987) also provide facilities for concurrent programming. ASTRAL provides an explicit transaction construct and a selection mechanism similar to that of Modula/R. RAPP extends the process of PascalPlus (Welsh and Bustard, 1979) to provide a transaction mechanism, and provides a locking facility through instances of a built-in monitor *type*. This is similar in form to the Modula-2 monitor described above, but an important point to note is that it is a type and not an object as in Modula-2. Thus rather than construct a new monitor for every relation as we must do in

Modula-2, we may in RAPP simply declare an instance of the built-in monitor type for each relation.

8.3   RECOVERY

A database management system must provide the software tools necessary to implement recovery in the event of an *inconsistent state* arising in a database system. In a large multi-user database system inconsistent states may arise from a variety of diverse sources. For example:

1. A deadlock situation in a concurrent usage environment. This problem, and some possible strategies for its solution were outlined in the previous section.
2. Failure of an updating transaction before it has completed its update but after it has written some changes to the database.
3. A software failure in the database management system which causes some or all transactions executing at the time of the failure to abort.
4. A hardware failure, such as corruption of a disc.
5. Corruption of the database by a faulty transaction, i.e. a transaction with faulty logic which writes incorrect or inconsistent data to the database.

Clearly, maintaining consistency is the responsibility of the database administrator and many modern database management systems provide a variety of facilities for protecting against inconsistent states, or for resolving inconsistencies when they arise. Some of these facilities are discussed below.

Back-up copies and snap-shots

Taking back-up copies of a large database system is obviously an expensive and time-consuming operation, and can only be taken as frequently as is cost-effective. Obviously it is important that the copy represent a consistent state, so in general no updating transaction must be in progress at the same time as the copying utility (the copying utility read-locks the database). In a highly volatile environment (i.e. one in which the information in the database is constantly being updated), frequent 'snap-shots' of highly active areas of the database are desirable.

The journal file

Many database management systems maintain a transaction logging file, or *journal file*, which records a history of every transaction which has updated the database since the last back-up copy was made. Entries for each transaction in the journal file typically consist of the following:

1. A unique transaction identifier.
2. The address of every item updated (or created) by the transaction

together with the old value of the item (preimage) and its new value
(postimage).
3. Key points (checkpoints) in the progress of a transaction.

It is particularly useful if the journal file records the point at which a
transaction *commits*, i.e when it has successfully recorded in the journal
file *all* its changes to items in the database. In these circumstances the following restriction on transactions greatly facilitates recovery in the event of
a crash.

The two-phase commit policy

*The updates of a transaction cannot be transmitted to the database until it
has committed.*

Thus an updating transaction which obeys the two-phase commit policy,
(*not* to be confused with the two-phase locking protocol) has two phases as
illustrated in Figure 8.2.

Phase 1
The transaction writes to the journal file details of changes which it requires
to make to items in the database. When all such changes have been
recorded in the journal, the transaction issues a COMMIT message.

Phase 2
The database management system transmits the changes from the journal to
the database.

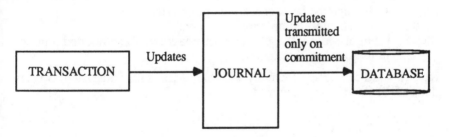

Figure 8.2   The journal file

If transactions do not obey this policy, but are instead permitted to write
directly to the database before committing, then in the event of a transaction
failure or system crash, recovery is difficult for two reasons:

1. A transaction which is uncommitted when it fails, or when a crash
    occurs, must have any updates which it has written to the database un-
    done ;
2. Any transaction which has read a value which was updated by a trans-
    action that is undone, must also be undone. Clearly, this effect can
    propagate, causing a large number of transactions to be undone.

Recovery from inconsistent states

Recovering from an inconsistent state may involve either undoing the changes made by a transaction (*roll-back*), or redoing the update of a committed transaction (*roll-forward*). If the journal file maintains both pre- and post-images then each operation may be carried out as follows:

Roll-Back

Step1:   The journal is scanned to identify the pre-images for the transaction.

Step 2:   These pre-images are applied to the database.

In addition it may be necessary to update any internal system tables which record information on transactions. Also, as described above, if a committed transaction is rolled back it will be necessary to undo other transactions which read a value written by the rolled-back transaction. Roll-back can deal effectively with deadlock, with a faulty updating transaction, or with certain classes of DBMS software failure which have affected only a small number of transactions.

Roll-Forward

Roll-forward requires the journal to record *checkpoints*. These are simple markers written to the journal indicating a point in time to which the system can return and be consistent. This usually means a point in time during which no updating transactions are active. The steps involved in rolling forward are then:

Step 1:   Determine the latest checkpoint prior to the crash.

Step 2:   Load the latest dump prior to the crash.

Step 3:   Using the journal, apply the post-images of all committed transactions up to the checkpoint.

Roll-forward can cope effectively with hardware faults and system crashes due to DBMS software failure.

8.4   PRIVACY PROTECTION

Any DBMS installation must protect against undesired destruction or modification of data and against unauthorised access to confidential data. Such security problems of course are not unique to database systems and many operating systems for example, provide facilities for controlling access to a computer system and for protecting users' files. Also, the most fundamental aspect of security, namely that of the physical protection of computers and storage devices against damage or theft, is a problem that must be faced by all computer installations whatever their size and function. Such *external* security controls shall not concern us here.

In this section however we shall concern ourselves with a number of security mechanisms which are of particular relevance to database systems and whose implementation and maintenance is largely in the hands of the software engineer. These *internal* security mechanisms involve for example, user identification and password management, control of access to the stored data, encryption (or coding) of confidential data, and measures to prevent confidential information being inferred from the stored data.

8.4.1 User identification and access constraints

In a multi-user database environment it is usually desirable to restrict access to certain parts of the database. The most common scheme is to identify a user with a password which is known only to the user and to the system and this password defines the user's global access rights to the database. These rights will generally be concerned with the user's freedom to obtain read access to certain portions of the database, and his level of authorisation to perform insertions, deletions and modifications. Additional passwords may be required to access specially protected areas of the database, or to execute certain powerful commands which, if used incorrectly, may have a catastrophic effect on the system.

Views as protection mechanisms

Views, as described in Chapter 5, promote data independence and offer a powerful means for simplifying access to the database and implementing integrity constraints. However, they also serve as convenient protection mechanisms. For example, we may have:

1. *Read-only views* in which users are given access to part (or even all) of the database, but no updating operations are permitted. This is a very common and useful form of protection since there are many practical situations where it is desirable to give a large body of users read-only access to a database, but prevent those users from performing any modifications on the database.

2. *Read-write views* through which users may access and update only that portion of the database represented by their view. This kind of view presents problems for the implementor, since updating a view may have an effect on parts of the database which do not lie within the view. For example, a new or updated record may not satisfy the predicate in the view definition and would thus disappear from the view but be present in the underlying relation. Also, when a record is inserted into a view any fields of the underlying relation not present in the view must be set to null, possibly violating referential and/or key integrity. Deletion operations on views may also have serious consequences since after a tuple has been deleted, referential integrity rules may spawn the deletion of other tuples which are outside the scope of the view. Some of these problems have already been discussed in Chapter 5 in relation to integrity.

Views in the relational model

Consider the following relations representing employees and their departments:

EMPLOYEES (EMP#, ENAME, ADDRESS, SALARY, DEPT#)

DEPTS (DEPT#, DNAME, MANAGER#)

We may define views on these relations, in order to hide sensitive data from unauthorised users, as the following examples illustrate.

Examples
1. We require a view for a user allowed access to employee records but not to their salaries. In relational algebra we could define a new relation EMPVIEW which is simply a projection on EMPLOYEES. The user is then given access to EMPVIEW rather than employees.

    EMPVIEW := EMPLOYEES [EMP#, ENAME, ADDRESS, DEPT#] ;

    In SQL we could define such a view in the following manner:

        CREATE VIEW EMPVIEW
            AS SELECT EMP#, ENAME, ADDRESS, DEPT#
            FROM EMPLOYEES ;

    In this view the users see only a *vertical fragment* of the relation.

2. We require a view for a user allowed access to complete employee records but only for those employees in dept #D3. In relational algebra we may define this view as:

    EMPVIEW := EMPLOYEES *where* DEPT# = D3 ;

    In SQL:

        CREATE VIEW EMPVIEW
            AS SELECT EMP#, ENAME, ADDRESS, SALARY, DEPT#
            FROM EMPLOYEES
            WHERE DEPT# = D3 ;

    In this case the view is a *horizontal fragment* of the relation.

3. We require a view for a user allowed access to records only for employees in the department for which he is the manager. In relational algebra:

    USERDEPT := DEPTS *where* MANAGER# = USER# ;

    USERVIEW := EMPLOYEES *join* USERDEPT ;

    In SQL we may write:

        CREATE VIEW EMPVIEW
            AS SELECT EMP#, ENAME, ADDRESS, SALARY, DEPT#
            FROM EMPLOYEES

```
WHERE DEPT# IN
  ( SELECT DEPT#
    FROM DEPTS
    WHERE MANAGER# = USER# ) ;
```

As can be seen in the above examples, the view mechanism provides an important and flexible measure of security. However, the difficulties which arise if the user is allowed to update his view must be carefully considered (see discussion on views in Chapter 5).

Access privileges

The view mechanism just described does not allow for the specification of *access privileges*, i.e. operations that authorised users may apply to relations or views. In SQL this function is performed by the GRANT command:

```
GRANT <privilege>{,<privilege>} ON <relation>{,<relation>}
  TO <user-name>{,<user-name>}
```

The privileges that may be granted on relations (or views) include SELECT, UPDATE, DELETE and INSERT. For example,

```
GRANT SELECT, DELETE, UPDATE ON EMPLOYEES TO
  'ABCD1234' ;

GRANT SELECT ON EMPVIEW TO 'ABCD1234' ;

GRANT SELECT ON DEPTS TO PUBLIC ;
```

where 'ABCD1234' identifies a particular user, and PUBLIC is a keyword representing *all* users. Access privileges which have been granted can be subsequently withdrawn using the REVOKE command:

```
REVOKE <privilege>{, <privilege>} ON<relation>
  {, <relation>} FROM <user-name>{,<user-name>}
```

The view definition mechanisms of database programming languages, as described in Chapter 5, offer very powerful facilities for defining access privileges. Recall that in these programming languages, views may be defined by module interfaces which specify precisely the data structures pertaining to the view together with the operations which may be applied to data objects which fall within the view. For example a view definition module (using Modula-2 syntax) might take the following general form:

```
DEFINITION MODULE ViewName ;

  { Data declarations for view definition }

  { Interfaces of exported procedures }

END ViewName.
```

The user of the view is restricted to the high-level operations on the view provided by the exported procedures.

8.4.2   Data encryption

Data encryption is concerned with the storage and transmission of data in encrypted (coded) form. It is possibly the most effective countermeasure against all security threats. The data to be stored or transmitted is encrypted and only authorised users or receivers are aware of the appropriate decryption algorithm to apply to the encrypted data to retrieve the original text. The large volume of personal and sensitive data currently held in databases and transmitted over telecommunication lines has made encryption increasingly important.

The original data is called the *plaintext*. The plaintext is *encrypted* (the terms enciphered, scrambled, transformed and coded are also used) by subjecting it to an *encryption algorithm*. The encrypted form of the data is called the *ciphertext*. To illustrate the main ideas and the problems that can arise with encryption, we begin with an example of a simple, unsophisticated encryption algorithm. We then consider the more elaborate scheme called 'public-key encryption' which is widely used in practice.

Encryption Algorithm

Input   : Plaintext, Encryption Key

Output   : Ciphertext

The encryption key is kept secret. The ciphertext is the data that is stored or transmitted. Consider the following simple example:

Plaintext   : GOLDILOCKS

Encryption Key : ELIZA

Step 1
Divide the plaintext into blocks of equal length to that of the encryption key:

GOLDI I LOCKS

Step 2
Replace each character by an integer, using ASCII codes or, for simplicity, the scheme, space = 00, A = 01, . . . Z = 26.

0715120409 I 1215031119

Step 3
Repeat step 2 for the encryption key:

0512092601

Step 4
For each block of the plaintext, replace each character by the sum (mod 27) of its integer encoding and the integer representation of the key:

0715120409 | 1215031119
0512092601 | 0512092601
1200210310 | 1700121020

Step 5: Replace each integer encoding in the result of Step 4 by its character equivalent :

LV UCJ | QV LJT

Decryption

For this simple example, decryption is straightforward if given the key. (Exercise : Decrypt the ciphertext shown above.) The important question is: 'Given matching plaintexts and ciphertexts, how difficult is it to determine the key?' For the example given above, the answer is clearly 'very easy'. However, more sophisticated schemes can be devised based on the ideas of public-key encryption (Diffie and Hellman, 1976; Rivest et al., 1978).

Public key encryption

In public key encryption, both the encryption function E and the encryption key are made public but the decryption function D is kept secret. Thus anyone can encrypt data but only those who know the decryption key can decrypt. The functions E and D should have the following properties:

1. Decrypting a ciphertext C yields the plaintext P. That is

$$D (E (P)) = P.$$

2. If a ciphertext C is first decrypted and then encrypted, the ciphertext C results. That is,

$$E (D (C)) = C.$$

3. Both E and D are easy to compute.
4. A knowledge of E does not provide an easy way of determining D.

Obviously if a user knows E and the encryption key and he wishes to decrypt a ciphertext C, he could write a program to test all possible plaintexts P until one is found such that E(P) = C. However if property (4) above is satisfied then the number of such plaintexts to test will be so large as to make this approach infeasible.

The encryption and decryption functions described above are examples of *trap-door one-way functions* (Diffie and Hellman, 1976). Such a function f has the properties:

1. For all positive integers x, $f(x)$ exists, is positive, and is unique ;
2. There exists an inverse function g such that $g(f(x)) = x$;
3. Efficient algorithms exist for computing f and g ;
4. It is computationally infeasible to discover g given f.

The functions are termed 'one-way' because they are easy to compute in one direction but difficult to compute in the other direction. The 'trap-door' term applies because the inverse functions are easy to compute once certain private ('trap-door') information is made known.

The best known scheme for public-key encryption is based on the following two facts:

1. There is a known fast algorithm for determining whether a given (large) number is prime.
2. There is *no* known fast algorithm for determining the prime factors of a given (large) non-prime number.

The scheme may be described as follows (Rivest et al., 1978). First reduce the plaintext to an integer P in the range 0 to $n-1$ (or a series of such integers). Any standard method, such as that described above, may be used. The purpose at this stage is simply to reduce the plaintext to an integer, not to encrypt it. To encrypt the plaintext we raise P to the power of e, modulo n. To decrypt a ciphertext C we raise it to the power of d modulo n. The encryption key is therefore the pair of integers (e, n), which are made public, while the decrytion key is the pair (d, n) which are kept private.

Making use of the above two facts concerning large prime numbers, we choose e, d and n as follows:

1. Choose randomly two distinct large primes p and q (~100 digits each) and compute their product $n = p*q$.
2. Choose the encryption key e to be any prime greater than p and q.
3. Take the decryption key d to satisfy the formula,

$$(d * e) \bmod ((p-1) * (q-1)) = 1$$

The algorithm for computing d is straightforward if p and q are known. Rivest et al. show that this choice of d guarantees that properties (a) and (b) above hold, i.e. that the encryption algorithm E and the decryption algorithm D are inverse permutations.

4. To encrypt a piece of plaintext, reduce it to a sequence of integers less than n and replace each integer P by the ciphertext C, where

$$C = P^e \bmod r$$

5. To decrypt, use the formula

$$P = C^d \bmod r$$

Example.
Obviously it would be impractical to illustrate the above scheme here using 100-digit primes. However in order to demonstrate that the scheme works we present a simple example, using small primes.

Let $p = 3$, $q = 5$ and $e = 11$. Then $n = 15$ and $(p-1)*(q-1) = 8$. To compute d, we have that

$$(d * 11) \bmod 8 = 1$$

giving $d = 3$.

Suppose that $P = 2$, then the ciphertext is given by the following:

$$C = 2^{11} \bmod 15 = 2048 \bmod 15 = 8$$

and the plaintext P is retrieved by the formula,

$$P = 8^3 \bmod 15 = 512 \bmod 15 = 2$$

Disadvantages of encryption

1. Key management (i.e. keeping keys secret) is a problem. Even in public-key encryption the decryption key must be kept secret.
2. Even in a system that supports encryption, data must often be *processed* in plaintext form. Thus sensitive data may still be accessible to transaction programs.
3. Encrypting data gives rise to serious technical problems at the level of physical storage organisation. For example indexing over data which is stored in encrypted form can be very difficult.

8.4.3 Security of statistical databases

Statistical databases typically contain sensitive data about individuals. Examples include census data and medical records. The problem with such systems is to guarantee the confidentiality of information about individuals, yet at the same time provide statistical operations (e.g. counts, averages, totals, etc.) on the data. As we shall see, this problem cannot be solved by access control mechanisms alone.

In the following discussion we say that a statistical database has been *compromised* if the value of an individual field has been determined. The term *query set* is used to refer to a subgroup of the population satisfying a query.

Example.
Consider a payroll database containing the records shown in Table 8.1.

Name	Sex	Location	Salary
Abel	M	London	20000
Burns	F	Glasgow	12000
Collins	M	Cardiff	15500
.	.	.	.
.	.	.	.
Smith	F	Belfast	15000
.		.	.

Table 8.1

An individual tracker

Assume that the only operations that we may perform on this database are statistical operations such as COUNT and SUM, which have the following formats:

(i) COUNT (<predicate>), returns the number of records satisfying the specified predicate.

(ii) SUM (<attribute name> : < predicate>), returns the sum of the values of the specified attribute for all records satisfying the given predicate.

Suppose that we know that Smith is female and is located in Belfast and we wish to compromise the database by determining her salary. Suppose that the query:

COUNT (Location = 'Belfast' *and* Sex = 'F') = 1

confirms that these attribute values *uniquely* identify Smith. Once we have determined a set of attribute values that uniquely identify a particular individual we may use statistical operations to compromise the database. For example, the following query provides the salary of Smith:

SUM (Salary : Location = 'Belfast' *and* Sex = 'F') = 15000

We may inhibit such compromise by imposing restrictions on the allowable query set size (i.e. a query is not answered unless its query set is greater than some limit). However, large query sets also allow compromise. For example, the queries:

COUNT (Location = 'Belfast' *or not* (Location = 'Belfast')) = 527

and

COUNT (*not* (Location = 'Belfast' *and* Sex = 'F')) = 526

again provides the information that only one female is located in Belfast. Then the results,

SUM (Salary : Location = 'Belfast' *or not* (Location = 'Belfast'))
= 575000

SUM (Salary : *not* (Location = 'Belfast' *and* Sex = 'F'))
= 560000

provide the salary of that female by subtraction of the totals.

Suppose we now impose the restriction that the query set cardinality c must lie in the range:

$$m \leq c \leq n - m$$

where n is the number of records in the database and m is an integer satisfying the inequality $0 \leq m \leq n/2$. Once again, this restriction is not sufficient to guard against compromise, since queries of the form:

COUNT (Sex = 'F' *and not* (Location = 'Belfast')) = 256

COUNT (Sex = 'F') = 257

might again confirm that Smith is uniquely identified by the attribute values, Location = 'Belfast' *and* Sex = 'F', without violating the above restriction on query set cardinality (assuming that $m < 256$ and $n - m > 257$).

The predicate (Sex = 'F' *and not* (Location = 'Belfast')) is called an *individual tracker* because it enables a user, in conjunction with a more general predicate, to track down information about a specific individual. In general, suppose that an individual is uniquely identified by a predicate C (called a *characteristic formula*), and we can decompose C into two predicates C_1 and C_2 such that

$$C = C_1 \text{ } and \text{ } C_2.$$

To allow compromise we choose C_1 and C_2 such that

$$m \leq \text{COUNT} (C_1 \text{ } and \text{ } not \text{ } C_2) \leq n - m$$

and

$$m \leq \text{COUNT} (C_1) \leq n - m$$

Then the predicate (C_1 *and not* C_2) is an individual tracker.

The general tracker

In general, a database which restricts query set cardinality as described above, may be compromised using a *general tracker* T for which,

$$2m \leq \text{COUNT} (T) \leq n - 2m$$

Then if we require a count for a query C, where COUNT(C) $< m$, the strategy for compromise is to use the relationship:

$$\text{COUNT (C)} = \text{COUNT (C } or \text{ T)} + \text{COUNT (C } or \text{ not T)}$$
$$- \text{COUNT (T)} - \text{COUNT (} not \text{ T)}$$

In this formula, it is easy to show that the query sets of all the counts on the right hand side will lie in the appropriate range to be answered. For example, suppose that $m = 100$, and we know that COUNT(Sex = 'F') is greater than $2m$ and less than $n - 2m$ (i.e. that the number of females in the database lies between 200 and 327). Then the predicate T = (Sex = 'F') is a general tracker and the above formula may be used to compromise the database.

Query overlap

One of the reasons that we can compromise the database is that the query sets overlap. Suppose that we are only allowed to make queries where:

(i) $m \leq$ query set cardinality $\leq n - m$.
(ii) No two queries involve more than k common fields.

Assume that p field values are known for a record. Then it can be shown (Ullman, 1982) that to compromise the database we must make at least

$$1 + (m - 1 - p)/k$$

queries. Thus we may conclude that total security against compromise is impossible but a large m and a small k make it very difficult. However, such restrictions may place intolerable burdens on legitimate users.

A comprehensive description of trackers may be found in the paper by Denning et al. (1979), and an overview of statistical database security in Denning (1978).

8.5   DISTRIBUTED DATABASES

In a distributed database the data are held on a network of computers across different sites (or nodes) which are geographically remote from each other. Each site holds a partition of the database and these partitions may overlap, i.e. some relations or parts of relations may be replicated at different sites. Typically, each site runs its own version of the DBMS which is responsible for handling the necessary communications across the network. (In fact the local DBMSs could be different systems leading to what is known as a heterogeneous distributed system, but we shall not concern ourselves with such systems here.)

Ideally, a *distributed database management system* should absolve the user of the responsibility for dealing with the significant additional problems which arise due to distribution. That is, the *location, replication* and *fragmentation* of data should be transparent to the user.

Location transparency and efficient query processing

Location transparency absolves the user of the responsibility of knowing at which site a particular item of data is stored. Thus he may retrieve data from multiple sites simultaneously without restrictions. Obviously, due to the relative slowness of communication links, response times for accessing data stored at remote sites may be much greater than for accesses to locally held data. Except for this difference however, it should appear to the user that the entire database (or at least his view of it) is stored at his location.

The provision of location transparency presents the system with the very considerable problem of devising and implementing efficient query processing strategies. A particularly difficult problem in this regard is how best to perform a join operation when the operand relations are stored at different sites. If the relations are very large then transferring one of them in its entirety from one site to another, in order to compute the join at a single site, may result in significant delay. This delay will of course depend on the bandwidth of the communication links, but will typically be significantly larger than the computation time required to perform the join. One important technique which has been proposed to deal with this problem involves the use of the *semi-join* operation (Wong, 1977; Bernstein and Chiu, 1981).

In terms of the other algebraic operators, the semi-join of relations R_1

and R_2 is defined as:

$$R_1 \; \textit{semi-join} \; R_2 \equiv (R_1 \; \textit{join} \; R_2) \,[\text{ attributes of } R_1 \,]$$

That is, the semi-join yields the subset of tuples of R_1 which contributes to the join with R_2. The main advantages of the semi-join are as follows:

1. Its evaluation only requires the transmission of a *vertical fragment* of a relation (i.e. the common attributes), rather than the entire relation.
2. It has a *reductive* effect since the result of R_1 *semi-join* R_2 is a subset of R_1, whereas the join may yield the Cartesian product in the worst case.

For example, suppose we require the join of relation $R_1(A, B)$ which is at site 1, with relation $R_2(B, C)$ at site 2. A sequence of operations to evaluate the join while (possibly) reducing data transfer time is as follows:

1. Send from site 2 to site 1 the result, S_1, of R_2 projected on the common attributes, i.e.

$$S_1 \; := \; R_2 \,[B]\,;$$

2. Compute at node 1, the relation S_2 which is the result of the join of R_1 and S_1. That is,

$$S_2 \; := \; R_1 \; \textit{join} \; S_1 \,;$$

S_2 is in fact the semi-join of R_1 and R_2. That is, it contains those tuples of R_1 which participate in a join with R_2.
3. Send the relation S_2 to site 2 and compute the join of S_2 with R_2. This gives us the required result relation, i.e.

$$\text{Result} \; := \; S_2 \; \textit{join} \; R_2 \,;$$

This strategy will reduce the data transfer costs only if

$$\text{Size} \,(S_1) \; + \; \text{Size} \,(S_2) \; < \; \text{Size} \,(R_1)$$

where the function Size is defined to be the number of tuples in the operand relation multiplied by the width of a tuple in bits. Experience shows that this condition is frequently satisfied in practice.

Replication transparency and concurrency control

In providing replication transparency the system takes responsibility for maintaining duplicate copies of relations which are held at multiple sites to facilitate query processing. This means that updates to replicated data must be propagated automatically (and transparently to the user) to secondary copies, ideally at the same time as the primary update. If updates are delayed then out-of-date retrievals may result, leading to inconsistent states.

Problems obviously arise if a site holding a copy of an updated data item is temporarily unavailable. One possible strategy would be to reject any update operation on an item which cannot be broadcast immediately to all copies of that item. However this leads to a loss of local autonomy since transactions are rejected due to non-local factors. Also the probability of an update transaction failing may be quite high if there is a lot of replication across many sites. A better strategy is to leave pending (at some available site) any updates which cannot be applied immediately. A restart procedure for a site is then responsible for applying any pending updates to its local data upon reconnection to the network.

Data replication also has significant consequences for concurrency control in a distributed system. As shown by Traiger et al. (1979), a distributed system with data replication which enforces the following protocol will be guaranteed serialisability:

1. Before reading an item a transaction must acquire a (shared) read-lock on *at least one* copy of the item.
2. Before updating a data item a transaction must acquire an (exclusive) write-lock on *every* copy of the item.
3. Once a transaction has acquired a lock (of either kind) it must not release that lock until it has *committed*.

This protocol may be regarded as a distributed version of the two-phase locking protocol described in Section 8.3. However complications arise if a write-lock cannot be granted because a site containing a copy of the relevant item is unavailable. Also note that the commitment of a transaction in the distributed case requires that *all* sites have recorded the updates of that transaction relevant to their local data items. That is either all sites accept the transaction or they all reject it (roll it back).

A problem with locking in a distributed environment is that it may considerably reduce response time in view of the amount of message traffic it generates on the network (e.g. lock and unlock requests, lock and unlock grants, commit messages etc.). There is also the problem of *global deadlock* arising, i.e. deadlock involving more than one site. It may be impossible for a single site to detect such deadlock since it does not have all the relevant information available locally. Thus detection and resolution of global deadlock can generate further message traffic. In many distributed systems therefore, deadlock is detected by a timeout mechanism, by which a transaction is aborted if it exceeds some specified waiting time.

Timestamping in a distributed environment avoids deadlock and incurs less communication overheads. However this technique tends to provide a lesser degree of concurrency than locking.

Fragmentation transparency

With this form of transparency, the system supports the fragmentation of a relation among the different sites in the network, and hides the details of such fragmentation from the user. The purpose of fragmentation is, of course, to place data more precisely at the site where it is most often accessed.

Fragmentation may be *horizontal* or *vertical*. With horizontal fragmentation, subsets of tuples of a relation may be stored at different sites. For example, if our college database of Chapter 2 were distributed throughout the various departments, each department might store a horizontal fragment of the STUDENT relation, consisting of records for those students taking courses in that department. With vertical fragmentation, the set of domains of a relation may be partitioned across the network. (Note however that in order to avoid loss of information each vertical fragment of a relation must include a candidate key.) An example of a vertical fragment might arise in the college database if the faculty office required, from each department, the number and title of each course but not the lecturer giving the course. Thus the faculty site on the network might store a vertical fragment of the COURSE relation consisting of the COURSE# and COURSE-TITLE attributes. An additional complication is added if a fragment of a relation is replicated at different sites.

Strategies for fragmentation in distributed database systems have been proposed (see for example Ceri et al., 1984), but obviously they depend to a large extent on the characteristics of the individual database.

EXERCISES

8.1   Consider a schedule S of four concurrently executing transactions T_1, T_2, T_3, and T_4 consisting of the following steps:

1. T_1 :   read-lock (A) ;
2. T_3 :   read-lock (A) ;
3. T_1 :   write-lock (B) ;
4. T_1 :   unlock (A) ;
5. T_3 :   write-lock (A) ;
6. T_1 :   unlock (B) ;
7. T_4 :   read-lock (B) ;
8. T_3 :   unlock (A) ;
9. T_2 :   read-lock (B) ;
10. T_4 :   read-lock (A) ;
11. T_2 :   unlock (B) ;
12. T_4 :   unlock (A) ;
13. T_2 :   write-lock (A) ;
14. T_2 :   unlock (A) ;
15. T_4 :   unlock (B) ;

By constructing the precedence graph, determine whether this schedule is serialisable and if so, give an equivalent serial schedule.

8.2   Discuss the relative advantages and disadvantages of *locking*, *optimistic scheduling* and *timestamping* with regard to the following criteria:

(i)   The degree of concurrency provided.
(ii)   The processing time overheads.
(iii) The storage overheads.

8.3 (a) The simple encryption scheme given in Section 8.4.2, with the key AMBER, has been produced the following ciphertext:

EREWP I QFKTE I AVUEJ I UDCNY I IFHTI I XNTIR

Decrypt this message.

(b) The same scheme but with a different 5-character key has produced the following matching plaintext and ciphertext:

Plaintext: KEEP SECRETS HIDDEN

Ciphertext: NTΔUR I VTYWW I WGVMΔ I GSΔSR

where the character 'Δ' denotes a space. Determine the key.

8.4 Consider the following relational schema representing doctors, patients and consultations between doctors and patients:

DOCTOR (DNAME, PHONE#, SPECIALITY)
PATIENT (PATIENT#, PNAME, SEX, DNAME)
CONSULTATION (DNAME, PATIENT#, DATE, TIME, NOTES)

In this schema the foreign key DNAME in the PATIENT relation represents the fact that each patient is assigned to a particular doctor. A patient may have a consultation with any doctor (e.g. if his or her own doctor is unavailable).

Using SQL, define views on this database for the following users:

(i)   A patient who is allowed to read-only access to his or her own consultation records.

(ii) An administrator who requires read and write access to the details of all consultations, excluding the doctor's notes.

(iii) A doctor who is allowed read and write access to consultation records associated with his own patients.

9

Commercial Systems and Database Machines

9.1 CRITERIA FOR DBMS EVALUATION

In order to critically assess the large number of commercial database management systems currently available, it is necessary to define the most important characteristics which one should look for in selecting and acquiring such a system. The following subsections outline some of the most important criteria. We shall concentrate on relational systems.

Data definition facilities

The relational model of data is now the dominant model in the commercial environment. Although some network and hierarchical systems still have the edge on performance for certain applications, they impose too many restrictions at the data modelling level, support only pre-defined transactions against the database and are difficult to modify and upgrade. In addition, as described in Chapter 1, such systems provide only a minimal amount of data independence, whereby the logical database structure is buffered from the physical database organisation.

Although the issue of performance has to be considered very carefully, modern relational systems provide an abundance of tools (e.g. fourth generation languages) which can significantly reduce both development time and maintenance costs. They are also well-suited to handling ad hoc queries. It should be pointed out however that a marketing description of a DBMS as 'relational' does not necessarily imply that the system will support a fully functional data independent environment at all. There are many systems on the market which are simply old-fashioned network or hierarchical systems with a crude semi-relational user interface placed on top. Even the 'respectable' relational systems are not fully relational in the strict theoretical sense. For example, most provide only very limited domain

213

types and few enforce key uniqueness and referential integrity. The minimum requirements of a relational system must be that it supports the tabular data structure known as a relation, and that it provides a data manipulation language which is at least as powerful as the relational algebra (i.e. the language should be *relationally complete*).

Data manipulation facilities

A DBMS should provide data manipulation languages of various types, both procedural and non-procedural, for end-users as well as for system programmers. SQL is rapidly emerging as an industry-wide standard query language for relational systems, and is often provided both as a stand-alone query language as well as embedded in a variety of programming languages. Easy-to-use natural language user-interfaces are of great benefit, and are becoming more widespread.

Data independence

As discussed in Chapter 1, support for data independence is arguably the most important feature of a relational DBMS. The ability of a DBMS to separate the logical database definition from its physical storage organisation increases the capabilities to redefine and restructure the database. Similar benefits are derived from a DBMS that separates the global logical database definition from the many user views, whether those of terminal users or application programs. Flexible and efficient mechanisms for defining and manipulating views is highly desirable in a relational system. Views not only support data independence but as described in Chapters 5 and 8, they provide a convenient means for implementing integrity and security constraints.

Integrity control

Validation of transactions is a very important function of any database management system. In a relational DBMS this requires the system to maintain the many forms of integrity control described in Chapter 5, including domain integrity and referential integrity. Until recently, relational systems were very weak in the area of integrity control but this situation is rapidly improving. More sophisticated typing facilities, coupled with strong type checking, is becoming more common and a few systems also offer automatic control of referential integrity.

Data dictionary facilities

These are among the most essential data management tools, providing intelligence on data resources and database usage, and supporting data administration, systems development and maintenance. The data dictionary (sometimes called a system catalogue) may be regarded as a *meta-database*, i.e. a database which holds information on the databases which are managed by the DBMS. In particular, the dictionary maintains for each database a description of the schema and the various user views. Other information which is of importance to database administration is also held, including the data requirements and usage of individual users and transactions, and the frequency with which portions of the database are accessed. It should be possible for the database administrator and systems programmers to query the data dictionary just like any other database, but its maintenance should be the responsibility of the system software.

Concurrency control facilities

The DBMS should provide concurrency control with a degree of granularity down to the record level. In a highly concurrent-usage environment file/relation locking creates bottle-necks and unacceptable lengthening of response times. Optimistic concurrency control (see Chapter 8) has been employed successfully in a number of commercial systems and might prove to be a viable alternative to locking in some circumstances.

Back-up and recovery facilities

Ideally back-up and recovery facilities should be automatic and should not require the intervention of the database administrator. Both preimages and postimages of database items should be automatically maintained in the system journal for each transaction. Facilities for taking *snapshots* of highly active areas is desirable in that it reduces the need to invoke time-consuming back-up operations. Recovery should be possible from both hardware and software failures.

Database restructuring facilities

In order to allow for changes in the enterprise or in user requirements, support should be provided in a DBMS for database offloading, redefinition, and reloading. Facilities for adding new files (relations) to the schema and linking them to existing files are essential, as is the ability to add new attributes to a file or modify existing attributes.

Performance

If it is to be used to implement large multi-user databases, it is essential that the chosen DBMS has been proven to perform well in a high-transaction volume environment. Automatic query optimisation is essential. In addition, the applications programmer must be provided with tools such as B-tree secondary indexes which give him intimate control over the efficiency of his database transactions. The past few years has seen significant improvements in performance of commercial relational database management systems which has led to their widespread acceptance in transaction intensive application areas. Performance of course is influenced by the choice of both software and hardware, and each of these have to be carefully considered. In the latter part of this chapter we examine some of the most important hardware considerations which have an influence on database management.

Distributed data

If the data is to be dispersed geographically among different sites, a DBMS which directly supports distribution has important advantages. As discussed in Chapter 8, such a system should provide *transparency*, which insulates the user from the many complexities associated with data distribution. In particular the system should provide location transparency, replication transparency and fragmentation transparency. Special attention should be paid to the facilities in the system for concurrency control, update propagation and recovery, all of which are significantly more complex in distributed databases.

Standards

SQL has been developed to an international standard under the auspices of the American National Standards Institute (ANSI). As a result, most relational DBMSs now provide an SQL interface. ORACLE have provided SQL for some time and Version 5 of their database management system brings their implementation of the language into line with the ANSI standard. Relational Technology Inc. have followed by announcing an SQL interface to its INGRES database system which is compatible with that provided by IBM's DB2. Also, Software AG have introduced AdaSQL, an SQL interface which sits on top of their Adabas DBMS, and Cullinet have announced that the next version of IDMS/R will offer SQL compatibility. Despite this popularity, implementations of SQL often suffer from poor performance and require enormous resources for query optimisation. However this situation is improving rapidly.

9.2 CHARACTERISTICS OF COMMERCIAL SYSTEMS

9.2.1 ORACLE

ORACLE, which first appeared around 1979, was one of the first relational database management systems to be marketed commercially. The product has developed considerably since then, particularly in the areas of performance and integrity preservation.

ORACLE is relationally complete in that it provides all the relational operators for the manipulation of tables. The data types which it provides are: numeric, character strings, date, time and money. Database constraints may be implemented via *triggers*, i.e. database procedures which are invoked (or triggered) when a specified condition occurs. Key uniqueness and key integrity are supported.

ORACLE provides the SQL language as its main user interface, and its implementation of the language conforms fully to the ANSI standard. SQL statements may be embedded in programs written in C, COBOL, FOR-TRAN, Pascal and PL/1.

Besides SQL, the ORACLE system provides a number of tools for end-users. These include:

1. *EASY*SQL* - which uses a mouse and screen graphics to allow inex-pert users to exploit the power of SQL without having to learn the syn-tax of the language.
2. *SQL*Calc* - a spreadsheet system which allows data to be retrieved from the database to participate in the spreadsheet.
3. *SQL*Graph* - which automatically converts the data that results from a query on the database into graphical form.
4. *SQL*Plus* - which provides conversational interaction with an ORA-CLE database. Users can create and modify tables and views, enter and modify values for data items, and set up ad-hoc enquiries. Report-writing facilities are also included.

Data independence

The level of data independence in ORACLE is high. As with all good rela-tional systems, the end-user does not need to know how the data is physi-cally structured in order to interact with the database. The system provides automatic navigation to the relevant data. In addition, ORACLE provides a very flexible mechanism for defining views on a database, through which only selected data is visible to the user. Views are defined as dynamic vir-tual tables and defined by assigning a name to a retrieval command. They do not occupy additional storage space but they 'look like' and may be operated upon as if they were real tables. Both retrieval and update oper-ations are permitted, but it should be pointed out that updating views is a rather dangerous procedure unless carefully controlled. ORACLE, like most other systems, leaves such control largely in the hands of the user. Apart from this reservation however, there is no doubt that the view mech-anism is a powerful facility for simplifying interactions with the database and for providing data security and privacy.

Database administration in ORACLE

The SQL*Design Dictionary (SDD) of ORACLE allows the database administrator to define the structure of the database and to impose con-straints for security and integrity preservation. The SDD then holds infor-mation concerning the definition and storage implementation of tables in the database, together with authorised users and their access rights. The dictio-nary can be used to monitor database usage and fine tune its performance.

The lowest concurrency granularity is at the tuple (row) level. That is, as SQL statements are executed, rows are only locked while they are actu-ally being operated upon. If a user requires exclusive access to a number of tables he can construct a transaction which will lock each table specified until the transaction has ended. Transactions are automatically rolled back to resolve deadlock situations.

With regard to recovery in ORACLE, both pre- and post-images are maintained in the journal file. Failed transactions are automatically rolled back.

Database restructuring capabilities are provided. Table definitions can be expanded to include additional attributes and attribute field widths may be altered. New views may be defined at any time.

Performance

Version 5 of ORACLE claims to apply artificial intelligence to SQL query optimisation. Precise details of the optimising techniques are difficult to obtain but there is little doubt that ORACLE continues to be one of the leaders in this field. Multi-table operations, such as joins, may be optimised in ORACLE (in common with many other relational systems) using a technique known as 'multi-table clustering', through which data from different tables may be stored on the same physical disc page.

Distributed data

Recent additions to the ORACLE product family provide the tools for users on one machine to process data that is physically resident on another, even if the machines are of quite different types. With all of these products it is the user's responsibility to employ SQL security features to preserve the integrity of the data from the inconsistencies that can arise with multiple remote access.

SQL*Plus and Easy*SQL have facilities to link an ORACLE user, usually on a PC, to an ORACLE system on another machine in the same network. Data may be extracted from the remote machine and processed locally.

SQL*Star gives interactive users or application programs transparent access to data on any ORACLE system on the same network. That is, they can process the data as if it were local, regardless of the host system on which it actually resides.

SQL*Connect allows ORACLE users on one machine to access data held in non-ORACLE databases on another. The non-ORACLE databases system must be SQL-compatible.

9.2.2   INGRES

INGRES was originally an experimental relational database management system developed during the seventies at the University of California, Berkeley (Stonebraker et al., 1976). Since 1980 a commercial version of INGRES has been marketed by a company called Relational Technology Inc. (RTI).

Data definition and manipulation

INGRES provides two non-procedural database languages: QUEL and

SQL. QUEL was developed at the same time as the experimental system and has gained widespread popularity in the scientific and engineering world. In 1986 however, RTI finally bowed to market pressure and provided an SQL interface to INGRES which is compatible with the proposed ANSI standard. Both languages may be used both for interactive querying and as database programming languages embedded in a variety of host languages (BASIC, C, COBOL, FORTRAN, Pascal and PL/1).

INGRES provides data types for integer and floating point numbers, money, dates, and both fixed length and varying length character strings. Key uniqueness is not supported by default, but the user may impose this constraint on a table. A table is initially created as a heap but the storage structure may be changed at any time to a more efficient organisation, such as an indexed (BTREE) structure or a hash-addressed structure.

For end users INGRES provides a family of tools through its 'Visual Programming' products. These include:

1. INGRES/REPORTS - a comprehensive and easy to use report writer;
2. INGRES/FORMS - for designing and modifying full-screen forms;
3. INGRES/QUERY - an interactive forms-based user interface for browsing and performing simple modifications;
4. INGRES/GRAPHICS - allows users to create good quality graphs from an INGRES database.

As with ORACLE, the facilities in INGRES for view definition and manipulation are very powerful.

Database administration in INGRES

In common with ORACLE, INGRES provides a comprehensive integrated data dictionary and extensive facilities for concurrency control and recovery.

Distributed data

With their product INGRES/STAR, RTI offer an open-architecture distributed database system which supports mixed hardware environments. In an INGRES/STAR environment local sites in the network run a standard version of INGRES, each with its own local data dictionary. A distributed data manager acts as an interface between applications and several back-end databases, allowing local INGRES DBMSs to operate autonomously.

The first release of INGRES/STAR runs under Unix™ and VMS, and includes:

1. Location transparent retrieval. Users can retrieve data from multiple sites simultaneously without restriction.
2. Distributed transactions with *single-site* update. Updates in any one single transaction must only affect data at one site. Separate transactions in the same application may update different sites. Future releases of INGRES/STAR promise full multiple-site update capabilities.
3. A degree of replication transparency, in that the *primary* copy of a relation is updated directly by a transaction, while updates to copies will

be automatically propagated through background tasks. Concurrent updating of copies is promised for a future release.
4.   Distributed query optimisation. The first release appears to provide only a moderate amount of optimisation.

Performance

Performance is an area to which RTI have devoted a great deal of effort in recent years. INGRES Release 5.0 gave performance improvements of up to 50 per cent over Release 4.0. Enhancements included major improvements in B-tree storage structures, extensions to SQL aimed at improved query processing, and modifications to locking to improve transaction throughput.

9.2.3   DB2

During the past decade IBM have produced a family of relational DBMS products largely based on the research and development carried at at San Jose during the seventies on the prototype 'System R'. Three products of that research are now commercially available and are known as DB2, SQL/DS and QMF. All three products run on the IBM System/370 and similar machines. DB2 is a DBMS for the MVS/370 and MVS/XA operating systems; SQL/DS is a DBMS for the VM/CMS and DOS/VE operating systems; and QMF is an ad hoc query and report-writing front-end product for both DB2 and SQL/DS.

Data definition and manipulation in DB2

DB2 provides data types for integer, decimal and floating point numbers, and also for fixed- and varying-length character strings. Data manipulation is of course provided through SQL, which may be embedded in a wide variety of programming languages.

Database administration in DB2

DB2 maintains a *system catalogue* for each database which itself consists of relations or tables. Thus the catalogue may be queried through the same interface as a normal database, namely SQL. A user who is not familiar with the structure of the database may query the system catalogue to discover that structure. Catalogue information is also used extensively by the system. For example, the query optimiser uses catalogue information about indexes to choose a specific access strategy, while the authorisation subsystem uses catalogue information about users and access privileges to grant or deny specific user requests.

DB2 databases may be accessed concurrently by the IMS/VS data communication feature, by CICS/OS/VS, and by TSO users. Normally each SQL statement is treated as a transaction although facilities also exist for a user to group together several SQL statements as a single transaction.

Locks are at the record level.

DB2 has comprehensive recovery mechanisms fully integrated with the system. After a system failure, a restart of DB2 automatically restores data to a consistent state by rolling back uncommitted transactions and redoing those which had been committed at the time of the crash. Single failed transactions are automatically rolled-back. Disc logging and incremental image copying is provided.

DB2 allows new tables or indexes to be added to the database at any time. Also, tables or indexes no longer required may be deleted. It is not clear if new attributes may be added to an existing relation, or if attribute types may be modified. The view definition mechanism in DB2 is quite sophisticated.

Performance

Users may define indexes in DB2 to provide for faster access to data in a relation. The system provides automatic access path selection, using information about data placement and indexes held in the system catalogue. Programmers never reference indexes in their programs. A 'binding' procedure following compilation selects the optimal access paths taking into account any indexes which exist.

9.2.4   Other relational systems

Other relational systems worthy of consideration include *Informix* from Sphinx Inc., and *Unify* from Unify Corporation. Unify now has a fourth generation language called ACCELL built around it and this system will be discussed in the next section.

Informix is a very popular DBMS, especially on mini- and micro-computers, and is geared mainly for the Unix environment. It has an SQL interface (Informix-SQL) and a fourth generation language (Informix-4GL) similar to Query-by-Example. The ACE report-writer of Informix is quite sophisticated in that it embodies program control structures, such as if-then-else statements, and allows C programs to be called from within a report. Informix provides fairly sophisticated facilities for concurrency and for data security and integrity. These include record-level locking, transaction logging and recovery through both roll-forward and roll-back. In many important areas Informix is on a par with the three systems described in the previous sections.

9.3   FOURTH GENERATION SYSTEMS

Fourth Generation DBMSs are characterised by their *integrated* approach to end user requirements and the nonprocedural nature of the language used. Integration of end user requirements consists of providing a complete set of functions using a common and consistent command syntax. Nonprocedural languages allow the user to simply describe the desired result from the database and eliminates the necessity to describe how the data is to be accessed.

The advantage of fourth generation languages (4GLs) lies in their ability to produce new application systems much faster than can be achieved with third generation languages such as COBOL. Often the end user can program the application directly without the assistance of data processing personnel. The drawback is that the performance of 4GL applications is usually considerably inferior to the performance of a procedural-based version of the same application. However, the efficiency of 4GL systems is improving steadily and this disadvantage is rapidly becoming less important.

Some 4GLs, such as Natural from Software AG, and ADS/O from Cullinet are designed for the professional programmer who builds complex systems. Others, such as APS from Sage Systems, generate COBOL data processing procedures. Those geared to database applications include FOCUS from Information Builders Inc., ACCELL from Unify Corporation, Ramis II from Martin Marietta Data Systems Inc., NOMAD2 from D&B Computing Services Inc., and FACTS from Deductive Systems Ltd. Each of these systems uses a somewhat different approach, and to illustrate the varying concepts of 4GL systems the principal features of FOCUS, ACCELL and FACTS are described below.

9.3.1   FOCUS

FOCUS is perhaps the best known 4GL system for database users and has been on the market longer than most. It is an integrated DBMS product since it includes all the basic functions required by an end user of a DBMS, including data base manager, a query/update language, a sophisticated report writer, graphical routines and other utilities, and data dictionary facilities.

The FOCUS database manager is capable of reading a wide variety of foreign data sources including files from a number of commercial DBMSs (e.g. IMS, TOTAL, IDMS and ADABAS). The system has its own data model, which is called the *shared-relational* structure, which might be considered as a combination of all three popular models (hierarchical, network and relational). As far as relational structures go, FOCUS databases can be created as tables which can then be logically linked using a type of join operator to produce composite tables. Files other than FOCUS shared-relational databases may participate in the relational operations. Any field in a FOCUS shared-relational file can be indexed.

End users may access a FOCUS database concurrently. In concurrent mode, end user requests are dealt with by a central FOCUS supervising program that processes the requests and returns the responses to the end user's copy of FOCUS. The concurrency is transparent, absolving the end user of the responsibility of understanding and managing the complexities of data sharing and access control. The system provides quite sophisticated data protection mechanisms, with data access security granularity can be at the file, segment, field, or field value level. That is, access constraints may be specified at any of these levels

The feature that distinguishes FOCUS from the more traditional DBMS products (especially network and hierarchical systems) is its highly non-procedural query language. With this 4GL, considerably less knowledge of the database structures, and very little programming expertise is required to generate applications. While the strength of this language lies in its querying capability, it can also be used to update a database. In addition, FOCUS provides a database editor to simplify the process of updating fields in a file without writing a detailed program. A transaction construct is also available.

FOCUS provides a host language interface for its query language, which allows programs written in COBOL, FORTRAN, PL/1 and assembler to access FOCUS databases. Most of the fourth generation language constructs are available to the programmer, and this approach is intended for the implementation of applications which demand better performance than is possible with FOCUS 4GL programs.

The report-writing capabilities of FOCUS are quite sophisticated and can significantly reduce the time it takes to produce a formatted report. Of course, any data request will be automatically formatted according to a set of defaults, but customised reports can be produced with full control page headings and footings, column positioning, grand totals, etc. The graphical routines include bar charts, histograms, connected point plots, pie charts and scatter diagrams. Graphical output can be refined via the 4GL.

9.3.2   ACCELL

ACCELL from Unify Corporation is a relative newcomer to the 4GL market. It is described as an integrated development system and incorporates an applications generator, a 4GL, and a relational database. The applications generator is an interactive, menu-driven system while the 4GL is built around standard SQL. The 4GL allows the more experienced user to build on applications produced by the generator.

The architecture of the relational database component is based on that of the Unify DBMS which has been around for some years and which has a particularly good reputation for efficient transaction processing under Unix. The 'PathFinder' architecture of the Unify DBMS provides several access methods in addition to the usual B-tree indexes, and ACCELL claims to be able to automatically select the most efficient method for any task. ACCELL is also very strong in the areas of data integrity and security. It provides a lock manager which offers concurrency control and locking consistency, with a granularity at the record level. It is also one of the few systems to offer automatic referential integrity, which it provides via its integrated data dictionary.

The fact that it is built on top of an efficient relational DBMS is likely to give ACCELL rather better performance than other 4GLs, particularly in applications requiring large databases.

9.3.3   The FACT system

The FACT system from Deductive Systems Ltd. is a commercial product based on the work of McGregor and his co-workers at the University of Strathclyde. The principle idea behind the system, namely that of a *generic associative network*, is described in a number of published papers (McGregor et al., 1976; McGregor and Malone, 1982).

FACT actually claims to be a *fifth* generation language, which minimises the requirement for a user to have prior knowledge of the structure of the database he wishes to query. The system combines rule-based inference with relational database capabilities, and incorporates a novel indexing technique which the designers call the Generic Associative Technique (GAT). GAT is supported by specialised hardware, a device called the *Generic Associative Memory* (GAM) which has been developed at the University of Strathclyde.

The key to this system lies in the fact that it automatically maintains a comprehensive description of the entities and inter-relationships in each database. The existence of this 'generic data structure' means that a user does not need to know how the data is laid out in the tables in order to use it effectively. Nor does he have to explicitly index the data. Indexing is handled transparently through 'generic association'. The resulting associative network is directly implementable as an electronic circuit, and can provide flexible access to a database held as a semantic network. The circuit is used to expand the range of terms stated in a query, and to access information by deduction using set membership linkages.

The FACT system treats all information in the same manner, so that there is no difference in terms of storage or access method between database schema and actual data. Thus there is no separate data dictionary as in most other systems. This feature, coupled with the automatic deduction capabilities gives the system a unique degree of data independence.

One of the most interesting aspects of the FACT system is the GAM. This is a customised chip designed to accelerate the generic associative technique, and it can be incorporated into a conventional computer system. If the chip has a major influence on the speed of operations then the FACT system may go a long way towards making expert system functionality immediately and efficiently available in a database environment.

9.4   DATABASE MACHINES

By the term database machine we mean any specialised hardware which is designed to enhance the performance of database operations. The subject has been investigated from many different angles for many years, but commercially available database machines have evolved comparatively slowly. Any developments which have been made have been somewhat overshadowed by developments in software, particularly in the areas of query optimisation. That is, the development of sophisticated software query optimisers, coupled with new techniques for physical storage organisation, have to some extent reduced the need for expensive hardware enhancements. However, database machines are beginning to fulfil some of their early promise and there are several products on the market which are worthy of serious consideration. These products fall into two broad classes of configuration, associative memories and back-end database processors and these are described in detail below.

We also describe the significance of two relatively new computer architectures for database management. These are the RISC (Reduced Instruction Set Computers) architecture and parallel architectures. We end the chapter with a discussion of mass storage media.

9.4.1   Associative memories

The first step in constructing a database machine is to move input/output processing to an intelligent device controller which has its own memory and processing capability. Thus some hardware search logic may be applied to the data directly as it is read from disc, thereby reducing the amount of processing that must be done by the host computer. Recall from Chapter 6 that in a conventional database system the process of retrieving a record given a set of attribute values involves the use of data structures (such as indexes) which map the attribute values onto record addresses. Index construction and maintenance is a large and expensive overhead in database management systems. Associative memories remove the need for such structures in that they accept *logical* requests for data from the host computer.

In this category of database machine there are many experimental systems under development at universities throughout the world, but only the CAFS (Content Addressable Filestore) system from ICL appears to be available commercially . CAFS (Mitchell; 1976) is a filter device which is installed between an ICL host computer and the normal back-end disc system. The basic architecture is illustrated in Figure 9.1.

There are 16 key registers each of which can hold an attribute name and value. Each comparator determines its attribute by comparing the attribute name with those in the multiplexed data stream coming from up to 12 disc tracks. Whenever the correct attribute is located in the data stream, the comparison for the value part begins. The comparator results are sent to latches where the comparison requested in the user query is stored and the outcome of the key register comparison is compared with it. If a match is obtained the result is reported to the search evaluation unit. This unit combines individual comparisons into an overall query evaluation or to several evaluations for different queries. That is, the device can process several distinct user queries in parallel. The selection conditions can be quite complex and can involve nested Boolean expressions

ICL claim a search rate with CAFS of close to a megabyte per second, and its use has produced significant increases in productivity in a variety of applications (Addis, 1982). Babb (1979) describes two extensions to the CAFS architecture which can enhance the efficiency of projection and join operations.

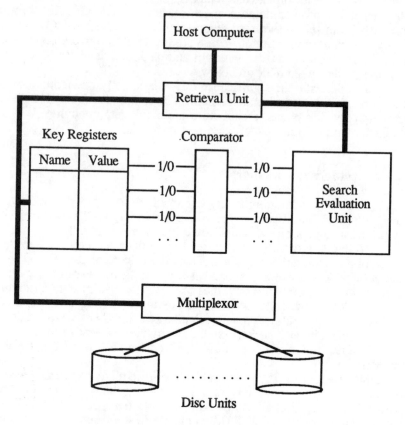

Figure 9.1   CAFS architecture

9.4.2   Back-end database machines

With back-end database machines the database management system is moved out of the computer with which the end users interact, and into a dedicated machine. This back-end machine may be a conventional computer, but often it will have special features suited to database management. In this category we shall describe in detail two specially built back-end systems which have been commercially successful over the past few years, namely the Intelligent Database Machine (IDM500) from Britton Lee Corporation, and the Data Base Computer (DBC1012) of Teradata Corporation. Other systems worthy of mention include the Cambex PCM (a software back-end system for IBM hosts developed by Software AG, the vendor of the ADABAS relational DBMS), and Amperif (a software back-end for the Unisys 1100 series which executes a form of relational query language (RQL) code).

Britton Lee's IDM500

The IDM architecture is based on DEC's minicomputers (PDP, VAX). The added components are the database accelerator and RAM cache units (Figure 9.2). The database accelerator performs fast access path searches and other DBMS primitives using B-trees for indexing. The RAM cache buffers disc I/O blocks and stores program code and data to process user queries. The I/O channel unit provides an interface between the host computer and the back-end system. The architecture is primarily aimed at fast execution of selection-type queries.

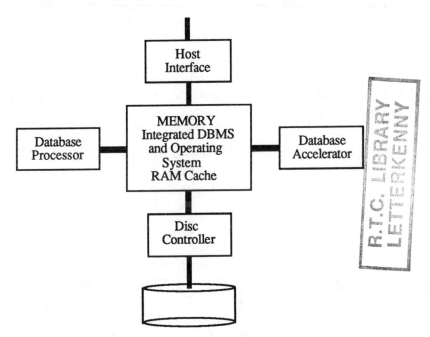

Figure 9.2   IDM architecture

Input to the IDM is a user request phrased in some high level query language such as SQL, or an IDM-specific language called IDL (Intelligent Database Language) which is similar to INGRES QUEL. Parsing of queries is performed on the host and the parse trees are passed to the IDM. Thus the software of the host machine is responsible for:

1. Accepting a user request and translating it into the appropriate encoded form.
2. Sending the encoded request to the IDM for execution.
3. Receiving the result back from the IDM.
4. Formatting and displaying the results to the user.

The IDM is responsible for the following functions:

1. Relational data management including query optimisation.

2. Data definition: databases, relations, views and indexes can be created and modified.
3. Transaction processing and concurrency control. The commands BEGIN TRANSACTION, END TRANSACTION, and ABORT TRANSACTION are provided.
4. Transaction logging (through a journal file) and recovery.
5. Data security and access control.

The IDM can support up to 32 gigabytes of on-line data. Britton Lee claims that the use of IDM can reduce host CPU usage by up to 90 per cent, and that database management functions can be accomplished in a third of the time needed on a conventional host-resident DBMS.

The Teradata DBC1012

The Teradata DBC1012 (Figure 9.3) is a database machine geared for IBM mainframes and marketed as an alternative to IBM's DBMS products.

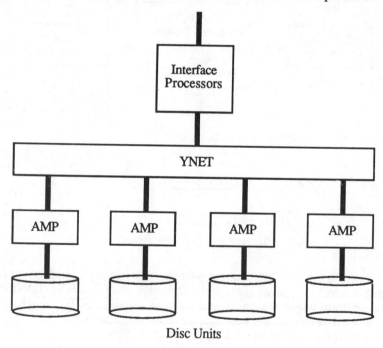

Figure 9.3   DBC1012 architecture

The interface processors are attached to the host through block multiplexer channels. There are four access module processors (AMPs) which are built around the Intel 16-bit 8086 microprocessor, and each AMP has its own dedicated 475 megabyte Winchester disc unit. The processors are interconnected through a high-speed logic lattice called YNet. The system can expand to a chain of 1,024 processors on YNet giving a total potential storage capacity of around 500 gigabytes. A database is distributed as evenly as possible over the storage units to maximise potential parallelism.

The DBC1012 can run on all IBM hosts with the MVS operating system. Teradata claim superiority of their system, in terms of performance, over IBM's IMS and DB2 software DBMSs. The system provides its own version of SQL which is called TEQUEL.

9.4.3 RISC architecture

Reduced Instruction Set Computer (RISC) architecture has become increasingly popular over the past few years, and there are now a significant number of machines based on this architecture ranging from the microcomputer level to the super-minicomputer level. The design of RISC-based processors differs considerably from one manufacture to another, but there are a number of commonly accepted properties which may be summarised as follows:

1. RISC machines execute one instruction per clock cycle. Analysis of computer programs shows that the most heavily used instructions are the primitives. With correct processor design, these primitives can be made to run in a single clock cycle, thereby simplifying pipelining, interrupts, and many other microprocessor functions. Providing only primitive instructions however, makes life much more difficult for systems programmers such as compiler writers who have a considerably reduced instruction set with which to work.
2. RISC machines use a fixed format for instructions which makes decoding easier, and facilitates hardwiring of the instructions. Thus microcode is avoided and speed is increased.
3. RISC machines are based on a load/store architecture. This means that the only instructions that are concerned with memory are simple load or store instructions. All other manipulations take place within the microprocessors. This requires a large number of on-chip registers, a common feature of RISC-based CPUs.

The RISC idea has had a huge impact on computer architecture and a number of companies are now marketing RISC machines which are considerably less expensive and faster than comparable machines based on traditional architecture. Some of the most successful of these RISC machines are those marketed by Pyramid Technology.

The Pyramid computers

The Pyramid Technology 9000 series is the second generation of superminis from this company based on an advanced RISC (Reduced Instruction Set Computer) architecture, and incorporating a high-speed intelligent I/O subsystem. These computers are particularly well-suited for on-line transaction processing and a large number of commercial database management systems are available for them, including ORACLE, INGRES and Informix. Also, Britton Lee provide data management software which enables Pyramid machines to be connected to their intelligent database machine, the IDM500. Pyramid supply optimising compilers for C, FORTRAN, Pascal and COBOL. Also available are an EMACS screen oriented editor, and a GKS graphics package.

The 9820 model incorporates dual symmetric RISC processors. Each CPU contains 528 32-bit registers, 16 Kbyte instruction caches, 64 Kbyte data caches, and a high-speed arithmetic accelerator unit to speed floating point operations. Each 9820 features a 5-MIP I/O processor and 14 parallel DMA channels to provide an aggregate I/O throughput of 11 gigabytes per second. The IOP disc controller supports up to four Pyramid disc drives each with a transfer rate of 2.5 megabytes per second. Overlapped seeks and rotational position sensing allow high transaction rates in multiple drive configurations. Main memory may be configured from 16 to 128 megabytes.

The 9280 CPUs communicate with main memory and with the IOP over a 40 megabyte per second, 32-bit XTEND bus. Since all of Pyramid's I/O and communications controllers have their own intelligent processors, the XTEND bus transfers only short, high-level messages between the CPUs and controllers. This message-based communication reduces bus activity and prevents I/O bottlenecks.

The 9820 includes a virtual disc facility which provides a transparent mapping between logical and physical disc volumes. You can combine several physical drives into one logical disc, allowing large databases to span multiple drives. Users can also increase the performance of disc I/O by evenly partitioning file access over several physical drives. The virtual disc facility also allows for the allocation of a portion of main memory to act as a virtual disc location for frequently accessed files or indexes. The system can be expanded to incorporate up to four Pyramid disc drives and a maximum system can support around 15 Gigabytes of disc storage.

9.4.4 Parallel architectures

There is little doubt that the future of computing lies, to a large extent, with parallel computers. Major performance improvements in single-CPU machines cannot be expected in the near future, as such machines are reaching fundamental physical limits. During the last decade, a number of different parallel architectures have been introduced, ranging from multiprocessing machines best suited to commercial transaction processing, to highly-parallel engines aimed at large-scale scientific calculations.

The advent of parallel processing as a commercially practical architecture has had, and will continue to have, a significant influence on relational database management. Relational database transactions are typically more CPU intensive than those of network or hierarchical systems where the access paths are well-defined and the physical structure of the database is designed to optimise path lengths. The almost unlimited flexibility provided by relational systems however, allows users to formulate complex queries which can cause excessive workloads and slow throughput for even the most powerful single-processor machines. This is, of course, particularly the case in multi-user environments. In a typical multi-user relational DBMS, transactions are handled by individual code modules assigned to each user. These user modules are natural candidates for concurrent execution in a parallel architecture. Also, if the database is stored on more than one disc, I/O bottlenecks can be significantly reduced if multiple disc operations can be carried out in parallel.

The Sequent computers

The Balance 8000 and Balance 21000 from Sequent Computer Systems Inc. are parallel computers with a variable number of 32-bit microprocessors sharing a common memory pool and a single copy of DYNIX, an enhanced version of UNIX™. The B8000 can have between two and twelve processors (two processors per board) giving a performance range of 1.4 to 8.4 MIPS (millions of instructions per second), and can support up to 96 users. The B21000 can have between four and thirty processors yielding between 2.8 and 21 MIPS, and supporting up to 256 users.

The processors are National Semiconductor 32032 microprocessors, each supported by a Floating Point Unit, Memory Management Unit and 8 Kbyte cache. The shared memory pool consists of up to 48 megabytes for the B21000, of which 28 megabytes is used by DYNIX and 4 megabytes for I/O. There is a 32-bit common system bus with a data transfer rate of up to 26.7 megabytes/second.

DYNIX is Sequent's enhanced version of UNIX™ which supports both 4.2BSD and System V applications. It makes the parallel architecture transparent to user software while automatically balancing the load across the multiple processors for maximum efficiency.

Sequent supply compilers for a large number of languages including C, FORTRAN 77, and Pascal, and a VERDIX ADA Development System (VADS) is also available. A variety of tools, including a subroutine library, provide the user with intimate control over the use of parallelism, from fine grain parallelism at the program statement level to coarse grain parallelism at the program level. At least four major relational data management systems are available for the Sequent computers: ORACLE, INGRES, Informix and Unify.

9.4.5 Mass storage media

In recent years intelligence has been migrating from the CPU to the disc storage unit which is being transformed from an isolated device into an intelligent, more modular subsystem. However, only optical technology has begun to seriously challenge magnetic discs as the principal mass storage medium for database (and all other) applications. Other promising electronic storage technologies such as charged-coupled devices (CCDs) and electronic beam-addressable memory have slipped into obscurity. After an initial flurry of expectation, magnetic bubble memories ran into production problems and have not yet challenged the magnetic disc market. A bubble memory stores data in the form of magnetic regions that are rotated by a magnetic field. Bubble detection and generation mechanisms are the equivalent of the read/write heads found in magnetic disc technology. Unlike discs there are no mechanical moving parts, and the advantages of bubble memories are therefore: greater reliability, smaller physical size and faster access times. Disadvantages of current bubble devices are that capacities are relatively small and data transfer rates low.

Optical disc technology has already opened up a wide range of new capabilities and novel applications. A typical optical disc records information in the form of pits or bubbles which have been etched by a laser. Resolution can be exceptionally high leading to large storage capacities. Advantages over magnetic media are often said to include high capacity, removability, and the ability to store images. However, optical drives are still slower than the best high capacity magnetic disc drives, and the longevity and reliability of optical media have yet to be proved. Optical products which have appeared on the market over the last few years range from multi-gigabyte write-once, read-many (WORM) discs intended mainly for archival purposes to smaller, easily replicable read-only discs based on video-disc and audio-disc technologies. The biggest disadvantages of the large WORM discs have been a lack of standards and high prices. Erasable optical technology is still at the laboratory development stage, although some prototypes have been shown in public by Hitachi and others.

Although all types of magnetic storage will feel the impact of optical memory systems, it is the small read-only discs which are likely to have the greatest impact over the next few years. These will challenge the low-capacity (less than 30 megabyte) end of the market, with easily replicable, inexpensive, read-only optical discs emerging as an alternative to some online database services. CD-ROM is, of course, an optical technology and as a read-only device it has applications as a publishing or reference tool where the data is relatively static, and where locations are widely distributed making networking expensive and difficult. CD-ROMs can be configured inexpensively as part of a larger system. Currently available CD-ROMs hold around 550 megabytes of digital data.

As the demand for increased magnetic disc recording densities escalates most of the industry is adhering to the proven longitudinal recording techniques, rather than adopting *vertical* recording methods. Longitudinal recording orients the magnetised areas that define each bit end-to-end; vertical recording increases surface densities by standing them up side by side. Unfortunately high density vertical recording works best with associated technologies which are both difficult and expensive to produce: thin-film media and very low-flying heads. Despite the fact that it is a very promising technology, relatively few companies are developing vertical magnetic media, and in terms of density, the best vertical technology still lags behind optical media.

In conclusion one may confidently say that large-capacity Winchester discs are unlikely to be superseded by optical technology, or any other, for quite some time. Winchester disc packs, developed by IBM during the 1970s, have the read/write heads and disc surfaces in a sealed unit thereby eliminating the problems of contamination and increasing reliability. Also, the heads are able to float close to the surface of the disc, permitting higher recording densities (currently up to 1,000 tracks per inch). With the growing capacities and capabilities of Winchesters, the fixed disc drives are evolving to fit new situations and are not being pushed aside by newer technologies. For applications in which storage requirements are large and access times are critical there are specially designed, high-end Winchester drives such as the Atlas Series marketed by Alpha Data. All Atlas drives use multiple heads and in the case of the 520 megabyte model, 76 heads move over four disc platters giving access times reported by the company to be less than 18 msec. Mini-Winchester drives have also been developed (3.5 and 5.25 inch diameters) which are suitable for attaching to microcomputers.

APPENDIX 1

An Overview of Modula-2

A1.1 INTRODUCTION

The following is not a comprehensive description of Modula-2. For that the reader is referred to the book by Wirth (1982), or that of Welsh and Elder (1987). Rather, this appendix describes those features of Modula-2 which have been used in this book to illustrate various aspects of Database Technology. In particular, we concentrate on the facilities in the language for type definition and modularity. The description should prove useful to someone already familiar with a well-structured language such as Pascal who wishes to become acquainted with Modula-2.

In presenting the syntax of the language we shall use the EBNF notation (Extended Backus-Naur Formalism) of Wirth. In this notation, square brackets [] denote that the enclosed object is optional, while chain brackets { } denote repetition (possibly zero times). Special symbols are enclosed in quotation marks.

A1.2 THE VOCABULARY OF MODULA-2

The vocabulary of Modula-2 consists of letters, digits and special symbols. A letter may be any of the 26 letters of the Roman alphabet in either upper-case or lower-case form:

letter = *'A'* | *'B'* | *'C'* | *'D'* | *'E'* | *'F'* | *'G'* | *'H'* | *'I'* | *'J'* | *'K'* |
'L' | *'M'* | *'N'* | *'O'* | *'P'* | *'Q'* | *'R'* | *'S'* | *'T'* | *'U'* | *'V'* |
'W' | *'X'* | *'Y'* | *'Z'* | *'a'* | *'b'* | *'c'* | *'d'* | *'e'* | *'f'* | *'g'* |
'h' | *'i'* | *'j'* | *'k'* | *'l'* | *'m'* | *'n'* | *'o'* | *'p'* | *'q'* | *'r'* | *'s'* |
't' | *'u'* | *'v'* | *'w'* | *'x'* | *'y'* | *'z'*.

A digit may be any one of the ten Arabic digits:

digit = *'0'* | *'1'* | *'2'* | *'3'* | *'4'* | *'5'* | *'6'* | *'7'* | *'8'* | *'9'*.

235

Sentences in the language are then constructed from this vocabulary according to the following syntax rules.

1. *Identifiers* are sequences of letters and digits in which the first character must be a letter:

    identifier = letter { letter | digit }.

    A distinction is made between upper and lower case letters. For example, the following identifiers are valid and considered distinct:

    someone   SomeOne   SOMEONE

    Certain upper case identifiers, known as standard identifiers, are predeclared in every Modula-2 implementation. These denote standard quantities and facilities provided by the language, such as data types and special functions. The following is a list of standard identifiers:

ABS	EXCL	INTEGER	ORD
BITSET	FALSE	LONGINT	PROC
BOOLEAN	FLOAT	LONGREAL	REAL
CAP	HALT	MAX	SIZE
CARDINAL	HIGH	MIN	TRUE
CHAR	INC	NIL	TRUNC
CHR	INCL	ODD	VAL
DEC			

2. *Numbers* may be integer constants or real constants. An integer constant is a sequence of digits. If the sequence ends with the letter B it denotes an octal constant, while if it ends with the letter H, it is a hexadecimal constant. Integer constants followed by the letter C denote the *character* with the specified (octal) ordinal number.

    number = *integer-constant | real-constant*
    integer-constant = *digit { digit }*
    | octal-digit { octal-digit} ('B' | 'C')
    | digit { hex-digit } 'H'.
    octal-digit = *'0' | '1' | '2' | '3' | '4' | '5'*
    | '6' | '7'
    digit = *octal-digit | '8' | '9'*
    hex-digit = *digit | 'A' | 'B' | 'C' | 'D' | 'E'*
    | 'F'
    real-constant = *digit { digit } '.' { digit }*
    [scale-factor]
    scale-factor = *'E' ['+' | '-'] digit { digit }*

Examples of valid integer constants are:

    38   0   99999   123B   6BH   0BEACH

Examples of valid real constants are:

    1.1   10.   7.06E15   2.E10   3.142E-21

3. *Strings* are sequences of characters enclosed in either single or double quote marks. The opening and closing marks must be the same and that mark cannot occur in the string. Some examples of strings are:

> "Hello!"
>
> "I'm your new neighbour."
>
> 'He said, "Come in", and opened the door wide.'

A single character string is of type CHAR.

4. Modula-2 has quite a large number of *special symbols* and *reserved words*. The reserved words must consist of capital letters and cannot be used as identifiers.

special-symbol =
'+' | '-' | '*' | '/' | ':=' | '&' | '.' | ',' | ';' | '(' | '[' | '{' | '^' |
'=' | '#' | '<' | '>' | '<>' | '<=' | '>=' | '..' | ':' | ')' | ']' | '}' | '|' |
'AND' | 'ARRAY' | 'BEGIN' | 'BY' | 'CASE' | 'CONST' |
'DEFINITION' | 'DIV' | 'DO' | 'ELSE' | 'ELSIF' | 'END' | 'EXIT' |
'EXPORT' | 'FOR' | 'FROM' | 'IF' | 'IMPLEMENTATION' |
'IMPORT' | 'IN' | 'LOOP' | 'MOD' | 'MODULE' | 'NOT' | 'OF' |
'OR' | 'POINTER' | 'PROCEDURE' | 'QUALIFIED' | 'RECORD' |
'REPEAT' | 'RETURN' | 'SET' | 'THEN' | 'TO' | 'TYPE' |
'UNTIL' | 'VAR' | 'WHILE' | 'WITH'.

5. *Comments* are character sequences deliminated by the brackets (* and *). (Chain brackets { and } cannot be used as comment delimiters.) Comments may be inserted between any two symbols in a program and have no effect on the meaning of the program.

A1.3   BASIC PROGRAM STRUCTURE

In Modula-2 an executable program is called a *program module*, which is formally defined as follows:

ProgramModule = 'MODULE' *identifier* [*priority*] ';'
    {*import-list*';'} *block identifier* '.'.
import-list = ['FROM' *identifier*] 'IMPORT' *identifier-list*.
identifier-list = *identifier* {',' *identifier*}

That is, a program module consists of a heading which names the module and specifies the names of imported objects and operations. This is followed by a *block* which is followed by an *identifier* and the module is terminated by a *period*.

A block is made up of a *declaration part* and a *statement part* as defined by the following syntax:

block = *declaration-part statement-part* 'END'.
declaration-part = {*declaration*}.

declaration = constant-declaration-part / type-declaration-part /
variable-declaration-part / procedure-declaration ';' /
module-declaration ';'.
statement-part = ['BEGIN' statement-sequence]

Every identifier occurring in a Modula-2 program must be introduced by a declaration unless it is a standard identifier (defined above). Declarations serve to specify certain permanent properties of the object which the identifier represents, such as whether it is a constant, a type, a variable, a procedure, or a module. An identifier may be qualified, in which case it is prefixed by another identifier which designates the module in which the qualified identifier is defined:

qualified-identifier = identifier { '.' identifier }.

A1.4   DATA TYPES AND DECLARATIONS

A1.4.1   Constant declarations

A constant declaration associates an identifier with a constant value.

constant-declaration-part = 'CONST' { constant-declaration ';' }.
constant-declaration = identifier '=' constant-expression.

A constant-expression is an expression in which all the operands are themselves constants (expressions will be considered in more detail below). Some simple examples of constant declarations are:

```
CONST
    Pi = 3.1415926 ;
    Order = 10 ;
    Limit = 2*Order + 1 ;
    FormFeed = 014C ;
    MyName = 'John Hughes' ;
```

A1.4.2   Type declarations

A data type defines a set of values. Modula-2, in common with most other high-level programming languages requires that every data item must have a single type associated with it, which determines the range of values that it may take and range of operations which may be applied to it.

type-declaration-part = 'TYPE' {type-declaration ';' }.
type-declaration = identifier '=' type.
type = simple-type / structured-type / pointer-type / procedure-type.
simple-type = qualified-identifier / subrange-type / enumerated-type.
structured-type = array-type / record-type / set-type.

The following simple types are predeclared and are denoted by standard identifiers:

1. INTEGER

   A variable of type INTEGER assumes as values whole numbers in the implementation-defined range, MinInt to MaxInt. Modula-2 defines a number of arithmetic operators which take integer operands and return integer results. These are:

+	addition
-	subtraction
*	multiplication
DIV	division with truncation
MOD	modulo (remainder after division)

   In addition + and - may be used as prefix operators (+A and -A) to denote sign identity and sign inversion.

2. CARDINAL

   A variable of type CARDINAL assumes as values the whole numbers in the range 0 to the implementation-defined maximum, MaxCard. Operators applicable to variables of type CARDINAL are the same as for the type INTEGER.

3. BOOLEAN

   A variable of type BOOLEAN may assume only the values TRUE or FALSE. Operators which take BOOLEAN values as operands and produce a BOOLEAN result are:

AND	logical *and* (also denoted by &)
OR	logical *or*
NOT	logical *not*

   BOOLEAN values may also be produced by applying *relational operators* to operands of other types. Modula-2 provides the following relational operators:

   relational-operator = '=' | '<>' | '#' | '<' | '>' | '<=' | '>=' | 'IN'.

4. CHAR

   A variable of type CHAR may assume values of the implementation-defined character set. As noted earlier, a value of type CHAR is denoted by either a string of length one, or by the octal-char notation. Examples are:

   'A'   '%'   '?'   '6'   '+'   014C

5. REAL

   A variable of type REAL may assume as values real numbers in some implementation-defined range. The arithmetic operators which take real operands and produce real results are:

+	addition
-	subtraction
*	multiplication
/	division

   As with integers, + and - may also be used as prefix operators to denote sign identity and sign inversion.

Enumerated types

An enumerated type is defined by a list of identifiers which denote the values which constitute the type. These identifiers are used as constants in the program. The values are ordered, the ordering being defined by their sequence in the enumeration.

enumerated-type = '(' identifier-list ')'.
identifier-list = identifier {', ' identifier}.

Examples of enumerated types are:

```
TYPE
    colour = (red, green, blue) ;
    DayOfWeek = (Monday, Tuesday, Wednesday, Thursday, Friday,
                    Saturday, Sunday) ;
    Suit = (Clubs, Hearts, Diamonds, Spades) ;
```

Subrange types

When a data item assumes a range of values which is a subrange of the values defined by some existing type, its type may be defined as a subrange of that host type:

subrange-type = [host-type-identifier] '[' constant-expression '..'
constant-expression ']'.

The first constant expression defines the lower bound and the second the upper bound. The lower bound must not be greater than the upper bound. A value assigned to a variable of the subrange type must be within the specified range. All the operators applicable to operands of the host type are applicable to operands of the subrange type.

Examples of subrange types are as follows:

```
TYPE
    itemrange = [0..Order] ;
    WorkDay = [Monday..Friday] ;
    LowerCaseLetter = ['a'..'z'] ;
```

Array types

For array types, components are of the same type and are indexed by values of an ordinal type (i.e. INTEGER, CARDINAL, CHAR, BOOLEAN, an enumerated type, or subranges of these types). Multi-dimensional array types, containing more than one index type, may also be defined.

array-type = 'ARRAY' simple-type{',' simple-type} 'OF' type.

Examples of array types are as follows:

```
TYPE
    name = ARRAY [1..30] OF CHAR ;
```

```
Rainfall  =  ARRAY DayOfWeek OF REAL ;
Board  =  ARRAY [1..8],[1..8] OF BOOLEAN ;
```

Record types

With record types, components of differing types are collected together into a unit. Each component has its own identifier, but when used in a program a component identifier must be qualified by the record name.

A record type may have a number of variant sections. In this case the first field of the section is called the tag field, and the value of this tag field indicates which variant is assumed by the section. Individual variant structures are identified by case labels which are constants of the type indicated by the tag field.

record-type = 'RECORD' field-list-sequence 'END'.
field-list-sequence = field-list {';' field-list}.
field-list = [fixed-part | variant-part].
fixed-part = identifier-list ':' type.
variant-part = 'CASE' [tag-field] ':' qualified-identifier 'OF'
            variant {'|' variant} ['ELSE' field-list-sequence]
            'END'.
tag-field = identifier.
variant = [case-label-list ':' field-list-sequence].
case-label-list = case-labels {',' case-labels}.
case-labels = constant-expression ['..' constant-expression].

An example of a record type containing a variant part is as follows:

```
TYPE
    Citizenship = (National, Alien) ;
    person  =    RECORD
                    Name : ARRAY [1..30] OF CHAR ;
                    Address : ARRAY [1..50] OF CHAR ;
                    Sex : (Male, Female) ;
                    DateOfBirth :   RECORD
                                        Day : [1..31] ;
                                        Month : [1..12] ;
                                        Year : [1900..1987];
                                    END ;
                    CASE Origin : Citizenship OF
                        National : PlaceOfBirth : ARRAY [1..30] OF CHAR ;
                        Alien :
                    END
                END ;
```

Set types

A set is an unordered collection of values chosen from the same base type. The domain of a set type is therefore the set of all sets which may be constructed from the base type (the power set of the base type). In Modula-2 the base type must be a subrange type, $[0..N-1]$, of the type CARDINAL, or an enumerated type with at most N values, where N is an implementation-defined constant.

set-type = 'SET' 'OF' simple-type ;

Examples of set type declarations are as follows:

```
TYPE
    Mixture = SET OF Colour ;
    Facilities = (television, telephone, restaurant, tennis, sauna,
                    swimming) ;
    Offered  = SET OF Facilities ;
```

The standard type BITSET is defined as follows:

```
TYPE
    BITSET = SET OF [0..W-1] ;
```

where W is an implementation defined constant (usually the wordsize of the computer).

Variables of the same set type may be combined using set operators. The symbols +,-,*, and / denote respectively the union, difference, intersection, and symmetrical set difference. The operator IN may be used to determine if a value is contained in a set instance.

Pointer types

All of the data types discussed so far describe static data structures. A dynamic data structure is one that can change during the lifetime of a program. That is, both the number of components and the relationships among them may change during the course of its existence, under program control. Such dynamic data structures may be created and managed in Modula-2 by the use of pointer types. Objects of a pointer type may be used to 'point to' (or address) objects of other types in main memory.

pointer-type = 'POINTER' 'TO' type.

A pointer variable may also assume the value NIL, whereby it points to no variable.

An example of a pointer type is as follows:

```
TYPE
    FamilyTree  =  POINTER TO PersonNode ;
    PersonNode  =  RECORD
                        name : ARRAY [1..30] OF CHAR ;
                        dateofbirth : datetype ;
                        father, mother : FamilyTree ;
                    END ;
```

Procedure types

In Modula-2 a variable may have a procedure type, and thereby may be assigned to actual procedure identifiers.

procedure-type = 'PROCEDURE' [formal-type-list [':' result-type]].

formal-type-list = '(' [[VAR] formal-type
{',' [VAR] formal-type}] ')'.
formal-type = type-identifier | 'ARRAY' 'OF' type-identifier.
result-type = type-identifier.

The standard type PROC denotes a parameterless procedure.
As an example of a procedure type, consider the following declaration:

```
TYPE
    TrigFunction = PROCEDURE (REAL) : REAL ;
```

The type TrigFunction represents all function procedures which have one
formal REAL value parameter and which return a REAL result.

A1.4.3   Variable declarations

Variable declarations introduce variables and associate with them a unique
identifier and a fixed data type. Such declarations are grouped into one or
more variable declaration parts which are defined as follows:

variable-declaration-part = 'VAR' {variable-declaration ';'}.
variable-declaration = identifier-list ':' type.

Examples of variable declarations are:

```
VAR
    Today : DayOfWeek ;
    Absent : BOOLEAN ;
    Xvalue, Yvalue : REAL ;
```

A1.5   STATEMENTS, EXPRESSIONS AND ASSIGNMENTS

The manipulation which a program performs on its data items is defined by
its *statement-part*. The *statement-part* defines the actions to be carried out as
a sequence of statements:

statement-part = ['BEGIN' statement-sequence].
statement-sequence = statement {';' statement}.

Modula-2 provides both simple and structured statements. Simple statements are not composed of any parts which are themselves statements.
Structured statements describe composite actions in terms of other component statements and are used to express sequencing, and conditional, selec-
tive and repetitive execution.

statement = simple-statement | structured-statement.
simple-statement = [assignment-statement | procedure-statement |
exit-statement | return-statement].
structured-statement = if-statement | case-statement | while-statement |
repeat-statement | loop-statement |
for-statement | with-statement.

Note that a statement may be empty, in which case it denotes that no action is to be taken. The procedure statement and return statement will be considered in Section A1.6. All other statement forms are described below.

An *assignment-statement* is used to assign a particular value to a variable, the value being specified by means of an *expression*, whose form we first consider.

A1.5.1   Expressions

An *expression* is a rule for the computation of a value, and consists of operands and operators. An operand may be a literal constant or a *designator*. A designator is an identifier (possibly qualified) referring to a constant, variable or procedure and it may be followed by selectors if the designated object is a component of a structured object:

designator = qualified-identifier { '.' identifier | '[' expression-list ']' |
'^'} .

expression-list = expression {',' expression}.

For an array structure A, the designator A[*e*] denotes the current value of the component of A whose index is given by the current value of the expression *e*. For multi-dimensional arrays an expression is required for each dimension in order to designate a specific element. If the structure is a record R, then the designator R.*f* denotes the current value of field *f* in record R. For a pointer variable P, the designator P^ denotes the current value of the variable which is referenced by P.

If the object is a function procedure, a designator without a parameter list refers to that procedure. If the procedure name is followed by an actual parameter list (possibly empty), then the designator implies a call of the procedure and refers to the value returned.

The syntax of expressions and the operator precedence rules governing their evaluation are defined by the following syntax rules:

expression = simple-expression[relational-operator simple-expression].
simple-expression = ['+' | '-'} term {addition-operator term}.
term = factor {multiplication-operator factor}.
factor = designator | number | string | constant-identifier |set |
    '(' expression ')' | 'NOT' factor.
relational-operator = '=' | '<>' | '#' | '<' | '>' | '<=' | '>=' | 'IN'.
addition-operator = '+' | '-' | 'OR'.
multiplication-operator = '' | '/' | 'DIV' | 'MOD' | 'AND' | '&'.*

A1.5.2   Assignment statements

The assignment-statement has the form:

assignment-statement = designator ':=' expression

The symbol ':=' is known as the assignment operator and is pronounced 'becomes'. The designator denotes a variable, and the effect of executing the assignment statement is to evaluate the expression to the right of the assignment operator, and to assign the resultant value to the designator on the left. The type of the variable (say T_1) must be *assignment compatible* with the type of the expression (T_2). This means that one of the following conditions must hold:

1. T_1 and T_2 are the same named data type.
2. T_1 is a subrange type of T_2, or T_2 is a subrange type of T_1, or both are subrange types of the same type.
3. T_1 and T_2 may be any combination of INTEGER and CARDINAL, or subranges of these types, provided that the expression value lies within the permitted range of values of the variable.

A1.5.3   The if statement

The syntax for the if statement in Modula-2 is as follows:

if-statement = 'IF' expression 'THEN' statement-sequence
 {'ELSIF' expression 'THEN' statement-sequence}
 ['ELSE' statement-sequence]
 'END'

The expressions which follow the IF or ELSIF keywords must yield a BOOLEAN result. If ELSIF clauses are present then the expressions following the IF and ELSIF clauses are evaluated in order of appearance until one yields the value TRUE, in which case the associated statement-sequence is executed. If none of the expressions is TRUE and an ELSE clause is present, then the statement sequence following ELSE is executed.
    Examples of if-statements are:

```
IF ch = EOL THEN EndOfLine := TRUE END

IF NOT finished THEN WriteChar(ch)
ELSE WriteString('End of data')
END

IF ch = 'I' THEN n := 1
ELSIF ch = 'V' THEN n := 5
ELSIF ch = 'X' THEN n := 10
ELSIF ch = 'L' THEN n := 50
END
```

A1.5.4   The case statement

The case statement has the following syntax in Modula-2:

case-statement = 'CASE' expression 'OF'case-limb {'|' case-limb}
 ['ELSE' statement-sequence] 'END'.
case-limb = [case-label-list ':' statement-sequence].

case-label-list = case-labels {',' case-labels}.
case-labels = constant-expression ['..' constant-expression].

The expression following the CASE keyword is known as the selector and must yield a value of an ordinal type. The constant expressions which prefix the statement sequence in each case limb are known as case labels, and their type must be compatible with the type of the selector. No value must occur more than once in the case label lists.

The action of a case statement is to evaluate the selector expression and then execute the statement sequence whose case label list contains the resulting value. If the value of the selector expression does not occur as a case label and an ELSE clause is present, then the statement sequence following ELSE is executed, otherwise an exception occurs.

An example of a case statement is as follows:

```
CASE ch OF
    'I'   : n := 1 ;
    'V'   : n := 5 ;
    'X'   : n := 10 ;
    'L'   : n := 50
END
```

A1.5.5   The while statement

The while statement specifies the repeated execution of a statement sequence depending on the value of a Boolean expression. Its syntax is:

*while-statement = 'WHILE' expression 'DO' statement-sequence
                    'END'.*

The expression following the WHILE keyword must produce a value of type BOOLEAN. The action of a while statement is as follows. The expression is repeatedly evaluated, and while it remains true, the statement sequence following the DO keyword is executed after each expression evaluation. The repeated execution of the statement sequence terminates as soon as the value of the expression becomes false.

Examples are:

```
WHILE ch <> EOL DO ReadChar(ch) END

WHILE m > 0 DO  m := m DIV 2 ; n := n + 1  END
```

A1.5.6   The repeat statement

Like the while statement, the repeat statement specifies the repeated execution of a statement sequence depending on the value of a Boolean result. The syntax is:

*repeat-statement = 'REPEAT' statement-sequence 'UNTIL'
                    expression.*

In this case the expression following the UNTIL keyword, which must yield a Boolean result, is evaluated after each execution of the statement sequence. Repeated execution of the statement sequence stops as soon as this expression yields the value TRUE.

An example is:

```
REPEAT
    NoOfSpaces := NoOfSpaces + 1 ;  ReadChar(ch)
UNTIL ch <> ' '
```

A1.5.7   The loop and exit statements

The loop statement is a generalisation of the while and repeat statements in that the termination condition may be specified and tested at any point within the body of the loop. The syntax of the loop statement is:

loop-statement = 'LOOP' statement-sequence 'END'.

Repeated execution of the statement sequence within the loop is terminated by the execution of an exit statement within the sequence.

exit-statement = 'EXIT'.

Execution of an exit statement causes control to pass to the statement immediately following the loop statement.

An example of a loop statement, for searching a binary tree, is as follows:

```
LOOP
    IF node^.keyvalue < k THEN temp := node^.left ;
        ELSIF node^.keyvalue > k THEN temp := node^.right
        ELSE found := TRUE
    END ;
    IF found OR (temp = NIL) THEN EXIT END ;
    node := temp
END
```

A1.5.8   The for statement

The for statement may be used for repeated execution of a statement sequence where the repetition is to be carried out a fixed number of times. The syntax for the for statement is:

for-statement = 'FOR' identifier ':=' expression 'TO' expression
['BY' constant-expression] 'DO' statement-sequence
'END'.

The identifier following the FOR keyword must denote a variable of some ordinal type, and is known as the *control variable*. It must not be a component of a structured variable, it must not be an imported variable, and it must not be a parameter of a procedure. The value of the control variable should not be changed by the statement sequence. The expressions separated by the TO keyword must yield values of the same ordinal type as the control variable. The constant expression following the BY keyword, if present, must yield a value of type INTEGER or CARDINAL.

The most general form of the for statement is therefore:

```
FOR v := i TO f BY inc DO ss END
```

The action of this statement is to repeatedly execute the statement sequence ss with v successively assuming the values i, i+inc, i+2*inc, ..., i+n*inc, where i+n*inc is the last term not exceeding f. If no increment is specified it is assumed to be 1. If f is greater than i then ss is not executed at all.

Examples of for statements are:

```
FOR Day := Monday TO Friday DO
    TotalHours := TotalHours + HoursWorked[Day]
END

FOR i :=10 TO 2 BY -1 DO A[i] := A[i-1] END
```

A1.5.9   The with statement

The with statement provides a statement for use with record variables that enables reference to record components without having to repeat the record variable identifier at each reference. The syntax of the with statement is defined as follows:

with-statement = 'WITH' record-variable 'DO' statement-sequence
'END'.

The effect of the with statement is to open a new scope which contains the corresponding field identifiers of the named record variable, thereby permitting the use of field identifiers as variables. With statements may be nested.

Examples of the use of with statements are as follows:

```
WITH node^ DO
    keyvalue := 0 ;
    left := NIL ;
    right := NIL
END

WITH aperson DO
    Name := ' Joe Smith' ;
    Address := '18 Main Street' ;
    Sex := Male ;
    WITH DateOfBirth DO
        Day := 28 ; Month := 8 ; Year := 1953
    END ;
    Origin := National ;
    PlaceOfBirth := 'Dublin'
END
```

A1.6   PROCEDURES AND FUNCTIONS

In Modula-2, in common with most programming languages, it is possible to define an action or group of actions in the form of a procedure, to which a name or *procedure-identifier* is given. This procedure may then be called by means of a *procedure-statement*, whose syntax is given by:

> *procedure-statement = procedure-designator*
> > *['(' actual-parameter-list ')'].*
> *procedure-designator = procedure-identifier | variable.*
> *procedure-identifier = qualified-identifier.*

(Parameters will be discussed later in this section.) A variable used as a procedure designator must be a procedure variable. The procedure statement may contain a list of actual parameters which are substituted for the corresponding formal parameters defined in the *procedure-declaration*.The syntax for a procedure declaration is as follows:

> *procedure-declaration = statement-procedure-declaration |*
> > *function-procedure-declaration.*
> *statement-procedure-declaration = statement-procedure-heading ';'*
> > *procedure-body identifier.*
> *statement-procedure-heading = 'PROCEDURE' identifier*
> > *['(' formal-parameter-list ')'].*
> *function-procedure-declaration = function-procedure-heading ';'*
> > *procedure-body identifier.*
> *function-procedure-heading = 'PROCEDURE' identifier*
> > *['(' formal-parameter-list ')'] ':' result-type.*
> *procedure-body = block.*
> *result-type = type-identifier.*

The identifier following the procedure body must be the same as that in the procedure heading. Statement procedures are activated by a procedure statement as described above. A function procedure is activated by a function designator as a constituent of an expression, and yields a result that is an operand in the expression

All constants, types, variables, procedures and modules declared within the block that constitutes the procedure body are local to the procedure. The values of local variables are undefined upon entry to a procedure. The rules for identifier scope in Modula-2 are as follows:

1. The scope of an identifier declaration is the block in which the declaration occurs, and all procedure blocks enclosed by that block, subject to rule 2.
2. When an identifier declared in block P is declared again in a block Q enclosed by P, then block Q and all blocks enclosed by Q are excluded from the scope of the identifier's declaration in P.

The return statement

Termination of execution of a procedure normally occurs as a result of executing the final statement of the procedure body. However, it is possible to terminate execution at any point in the procedure body by the use of a return statement, whose syntax is as follows:

   return-statement = 'RETURN' [expression].

When used in a statement procedure a return statement does not include an expression. In a function procedure a return statement must include an expression and the result of the expression must be assignment compatible with the result type specified in the procedure heading. Function procedures must include at least one return statement indicating the result value. There may be several but only one will be executed on any given call.

Procedure parameters

As described above, the declaration of a procedure in Modula-2 may include a *formal parameter list*:

   PROCEDURE identifier ['(' formal-parameter=list')'] [':' result-type].

When the procedure is activated, these formal parameters are replaced by corresponding actual parameters:

   procedure-identifier ['(' actual-parameter-list')'].

There are two classes of parameter in Modula-2, namely *value* and *variable* parameters. The class is indicated in the formal parameter list in the procedure declaration. Value formal parameters stand for local variables to which the result of the evaluation of the corresponding actual parameter is assigned as initial value. Variable formal parameters correspond to actual parameters that are variables and whose values may be altered by the execution of the procedure. Variable parameters are preceded in the procedure declaration by the symbol VAR. The syntax for a formal parameter list is as follows:

   formal-parameter-list =
         formal-parameter-section {';' formal-parameter-section}.
   formal-parameter-section = value-parameter-section |
                           variable-parameter-section.
   value-parameter-section = identifier-list ':' formal-type.
   variable-parameter-section = 'VAR' identifier-list ':' formal-type.
   formal-type = type-identifier | open-array-type
   open-array-type = 'ARRAY' 'OF' type-identifier.

Each actual parameter list used in a procedure statement or in a function procedure designator, must correspond with the appropriate formal parameter list. The number of parameters in the two lists must be the same and each actual parameter corresponds with the formal parameter occupying the same position in the formal parameter list. In the case of a variable formal parameter the actual parameter must be a designator denoting a variable of a compatible type. For a value formal parameter, the actual parameter must be an expression which is assignment compatible with the type of the formal parameter.

actual-parameter-list = actual-parameter {',' actual-parameter}.
actual-parameter = expression | variable.

If the formal parameter is an open array parameter the index range is mapped by the procedure onto the CARDINAL subrange 0 to $N - 1$, where N is the number of elements in the actual array parameter. Open array parameters may only be accessed element-wise by the procedure.

A1.7   STANDARD PROCEDURES

The standard procedures provided by Modula-2 are as follows:

ABS (x)   Returns the absolute value of x, where x is an integer or real expression. The result type is the same as the argument type.

CAP(ch)   If ch is a lower case letter, returns the corresponding capital letter.

CHR(x)   Returns the character with ordinal value x in the underlying character set. x is a CARDINAL expression.

FLOAT(x)   Returns the real number representation of the CARDINAL x.

HIGH(A)   Returns a CARDINAL indicating the high index bound of array A.

ODD(x)   Returns the BOOLEAN result of x MOD $2 <> 0$. x is INTEGER or CARDINAL.

ORD(x)   Returns the ordinal value of x, where x is of type CHAR, INTEGER, CARDINAL or any enumerated type. The result is of type CARDINAL.

TRUNC(x)   Returns the integral part of the real number x.

VAL(T,x)   Returns the value with ordinal number x and type T. x is a CARDINAL expression. T is an enumerated type, CHAR, INTEGER, or CARDINAL.

DEC(x)   Replaces x with its immediate predecessor: $x := x - 1$, where x is of an ordinal type (INTEGER, CARDINAL, CHAR, subrange, enumerated type).

DEC(x,n)   Replaces x with its nth predecessor: $x := x - n$, where x is of an ordinal type, and n is an INTEGER or CARDINAL expression.

EXCL(s,i)   Removes the member i from the set s: $s := s - \{i\}$.

HALT   Terminates program execution.

INC(x)   Replaces x by its immediate successor: $x := x + 1$, where x is of an ordinal type.

INC(x,n)   Replaces x by its nth successor: $x := x + n$, where x is of an ordinal type and n is an INTEGER or CARDINAL expression.

INCL(s,i)   Includes the member i in the set s: $s := s + \{i\}$.

A1.8   MODULES

The structuring of program systems in Modula-2 is based on the concept of *modules*. A module is a collection of data types, data objects and associated procedures. A main program is itself a module (a *program module*), and the data types, objects and procedures of a program module may be distributed among various *local modules*, each of which provides a solution to part of the overall problem. Modules of course must communicate with each other, and in Modula-2 all types, objects and operations which are provided by a module to the outside world must be explicitly declared in an *EXPORT clause*. Similarly, any type, object or procedure which is required by a module but is defined in some other module, must be declared in an *IMPORT clause*.

The syntax for a module declaration is as follows:

> *module-declaration = 'MODULE' identifier [priority] ';'*
> *{import-list ';'} [export-list ';']*
> *block identifier.*
> *import-list = ['FROM' identifier] 'IMPORT' identifier-list.*
> *export-list = 'EXPORT' ['QUALIFIED'] identifier-list.*

The identifier at the end of the module declaration must be the same as that in the module heading. If the EXPORT symbol is followed by the symbol QUALIFIED, then the listed identifiers must be prefixed with the module's identifier when used outside the module. Qualified export serves to avoid clashes of identifier names exported from different modules. The FROM clause in the import list has the effect of unqualifying the imported identifiers. That is, they may be used within the module in non-qualified form.

If a local module identifier is exported then that module's export list is also exported. If an identifier is exported which denotes a record type, then the field identifiers of the type are also exported. If a module exports an identifier which denotes an enumerated type, the constant identifiers which denote the values of the type are also exported.

A module whose declaration is imbedded in an enclosing program, procedure, or module block is called a local module. The statement sequence that constitutes the module body is executed when the procedure to which the module is local is called. Such a module serves to control the scope and visibility of identifiers declared inside and outside the module.

A1.8.1   Separately compiled modules

Modula-2 allows programs to be constructed from a number of separate compilation units which reflect the modular structure of the entire program. Such compilation units may be submitted to a compiler without the other units that make up the program. They take three forms, namely program modules, definition modules and implementation modules. These are described below.

Program module

A program module is a separately compiled sequence of statements that is capable of execution. It has the following syntactic form:

> *program-module =*
> *'MODULE' identifier [priority] ';' {import-list} block identifier '.'*

Thus a program module has no export list and imported objects are defined in other compilation units.

Definition and implementation modules

A definition module serves to *describe* the data types, objects and operations (procedures) exported by an implementation module. Its syntactic form is as follows:

> *definition-module = 'DEFINITION' 'MODULE' identifier ';'*
> *{import-list} {definition} 'END' identifier '.'.*
> *definition = 'CONST' {constant-declaration ';'} /*
> *TYPE' {type-definition ';'} /*
> *'VAR' {variable-declaration ';'} /*
> *procedure-heading ';'*
> *type-definition = type-declaration / opaque-type-declaration.*
> *opaque-type-declaration = identifier.*

Definition modules require the use of qualified export.

An implementation module is always paired with a definition module with the same name. It contains the detailed data declarations and logic corresponding to the exports specified in the definition module. The syntactic form of an implementation module is as follows:

> *implementation-module = 'IMPLEMENTATION' program-module.*

The implementation module contains the declarations of all non-exported objects together with all details of the implementation. The definition part acts like a prefix to the implementation part, and contains the list of all objects that are to be visible outside the module, and the declaration of all exported objects. Procedure declarations in the definition module consist of a heading only. The procedure body belongs to the corresponding implementation module. Variables declared in the definition module are visible and accessible only in those modules which import them. An importer of a module need only have available the definition module. Initialisation code is placed in the main body of the implementation module, and is executed when the procedure, to which the module is local, is called. If several modules are declared, then these bodies are executed in the sequence in which the modules occur.

A particularly powerful feature of the Modula-2 definition module is the ability to define *opaque types*. An opaque type is a type exported by a definition module, the internal representation of which is given only in the corresponding implementation module. Opaque types are very useful in that they allow for the definition of arbitrary, non-decomposable data objects, together with a set of operations which may be performed on those objects, while at the same time hiding details with regard to their representation and implementation.

A1.9   CONCURRENT PROGRAMMING

For concurrent programming, Modula-2 offers only some rather basic facilities which permit the representation of quasi-concurrent processes (or *coroutines*), which, although viewed as executing in parallel, actually share a single physical processor.

A new process is created in a Modula-2 program by a call to the procedure NEWPROCESS:

```
PROCEDURE NEWPROCESS ( p : PROC ; WorkArea : ADDRESS ;
        WorkSize : CARDINAL ; VAR ProcessName : PROCESS ) ;
```

where p denotes the procedure that constitutes the process. This procedure must be parameterless and must be declared at the outermost level of the module; WorkArea specifies the base address of the area in memory which will serve as the workspace for the process. This workspace is usually created by declaring an ARRAY OF WORD; WorkSize is the size of the workspace in bytes; ProcessName is the result parameter where its type, PROCESS, is imported from the system module.

A transfer of control between two processes is effected by a call to the procedure TRANSFER:

```
TRANSFER ( VAR p1, p2 : PROCESS ) ;
```

Such a call suspends the current process, assigning it to the variable parameter p1, and activates the process p2. A program terminates when control reaches the end of a procedure which forms the body of a process.

In many implementations of Modula-2 a Processes module supplies the procedures necessary for synchronising process execution using *signals*. The presence of a condition can be represented by variables of the type SIGNAL, and a signal can be sent through a call to the procedure SEND. By employing the procedure WAIT, a process can suspend its execution until it is informed, by a signal, that a particular condition has arisen. A common form for the Processes module, corresponding to the standard suggested by Wirth, is as follows:

```
DEFINITION MODULE Processes;

TYPE SIGNAL ;

PROCEDURE StartProcess ( P : PROC ;  WorkSize : CARDINAL ) ;
(* Defines and transfers control to a process*)

PROCEDURE SEND ( VAR Sent : SIGNAL ) ;

PROCEDURE WAIT ( VAR WaitingFor : SIGNAL ) ;

PROCEDURE AWAITED ( Check : SIGNAL ) : BOOLEAN ;
(* Indicates if any processes are currently waiting for a specified signal *)

PROCEDURE INIT ( VAR ASignal : SIGNAL ) ;
(* Initialises a signal *)

END Processes ;
```

APPENDIX 2

A Syntax for SQL

The following EBNF syntax for queries in SQL covers the subset of the language used in Chapter 4. It is similar to that used by Date (1986) and Gray (1984). Actual implementations of SQL will most likely provide additional constructs including update operations, and may restrict the complexity allowed in some operations (e.g. the depth of query nesting will usually be limited).

query	=	*query-exp /*
		query-exp 'ORDER' 'BY' sort-clause.
sort-clause	=	*order-spec {',' order-spec}.*
order-spec	=	*attribute-spec ['ASC' / 'DESC'].*
query-exp	=	*query-spec 'UNION' query-spec / query-spec.*
query-spec	=	*'SELECT' ['UNIQUE'] select-list*
		'FROM' table-list
		'WHERE' condition
		['GROUP' 'BY' attribute-spec
		{',' attribute-spec}
		['HAVING' condition]].
table-list	=	*table-spec {',' table-spec}.*
table-spec	=	*relation-name /*
		relation-name ['AS'] alias-name.
relation-name	=	*identifier.*
alias-name	=	*identifier.*
attribute-spec	=	*attribute-name /*
		table-name '.' attribute-name.
table-name	=	*relation-name / alias-name.*
select-list	=	*'*' / expression {',' expression}.*
expression	=	*['+' / '-'] term {add-op term}.*
term	=	*factor {mult-op factor}.*
factor	=	*constant / attribute-spec / function-spec /*
		'(' expression ')'.
add-op	=	*'+' / '-'.*

256

mult-op	=	*'*'	'/'.*
function-spec	=	*aggregate-function '(' simple-expression ')' |*
		'COUNT' '(' 'UNIQUE' attribute-spec ')'.
aggregate-function	=	*'COUNT'	'MAX'	'MIN'	'SUM'	'AVG'.*
simple-expression	=	*['+'	'-'] simple-term*
		{addition-op simple-term}.
simple-term	=	*simple-factor {mult-op simple-factor }.*
simple-factor	=	*constant	attribute-spec	*
		'(' simple-expression ')'.
condition	=	*boolean-term { 'OR' boolean-term }.*
boolean-term	=	*boolean-factor { 'AND' boolean-factor }.*
boolean-factor	=	*predicate	'(' condition ')'	*
		'NOT' boolean-factor.
predicate	=	*comparison	'EXISTS' nested-query.*
nested-query	=	*'(' query-spec ')'.*
comparison	=	*expression comparison-op expression |*
		*expression comparison-op ['ALL'	'ANY'	*
		['NOT'] 'IN'] nested-query.
comparison-op	=	*'='	'>'	'<'	'≤'	'≥'	'≠'.*

The above syntax includes some features that were not described in Chapter 4, specifically the use of the qualifier UNIQUE and the GROUP BY and HAVING clauses.

In common with many commercial database languages, implementations of SQL do not generally eliminate duplicate tuples from the relations resulting from queries or nested queries. Thus if the user requires the elimination of duplicates he must do so explicitly through the use of the keyword UNIQUE.

The GROUP BY and HAVING clauses may be best described by a simple example. Suppose that we have the relation,

REPORT (S#, C#, MARKS)

representing the many-to-many relationship between students (identified by S#), and courses (identified by C#). We wish to find the *total* marks obtained by each student, and the *average* mark over all the courses taken. We can perform this operation using the GROUP BY clause as follows:

SELECT S#, SUM (MARKS), AVG (MARKS)
FROM REPORT
GROUP BY S# ;

The GROUP BY operator logically reorders the tuples in the relation specified in the FROM clause into groups, such that within each group all tuples have the same value of the attribute or attributes specified in the GROUP BY clause. In the above example, the tuples of the REPORT relation are partitioned into groups so that each group contains all the tuples for a particular value of S#. The SELECT clause is then applied to each group rather than to each tuple. Thus each expression in the select clause must be single-valued for each group.

The HAVING clause allows us to impose selections on the resulting tuples of a GROUP BY operation so that we see only some of these tuples. For example, suppose that we wish to retrieve the total and average marks only for those students who achieved an average of 40 or more. We may write this in SQL as folows:

```
SELECT  S#, SUM (MARKS), AVG (MARKS)
FROM  REPORT
GROUP BY  S#
HAVING  AVG (MARKS) ≥ 40 ;
```

Again, expressions in the HAVING clause must produce a single value for each group.

APPENDIX 3

A Syntax for DAPLEX

The following is an EBNF syntax for an implemented dialect of DAPLEX (discussed in Chapter 5), called EFDM (Extended Functional Data Model), as described by Atkinson and Kulkarni (1984). It is adapted, with permission, from their user manual.

command	=	*'DECLARE' function-dec arrow 'ENTITY' /*
		'DECLARE' function-dec arrow type-ident /
		'DEFINE' function-dec arrow function-def /
		'CONSTRAINT' identifier 'ON'
		function-list '—>' constraint-type /
		'DROP' function-dec / 'DROP' view-ident /
		'DROP' identifier /
		'View' view-ident 'IS' deduce-clause
		{deduce-clause} 'END' /
		imperative-command.
function-dec	=	*function-ident '(' [argument-list] ')'.*
argument-list	=	*type-ident { ',' type-ident }.*
arrow	=	*'—>' / '—>>'.*
function-def	=	*expression / 'TRANSITIVE' 'OF' expression /*
		'INVERSE' 'OF' function-dec /
		'COMPOUND' 'OF' mtuple.
constraint-type	=	*"TOTAL' / 'FIXED' / 'UNIQUE' / 'DISJOINT' /*
		predicate.
deduce-clause	=	*'DEDUCE' function-dec arrow type-ident*
		'USING' function-def.
function-list	=	*function-spec {',' function-spec}.*
function-spec	=	*type-ident / function-dec.*
imperative	=	*'FOR' 'EACH' set imperative /*
		'FOR' single-var imperative-list /
		'PRINT' stuple /
		'LET' sv-function-call '=' singleton /

259

		'LET' mv-function-call '=' expression /
		'INCLUDE' function-call '=' set /
		'EXCLUDE' function-call '=' set /
		'DELETE' single-var /
		'DELETE' sv-function-call /
		'DELETE' variable-ident.
imperative-list	=	imperative {';' imperative}.
function-call	=	type-ident / sv-function-call /
		mv-function-call.
set	=	variable-ident 'IN' set-spec
		['SUCH' 'THAT' predicate] ['AS' type-ident].
set-spec	=	mv-function-call / type-ident /
		'{' stuple '}' / '(' set set-operator set ')'.
set-operator	=	'UNION' / 'INTERSECTION' / 'DIFFERENCE'.
expression	=	set / singleton.
singleton	=	constant / variable-ident /
		sv-function-call / single-var / predicate /
		a-expression / aggregate-call / '(' singleton ')'.
single-var	=	'THE' set / 'A' 'NEW' variable-ident 'IN'
		type-ident.
predicate	=	sv-function-call / boolean-term /
		quantifier set 'HAS' predicate.
quantifier	=	'SOME' / 'ALL' / 'NO' / 'EXACTLY' integer /
		'AT' 'LEAST' integer / 'AT' 'MOST' integer.
aggregrate-call	=	'COUNT' '(' set ')' / 'MAX' '(' set ')' /
		'MIN' '(' set ')' /
		'TOTAL' '(' 'OVER' mtuple singleton ')' /
		'AVERAGE' '(' 'OVER' mtuple singleton ')'.
boolean-term	=	boolean-factor / boolean-term 'OR' boolean-factor.
boolean-factor	=	boolean-var / boolean-factor 'AND' boolean-var.
boolean-var	=	boolean-prim / 'NOT' boolean-prim.
boolean-prim	=	a-expression comp-operator a-expression /
		variable-ident / boolean-constant / '(' predicate ')'.
comp-operator	=	'>' / '<' / '≤' / '≥' / '=' / '~'.
a-expression	=	['+' / '-'] unsigned.
unsigned	=	term / unsigned add-operator term.
add-operator	=	'+' / '-' / '++'.
term	=	factor / term mul-operator factor.
mul-operator	=	'*' / '/' / 'REM'.
factor	=	singleton ['AS' type-ident].
sv-function-call	=	function-ident '(' stuple ')'.
stuple	=	singleton {',' singleton}.
mv-function-call	=	function-ident '(' mtuple ')'.
mtuple	=	expression {',' expression}.
integer	=	singleton.
constant	=	integer-constant / boolean-constant / string-constant
variable-ident	=	identifier.
type-identifier	=	identifier.
view-ident	=	identifier.

The usage of the commands may be summarised as follows:

DECLARE — To declare new entity types and the functions which apply to entity types.

DEFINE — To define a derived function.

CONSTRAINT — To specify constraints on functions.

VIEW — To define views.

DROP — To drop an existing function, entity type, constraint or view.

FOR EACH — To range over each entity in a set.

FOR A NEW — To create a new entity.

DELETE — To delete an existing entity.

LET — To assign a single value to a function.

INCLUDE — To define a new value for inclusion in the set of values of a multivalued function.

EXCLUDE — To delete a value from the set of values of a multi-valued function.

PRINT — To print the results of retrieval operations.

R.T.C. LIBRARY
LETTERKENNY

References

Addis, T.R. (1982) A Relation-Based Language Interpreter for a Content Addressable File Store, *ACM Trans. on Database Systems* **7**, 125-63.

Allman, E., Held, G.D. and Stonebraker, M.R. (1976) Embedding a Relational Data Sub-Language in a General Purpose Programming Language, *Proc. ACM SIGPLAN/SIGMOD Conference on Data: Abstraction, Definition, and Structure.*

Amble, T., Bratbergsengen, K. and Risnes, O. (1976) ASTRAL: A Structured and Unified Approach to Database Design and Manipulation, *Proc. Database Architecture Conference Venice*, pp. 257-74.

Atkinson, M.P., Bailey, P.J., Chisholm, K.J., Cockshott, W.P., and Morrison, R. (1983) An Approach to Persistent Programming, *Computer J.* **26**, No. 4.

Atkinson, M.P. and Kulkarni, K.G. (1984) Experimenting with the Functional Data Model, in *Databases: Role and Structure*, (ed P.M. Stocker), Cambridge University Press.

Babb, E. (1979) Implementing a Relational Database by Means of Specialised Hardware, *ACM Trans. on Database Systems* **4**, No. 1.

Bayer, R. and McCreight, E. (1972) Organisation and Maintenance of Large Ordered Indexes, *Acta Informatica* **1**, 173-89.

Bernstein, P.A. and Chiu, D.W. (1981) Using Semi-Joins to Solve Relational Queries, *J. ACM* **28**, 25-40.

Bernstein, P.A. and Goodman, N.(1980) Timestamp-based Algorithms for Concurrency Control in Distributed Database Systems, *Proc. Int. Conf. on Very Large Databases*, pp. 285-300.

Blasgen, M.W. and Eswaran, K.P. (1976) On the Evaluation of Queries in a Relational Database System, *IBM Research Report RJ 1745*, IBM

Research Laboratories, San Jose, Calif.

Blasgen, M.W. and Eswaran, K.P. (1977) Storage and Access in Relational Databases, *IBM Syst. J.* **16**, 363-77

Brady, J. (1977) *The Theory of Computer Science: A Programming Approach*, Chapman & Hall, London.

Buneman O.P. and Frankel, R.E. (1979) FQL - A Functional Query Language, *Proc. ACM SIGMOD Int. Conf. on the Management of Data*, Boston, Mass.

Ceri, S., Pernici, B., and Wiederhold, G. (1984) An Overview of Research in the Design of Distributed Systems, *IEEE Database Engineering Bulletin* **7**, 46-51

Chamberlin, D.D. et al. (1976) SEQUEL 2: A Unified Approach to Data Definition, Manipulation and Control, *IBM J. R&D* **20**, No. 6.

Chen, P.P.S. (1976) The Entity Relationship Model: Towards a Unified View of Data, *ACM Trans. on Database Systems* **1**, No. 1.

CODASYL (1971) *Data Base Task Group April 71 Report*, ACM, New York.

CODASYL (1973) *Data Description Language Committee, Journal of Development*.

CODASYL (1978) *Data Description Language Committee, Journal of Development*.

CODASYL (1981) *Data Description Language Committee, Journal of Development*.

CODASYL COBOL (1978) *Journal of Development*.

Codd, E.F. (1970) A Relational Model of Data for Large Shared Data Banks, *Comm. ACM* **13**, 377-87.

Codd, E.F. (1972a) Further Normalisation of the Data Base Relational Model, in *Data Base Systems*, (ed R. Rustin), Courant Computer Science Symposia Series, **6**, pp. 33-64, Prentice Hall, Englewood Cliffs, N.J.

Codd, E.F. (1972b) Relational Completeness of Database Sub-Languages, in *Data Base Systems*, (ed R. Rustin), Courant Computer Science Symposia Series, **6**, pp. 69-98, Prentice Hall, Englewood Cliffs, N.J.

Codd, E.F. (1974) Recent Investigations into Relational Database Systems, *Proc. IFIP Congress*.

Codd, E.F. (1979) Extending the Data Base Relational Model to Capture More Meaning, *ACM Trans. on Database Systems* **4**, 397-434.

Date, C.J. (1981) Referential Integrity, *Proc. VIIth Int. Conf. on Very Large Databases*, Cannes, France.

Date, C.J. (1983) *An Introduction to Database Systems*, Vol. II, Addison-Wesley Publishing Co.

Date, C.J. (1986) *An Introduction to Database Systems*, Vol. I, 4th Edition, Addison-Wesley Publishing Co.

Denning, D.E. (1978) A Review of Research on Statistical Database Security, in *Foundations of Secure Computation* (eds R.A. DeMillo, D.P. Dobkin, A.K. Jones and R.J. Lipton), Academic Press, New York.

Denning, D.E., Denning, P.J. and Schwartz, M.D. (1979) The Tracker: A threat to Statistical Database Security, *ACM Trans. on Database Systems* 4, No. 1.

Diffie, W., and Helman, M.E. (1976) New Directions in Cryptography, *IEEE Trans. on Information Theory IT-22*.

Elder, J.W.G. (1984) *Construction of Data Processing Software*, Prentice Hall International, Hemel Hempstead.

Eswaran, K.P., Gray, J.N., Lorie, R.A., and Traiger, I.L. (1976) The Notions of Consistency and Predicate Locks in a Data Base System, *Comm. ACM* 19, No. 11.

Fagin, R. (1977) Multivalued Dependencies and a New Normal Form for Relational Databases, *ACM Trans. on Database Systems* 2, No. 3.

Fagin, R. (1979) Normal Forms and Relational Database Operators, *ACM SIGMOD Int. Symposium on Management of Data*, pp. 153-60.

Fernandez, E.B., Summers, R.C. and Wood, C. (1981) *Database Security and Integrity*, Addison-Wesley, Reading, Mass.

Fox, S., Landers, T., Ries, D.R., and Rosenberg, R.L. (1984) *DAPLEX Users Manual*, Report CCA-84-01, Computer Corporation of America, Cambridge, Mass.

Gray, J.N., Notes on Database Operating Systems (1978) in *Operating Systems: An Advanced Course.*, (eds R. Bayer, R.M. Graham, and G. Seegmuller), Springer-Verlag.

Gray, P.M.D. (1984) *Logic, Algebra and Databases*, Ellis Horwood.

Haerder, T. (1978) Implementing a Generalised Access Path Structure for a Relational Database System, *ACM Trans. on Database Systems* 3, 285-98.

Hammer, M.M. and McLeod, D.J. (1975) Semantic Integrity in a Relational Database System, *Proc. of 1st International Conference on Very Large Data Bases*, Framingham, Mass.

Heath, I.J. (1971) Unacceptable File Operations in a Relational Database, *Proc. ACM SIGFIDET Workshop on Data Description, Access and Control.*

Hoare, C.A.R. (1972a) Proof of Correctness of Data Representations, *Acta Informatica* 1, 271-81.

Hoare, C.A.R. (1972b) Notes on Data Structuring, in *Structured Programming*, (eds O.-J. Dahl, E.W. Dijkstra, and C.A.R. Hoare), Academic Press, New York, 83-174.

Hoare, C.A.R. (1974) Monitors: An Operating System Structuring Concept, *CACM* **17**, 549-57.

Hughes, J.G. and Connolly, M.M. (1987) A Portable Implementation of a Modular Multiprocessing Database Programming Language, *Software - Practice and Experience* **17**, 533-46.

Ichbiah, J.D. et al. (1979) Rationale for the Design of the Ada Programming Language, *ACM SIGPLAN Notices* **14**.

Jarke, M. and Koch, J. (1984) Query Optimisation in Database Systems, *Computing Surveys* **16**, 111-52.

Jarke, M. and Schmidt, J.W. (1982) Query Processing Strategies in the Pascal/R Relational Database Management System, *Proc. ACM SIGMOD Int. Conf. on Management of Data*, Orlando, Florida, pp. 256-64.

Kent, W. (1983) A Simple Guide to Five Normal Forms in Relational Database Theory, *CACM* **26**, No. 2.

Kim, W. (1980) A New Way to Compute the Product and Join of Relations, *Proc. ACM SIGMOD Conf. on Management of Data*, Santa Monica, Calif., New York, 179-87.

Knuth, D. (1973) *The Art of Computer Programming. Vol. III: Sorting and Searching*, Addison-Wesley Publishing Co.

Kung, H.T., and Robertson, J.T. (1981) On Optimistic Methods for Concurrency Control, *ACM Trans. on Database Systems* **6**, No. 2.

Liskov, B. and Zilles, S.N. (1974) Programming with Abstract Data Types, *ACM SIGPLAN Notices* **9**, 50-9.

McGetterick, A.D. (1982) *Program Verification Using Ada*, Cambridge Univ. Press, Cambridge.

McGregor, D.R., Thompson, R.G., and Dawson, W.N. (1976) High Performance Hardware for Database Systems, *Proc. Int. Conf. on Very Large Databases*, pp. 103-16.

McGregor, D.R., and Malone, J.R. (1982) The FACT Database: A System Using Generic Associative Networks, *Inf. Tech. Research and Development* **1**, 55-72.

Merrett, T.H. (1981) Why Sort-Merge Gives the Best Implementation of the Natural Join, *ACM SIGMOD Rec.* **13**, 39-51.

Mitchell, R.W. (1976) Content Addressable File Store, *Proc. of the Online Database Technology Conf.*, London.

Morrison, R. (1982) S-Algol: a Simple Algol, *Computer Bulletin* **II**, No. 31.

Navathe, S. and Cheng, A. (1983) A Methodology for Database Schema Mapping from Extended Entity-Relationship Models into the Hierarchical Model, in *Entity-Relationship Approach to Software Engineering*, (eds G.C. Davis et al.), Elsevier North-Holland, New York.

Palermo, F.P. (1972) A Database Search Problem, *Fourth Computer and Information Science Symposium*, Miami Beach, pp. 67-101.

Parnas, D.L. (1972a) A Technique for Software Module Specification with Examples, *CACM* **15**, 330-6.

Parnas, D.L. (1972b) On the Criteria to be Used in Decomposing Systems into Modules, *CACM* **15**, 1053-8.

Pomberger, G. (1984) *Software Engineering and Modula-2*, Prentice Hall International, Hemel Hempstead.

Reimer, M. (1984) Implementation of the Database Programming Language Modula/R on the Personal Computer Lilith, *Software - Practice and Experience* **14**, 945-56.

Rivest, R.L., Shamir, A., and Adleman, L. (1978) A Method for Obtaining Digital Signatures and Public-Key Cryptosystems, *CACM* **21**, No. 2.

Rowe, L.A. and Shoens, K.A. (1979) Data Abstraction, Views and Updates in RIGEL, *Proc. ACM SIGMOD Conf.*, Boston, Mass., 71-81.

Rowe, L.A. (1981) Issues in the Design of Database Programming Languages, *Proc. of Workshop on Data Abstraction, Databases and Conceptual Modelling*, Pingree Park, Co. U.S.A. Part 74, 180-2.

Sakai, H. (1983) Entity-Relationship Approach to Logical Database Design, In *Entity-Relationship Approach to Software Engineering*, (eds C.G. Davis, S. Jajodia, P.A. Ng, and R.T. Yeh), Elsevier North-Holland, New York, pp. 155-87.

Scheuermann, P., Scheffner, G. and Weber, H. (1980) Abstraction Capabilities and Invarient properties Modelling within the Entity-Relationship Approach, in *Entity-Relationship Approach to Systems Analysis and Design*, (ed P. Chen), North-Holland, pp. 121-40.

Schmidt, J.W. (1977) Some High Level Language Constructs for Data of Type Relation, *ACM Trans. on Database Systems* **2**, 247-61.

Schmidt, J.W. and Mall, M. (1980) *Pascal/R Report Bericht Nr. 66*, Inst. fur Informatik, Univ. Hamburg, Hamburg, West Germany.

Schoman, K.and Ross, D.T. (1977) Structured Analysis for Requirements Definition, *IEEE Trans. on Software Eng.* **SE-3**.

Shapiro, L.D. (1987) Join Processing in Database Systems with Large Main Memories, *ACM Trans. on Database Systems* **11**, 239-64.

Shipman, D.W. (1981) The Functional Data Model and the Language DAPLEX, *ACM Trans. on Database Systems* **6**, No. 1.

Shopiro, J.E. (1979) Theseus - A Programming Language for Relational Databases, *ACM Trans. on Database Systems* **4**, 493-517.

Sibley, E.H., and Kerschberg L. (1977) Data Architecture and Data Model Considerations, *Proc. AFIPS National Computer Conf.*, Dallas, Texas.

Smith, J.M. and Smith, D.C.P. (1977) Database Abstractions: Aggregation and Generalisation, *ACM Trans. on Database Systems* 2, No. 2.

Smith, J.M., Fox, S. and Landers, T.A. (1981) *Reference Manual for ADAPLEX*, Computer Corporation of America, Cambridge, Mass.

Stonebraker, M., Wong, E., Kreps, P., and Held, G. (1976) The Design and Implementation of INGRES, *ACM Trans. on Database Systems* 1, 189-222.

Teorey, T.J., Yang, D. and Fry, J.P. (1986) Logical Design Methodology for Relational Databases, *Computing Surveys* 18, No. 2.

Traiger, I.L., Gray, J.N., Galtieri, C.A., and Lindsay, B.G. (1979) Transactions and Consistency in Distributed Database Systems, *IBM Research Report RJ2555*.

Tsichritis, D.C. and Klug, A. (eds) (1978) *The ANSI/X3/SPARC DBMS Framework: Report of the Study Group on Database Management Systems Information Systems* 3.

Ullman, J.D. (1982) *Principles of Database Systems*, 2nd Edition, Pitman, London.

Van de Reit, R.P., Wasserman, A.I., Kersten, M.L. and De Jonge, W. (1981) High Level Programming Features for Improving the Efficiency of a Relational Database System, *ACM Trans. on Database Systems* 6, 464-85.

Wasserman, A.I. (1979) Design Goals for PLAIN, *Proc. ACM SIGMOD Conf. Boston*, pp. 60-70.

Wasserman, A.I. (1980) The Design of PLAIN - Support for Systematic Programming, *Proc. AFIPS*, NCC Vol. 49, pp. 731-40.

Wasserman, A.I. et. al. (1981) Revised Report on the Programming Language PLAIN, *ACM SIGPLAN Notices* 16, 59-80.

Welsh, J. and Bustard (1979) D.W., Pascal-Plus: Another Language for Modular Multi-Programming, *Software - Practice and Experience* 9, 947-57.

Welsh, J. and Elder, J.W.G. (1987) *An Introduction to Modula-2*, Prentice Hall International, Hemel Hempstead.

Wirth, N. (1977) Modula: A Language for Modular Multi-Programming, *Software - Practice and Experience* 7, 3-35.

Wirth, N.(1982) *Programming in Modula-2*, Springer-Verlag, Berlin.

Wirth, N. (1986) *Algorithms and Data Structures*, Prentice Hall, Englewood Cliffs, N.J.

Wong, E. (1977) Retrieving Dispersed Data from SDD-1: A System for Distributed Databases, *Proc. 2nd Berkeley Conf. on Distributed Data Management and Computer Networks*, Lawrence Berkeley Laboratory, Calif.

Yang, C.-C. (1986) *Relational Databases*, Prentice Hall, Englewood Cliffs, N.J.

Yao, S.B. (1979) Optimisation of Query Evaluation Algorithms, *ACM Trans. on Database Systems* **4**, 133-55.

Zloof, M.M. (1975) Query-By-Example, *Proc. of the National Computer Conf.* **44**, 431-7, AFIPS Press.

Index